TRANSFER PRICING AND VALUATION IN CORPORATE TAXATION:
Federal Legislation vs. Administrative Practice

TRANSFER PRICING AND VALUATION IN CORPORATE TAXATION: Federal Legislation vs. Administrative Practice

by

Elizabeth King
Harvard University

Kluwer Academic Publishers
Boston/Dordrecht/London

Distributors for North America:
Kluwer Academic Publishers
101 Philip Drive
Assinippi Park
Norwell, Massachusetts 02061 USA

Distributors for all other countries:
Kluwer Academic Publishers Group
Distribution Centre
Post Office Box 322
3300 AH Dordrecht, THE NETHERLANDS

Library of Congress Cataloging-in-Publication Data

King, Elizabeth A., 1956-
Transfer pricing and valuation in corporate taxation : federal legislation vs. administrative practice / by Elizabeth King.
p. cm.
ISBN 0-7923-9392-9
1. International business enterprises--Taxation--Law and legislation--United States. 2. Transfer pricing--Taxation--Law and legislation--United States. 3. Transfer pricing--Accounting. 4. Intangible property--Taxation--United States. 5. Intangible property--Valuation--United States. I. Title.
KF6464.K56 1994
343.7306'8--dc20
[347.30368] 93-28693
CIP

Printed on acid-free paper.

Printed in the United States of America

For Gary

Contents

Preface **xv**

I Legislation and Regulations **1**

1 Introduction **3**

2 Transfer Pricing and Valuation Regulations **9**

2.1 Transfer Pricing Regulations: Internal Revenue Code Section 482 10

2.1.1 The 1968 Regulations 11

2.1.2 The Tax Reform Act of 1986 24

2.1.3 The White Paper 26

2.1.4 The 1992 Proposed Regulations 32

2.1.5 The 1993 Temporary Regulations 40

2.1.6 The 1993 Proposed Regulations 53

2.2 Transfer Pricing Regulations for Possessions Corporations: Internal Revenue Code Section 936(h) 56

2.3 Concurrent and Subsequent Developments in Transfer Pricing 59

2.4 Institutional Dispute Resolution Procedures and Competent Authority Proceedings 67

2.5 Valuation of Acquired Assets for Tax Purposes: Internal Revenue Code Section 338 73

2.5.1 The Key Controversy Before 1993: Where Goodwill Begins and Ends 74

2.5.2 Areas of Broad Consensus: Valuation and Lifing Methodologies 79

Appendix A: Summary of Coordinated Issue Papers 82

II Transfer Pricing and Valuation Regulations in Practice **87**

3 The Cost-Plus Method **91**

3.1 Background 91

3.2 Cost-Plus Case 1: Leather Goods 93

3.2.1 Summary Functional Analysis 93

3.2.2 Intra-Company Transfer Pricing Policy 94

3.2.3 Potential Issues 95

3.2.4 Adjustment Methodology under the 1968 Regulations 96

3.2.5 Possible Adjustment Methodology under the 1993 Temporary Regulations 99

3.2.6 Taxpayer's Position 108

3.2.7 Resolution 108

3.3 Cost-Plus Case 2: Consumer Electronics 110

3.3.1 Summary Functional Analysis 110

3.3.2 Intra-Company Transfer Pricing Policy 111

3.3.3 Potential Issues 112

3.3.4 Adjustment Methodology under the 1968 Regulations 113

3.3.5 Possible Adjustment Methodology under the 1993 Temporary Regulations 113

3.3.6 Taxpayer's Position 113

3.3.7 Resolution 114

3.4 Critique of the Cost-Plus Method: 1968 Regulations and 1993 Temporary Regulations 115

3.4.1 Comparability Issues 115

3.4.2 The Cost Base Question 117

3.4.3 Adjustments for Differences between Comparables and Controlled Manufacturing Affiliate 118

3.4.4 Summary 119

3.5 The Broader Setting 120

4 The Resale Price Method 123

4.1 Background 123

4.2 A Resale Price Issue: Electronic Home Entertainment Products 125

4.2.1 Summary Functional Analysis 125

4.2.2 Intra-Company Transfer Pricing Policy 126

4.2.3 Potential Issues 126

4.2.4 Adjustment Methodology under the 1968 Regulations 130

4.2.5 Possible Adjustment Methodology under the 1993 Temporary Regulations 139

4.2.6 Taxpayer's Position 143

4.2.7 Resolution 145

4.3 Critique of Resale Price Provisions 147

5 Cost-Sharing Agreements 151

5.1 Background 151

5.2 Cost-Sharing Case 1: Scientific and Analytical Instruments 155

5.2.1 Summary Functional Analysis 156

5.2.2 Intra-Company Transfer Pricing Policy 157

5.2.3 Potential Issues 157

5.2.4 Adjustment Methodology under Section 936(h): Possessions Corporation (S_1) to U.S. Parent (P) 158

5.2.5 Adjustment Methodology under the 1968 Regulations: To and from the Scottish Subsidiary (S_2) 161

5.2.6 Possible Adjustment Methodology under Section 936(h) and the 1993 Temporary Regulations: Possessions Corporation (S_1) to U.S. Parent (P) 170

5.2.7 Possible Adjustment Methodology under the 1992 Proposed Regulations: From Scottish Subsidiary (S_2) to U.S. Parent (P) 171

5.2.8 Taxpayer's Position 173

5.2.9 Resolution 174

5.3 Cost-Sharing Case 2: Specialized Medical Equipment 175

5.3.1 Synopsis of Facts and Circumstances 176

5.3.2 Potential Issues 177

5.3.3 Intangibles Embodied in the Medical Equipment at Issue 178

5.3.4 Classification of Embodied Intangibles between Manufacturing and Marketing Types 183

5.3.5 Adjustment Methodology under the 1968 Regulations 188

5.3.6 Possible Adjustment Methodology under the 1993 Temporary and Proposed Regulations . . 189

5.3.7 Taxpayer's Position 190

5.3.8 Resolution 190

5.4 Cost-Sharing Case 3: Telecommunications Products 191

5.4.1 Summary Functional Analysis 191

5.4.2 Intra-Company Transfer Pricing Policy 192

5.4.3 Potential Issues 192

5.4.4 Adjustment Methodology under the 1968 and 1993 Temporary Regulations: the Capital Employed Approach 193

5.4.5 Taxpayer's Position 204

5.4.6 Resolution 204

5.5 Critique of Proposed Section 482 Cost-Sharing Provisions 206

6 Intra-Company Royalty Agreements **211**

6.1 Background 211

6.2 An Intra-Company Royalty Issue: Licensed Process Technology 214

6.2.1 Summary Functional Analysis 215

6.2.2 License Terms and Intra-Company Charges . . 215

6.2.3 Potential Issues 216

6.2.4 Adjustment Methodology under the 1968 Regulations 220

6.2.5 Possible Adjustment Methodology under the 1993 Temporary Regulations: The Comparable Profits Method 227

6.2.6 Comparison of Results under the 1968 Regulations and the 1993 Temporary Regulations 240

6.2.7 Critique of the Comparable Profits Method . . 241

7 Valuation of Intangible Assets: Section 338 245

7.1 Valuation of Patient Relationships 247

7.1.1 Introduction 247

7.1.2 Appraisal Firm's Methodology 249

7.1.3 Critique 250

7.1.4 Resolution 254

7.2 Valuation of Advertiser and Subscriber Lists 254

7.2.1 Introduction 254

7.2.2 Appraisal Firm's Methodology 255

7.2.3 Critique 257

7.2.4 Resolution 257

7.3 Valuation of Product Endorsements 258

7.3.1 Introduction 258

7.3.2 Appraisal Firm's Methodology 258

7.3.3 Critique 259

7.3.4 Primary and Alternative Positions 262

7.3.5 Resolution 262

8 Conclusions and Policy Recommendations 263

8.1 The 1993 Temporary Regulations: Two Steps Forward, One Step Back 265

8.1.1 The Cost-Plus Method 265

8.1.2 The Resale Price Method 267

8.1.3 Cost Sharing 269

8.1.4 Intra-Company Licenses of Proprietary Intangible Property 271

8.2 Proposed Revisions to the 1993 Temporary and Proposed Section 482 Regulations 272

8.3 Lessons from Section 338 276

8.4 Proposed Institutional Changes 279

Index 282

Preface

Transfer Pricing and Valuation in Corporate Taxation analyzes the disparities between both federal statutes and regulations, and regulations and administrative practice, in a highly controversial area of corporate tax policy: intra-company transfer pricing for tax purposes. It addresses issues that often mean millions of dollars to individual corporations, and a significant fraction of the federal government's revenue base.

These disparities between law, regulations, and administrative practice are concerning on a number of grounds. First, they impose considerable economic costs by inducing corporations to engage in a variety of "rent-seeking" activities designed to reduce their expected tax liabilities, and by requiring the IRS to devote still more to enforcement efforts that are very often futile. Second, they are inherently undemocratic. Administrative practice is currently *ad hoc*; by relying on dispute resolution procedures that can and do yield very different settlements on disputed tax issues from one case to another, the IRS often ends up treating similarly situated corporations very differently. Moreover, to the extent that the disparity between statute and implementation reflects the IRS's failure to carry out Congress' will, the laws passed by duly elected officials are effectively being superseded by administrative procedure, developed incrementally by individuals who are not answerable to an electorate.

Through a series of theoretical case studies that merge limited information from actual cases, I develop specific policy proposals designed to reduce this lacunae between tax law and administrative practice. While the analysis presupposes that existing legislation will remain in place, and, consequently, that regulations and practice should conform thereto, tax laws could as well be changed to conform to regulations or practice. In this spirit, I do not advocate higher or lower effective (or statutory) corporate tax rates *per se*. Nor do I address the normative questions of whether corporations should pay a profits tax at all, or whether a unitary system is preferable to the current separate entity approach to taxing multinational corporations. Rather, I assume that governments will continue to levy corporate profits taxes based on the separate accounting framework.

Tax practitioners who are understandably frustrated in their efforts to divine the IRS's reasoning in transfer pricing issues should find this book very helpful. In addition, it will be an important source of information for elected representatives, IRS and other public officials, and tax lobbyists in the process of evaluating existing corporate tax policy or formulating (or advocating) alternative tax policies, and a useful reference for academics studying international taxation, public finance, and treaty compliance.

I have worked in the field of international corporate taxation since 1986, first as an industry economist with the U.S. Internal Revenue Service, subsequently as a consulting economist with a large public accounting firm, and currently as an academic and independent consultant. I drafted the first version of this book in 1990. (The manuscript has since been completely rewritten to incorporate the 1993 temporary and proposed Section 482 regulations, and changes in penalty provisions, Section 936(h), and other relevant legislative initiatives incorporated into the Omnibus Budget Reconciliation Act of 1993.) It has taken over three years to persuade the IRS to clarify the conditions under which I would be permitted to publish this manuscript. In all likelihood, the IRS would never have responded without the concerted effort that Congressman Barney Frank (D-Mass.) made on my behalf, for which I will be eternally grateful.

I was extremely fortunate to have been able to confer with some of the most knowledgeable people in the transfer pricing field in the course of writing this book. Michael Picariello gave very generously of his time and his extensive knowledge of Sections 482 and 936(h). Kevin Fay shared his considerable insights into the workings of IRS management and the IRS Economist Program. Diane Kanakis, an expert in competent authority, was a very helpful resource. Joseph Boorstein served as an invaluable sounding board for my interpretations of the 1993 temporary transfer pricing regulations. I would also like to acknowledge with great warmth and respect my friends and former colleagues at the IRS, from whom I learned a great deal, including especially Ron Calitri, Don Coleman, Joe DeChristofaro, Wendy Jackson, Lee Keenan, Mike Lareau, Bob Majeau, Tom Mason, Denis McSweeney, Manny Melo, George Pallotta, Sam Sahagian, Frank Santos, Paul Blankfeld, Sandy Cohen, Barbara Gallagher, Marco Gonzales, Mar Haeussler, Ralph Harris, Siv Janger, Michael Poyntz, Milagro Richardson, Steve Steinberg, Mike Sweeney, Constance Tripp, Murray Tucker, Dave Wallenstein, Steve Zemsky, Seymour Zwick, and many others. And finally, I thank Gary for his insightful comments, unflagging support, and encouragement.

Part I

Legislation and Regulations

Chapter 1

Introduction

Intra-company pricing for tax purposes, the subject of this book, is governed by Section 482 of the Internal Revenue Code (IRC). Section 482 requires individual entities composing a "controlled group" (a multinational firm) to charge one another the same prices, fees, or royalty rates for goods, services, loans, and intangible property that they would charge unrelated parties. Multinational firms' intra-company pricing practices determine the allocation of their consolidated income across the separate taxing jurisdictions in which they operate and, hence, their worldwide effective tax rates.[1] Transfer pricing cases—in which the IRS and a given multinational firm with U.S. operations differ as to what constitutes an acceptable estimate of arm's length prices, fees, or royalty rates—are typically "large dollar" and highly contentious issues.

In this area of corporate taxation, statutory legislation and administrative practice diverge very substantially. Specifically, corporate tax liabilities under Section 482, as determined in practice by a combination of interpretive regulations, their application in specific instances, and dispute resolution procedures, are often less—and occasionally more—than the existing Section 482 statute mandates.

[1]Equivalently, the allocation of multinational firms' consolidated income determines individual taxing jurisdictions' revenue collections therefrom. Inasmuch as intra-company trade currently constitutes at least 40% of total international trade, multinational firms represent a significant portion of individual jurisdictions' potential corporate tax bases.

This disparity between legislation and implementation is explained by one of two possibilities:

- The Department of Treasury and the IRS are not effectively carrying out the will of Congress (and, by extension, the American people). The regulations that implement Section 482 legislation are highly (and, to some degree, unnecessarily) ambiguous, lending themselves to a wide variety of interpretations. One needs a certain level of expertise in economic and financial theory to apply these regulations effectively, and to rule out those interpretations that are incompatible with arm's length dictates. Unfortunately, the IRS does not always draw on such expertise to develop intra-company pricing issues, and rarely does so in resolving them, with the result that the range of potential interpretations is vastly wider, and the likelihood that a given application or resolution will be consistent with arm's length results commensurately smaller. Or,

- On balance, Congress intends that actual corporate tax liabilities under Section 482 fall short of those apparently mandated by statute (at least as regards U.S.-based multinationals), and ensures that this outcome is realized by providing the IRS ineffective enforcement tools and insufficient resources. Under this interpretation, the tax laws governing intra-company transfer pricing are merely for public consumption, designed to create the illusion that congressional representatives take a hard line with "big business."[2] Such behavior on the part of Congress may be motivated by a mix of political considerations, judgments as to the desirability of a corporate profits tax on economic grounds, or a perceived need to enhance the competitiveness of U.S. firms, individually or collectively. More pragmatically, it may simply represent the particular political compromise that Congress was able to craft in balancing the interests of individual members with regard to these issues.

What are the consequences of this disparity between Section 482 legislation and administrative practice? Certain possible conse-

[2]The rather striking difference in tools available for enforcing transfer pricing laws and regulations *vis-a-vis* domestic- and foreign-based multinational corporations, respectively, lends credence to this interpretation.

quences depend on the reasons for the disparity in the first instance. If the Treasury Department and the IRS are at fault for failing to carry out legislators' collective will, then administrative practice has largely superseded the relevant tax laws of the land. In a democracy, the elevation of administrative procedure over statutory legislation is intrinsically disturbing. Alternatively, if Congress is collectively content with the status quo, and intends that U.S.-based multinational firms' actual tax liabilities (under Section 482) fall short of those apparently mandated by statute, then the government's attempts to enforce existing laws and regulations—very often with minimal success—amount to a very costly form of window-dressing. As such, the considerable resources expended in this way could be put to more productive uses.

Additionally, the disparity between existing tax legislation and implementation entails certain costs, both in an economic sense and in terms of tax equity, that are entirely independent of the reasons for it. First, the IRS does not always treat similarly situated corporations uniformly (a problem that could in principle be diminished by more effective institutional coordination among technical specialists charged with enforcing Section 482—international examiners, IRS economists, attorneys, and Appeals officers[3]). Similar pricing cases may be developed along very different lines (some or all of which may bear little resemblance to arm's length results), and resolved through one-on-one negotiations that lead to highly idiosyncratic settlements. Second, to the extent that multinational firms stand to gain, in the form of reduced expected tax burdens, by "gaming the system," they will invest some portion (and potentially all) of the expected reductions in their tax liabilities in order to realize the remaining gains, a costly and unproductive use of limited resources.[4] Third, ineffective enforcement of the arm's length principle may cre-

---

[3]To date, IRS attorneys and, as of quite recently, international examiners, have somewhat more effective institutional channels for coordinating their positions on common issues than either IRS economists or Appeals officers.

[4]As the case studies in Part II will demonstrate, it may well have been *more* costly to comply with tax laws than to circumvent them until recently, both from the standpoint of up-front compliance costs and ultimate tax liabilities. However, this may change with regard to certain types of transfer pricing issues under the 1993 temporary regulations, and if the proposed penalty provisions are applied vigorously.

ate (or reinforce) incentives to integrate vertically and locate discrete activities in different (national) taxing jurisdictions, which may not be "welfare improving" from a societal standpoint.

Inasmuch as disparities between the Section 482 statute and administrative practice imposes substantial costs, the obvious solution is to eliminate it. This can be done in one of two ways:

- The interpretive regulations drafted by the Treasury Department and the IRS, and the latter's administrative dispute resolution procedures, can be modified to produce results that are more in line with those mandated by statute; or,

- Congress can rewrite the laws themselves, such that they produce results consistent with those one observes in actuality. (This revision would probably take the form of fairly crude profit split rules that could be applied unambiguously.[5])

In a procedural sense, the proper choice between these two courses of action ultimately depends on legislators' true intent. (That is, if Congress intends that U.S. multinational firms' actual corporate tax liabilities under Section 482 fall short of the amounts implied by the current statute, and brings this result about by providing the IRS with ineffective enforcement tools and insufficient resources, then the statute should be changed to accord with actual practice, and conversely.) However, as regards international tax laws in general, and Section 482 in particular, Congress is constrained by numerous bilateral tax treaties. The arm's length standard is clearly the dominant international norm, long championed by the United States. As such, Congress is unlikely to abandon it unilaterally at this stage (although such a development is not inconceivable). Hence, for purposes of discussion throughout this book, I take the current Section 482 statute as "fixed," and suggest how the IRS's interpretive regulations and

[5]While this approach would likely produce more consistent results across cases and reduce or eliminate rent-seeking behavior, it would not necessarily eliminate incentives to integrate vertically and diversify geographically. If vertically integrated (and geographically diversified) firms' tax burdens are consistently lower than their stand-alone counterparts' combined tax burdens—whether by virtue of more advantageous tax laws or ineffective enforcement of the arm's length standard—there will be tax benefits to integrating vertically, all other things equal.

administrative practices could be modified to bring the results that they produce more in line with arm's length results.

This book is organized into two parts:

- Part I contains an overview of IRC Section 482 and recent legislative, regulatory, and procedural initiatives and proposals. Because the valuation of intangible assets may figure increasingly prominently in intra-company pricing under the 1993 temporary and proposed regulations, Part I also reviews the (evolving) statutes and regulations governing such issues in connection with acquisitions of ongoing businesses.
- Part II consists of seven detailed transfer pricing case studies and three valuation case studies, and a concluding chapter that pulls together the separate critiques of specific pricing and valuation methodologies developed in these case studies. All of the case studies are composites, developed by merging limited information from actual cases and fleshing out this basic framework with additional fictional details. None deal with the affairs of any particular taxpayer. Likewise, the discussions of taxpayers' counter-arguments against proposed adjustments to their taxable income and the terms on which individual cases were resolved, while broadly realistic, are hypothetical. (As such, the case resolutions have no precedential value.)

The composite transfer pricing case studies reviewed in Part II represent a broad range of pricing issues. Each composite case is analyzed under two sets of Section 482 regulations: the 1968 regulations (in effect from 1968 to early 1993), and the 1993 temporary and proposed regulations (issued on January 21, 1993 and effective as of April 21, 1993 for a maximum of three years). This comparative approach will enable corporations long familiar with the 1968 regulations to gauge whether and how a given transfer pricing issue will be analyzed differently under the new 1993 temporary and proposed regulations. It will also demonstrate that the latter are probably as open to interpretation as the 1968 regulations on a number of important points. Hence, the divergence between statutory legislation and administrative practice will likely persist, and with it, the uneven tax treatment of similarly situated firms and the attendant economic costs described above.

As noted above, and as the composite transfer pricing case studies will demonstrate, the relative (or absolute) values of intangible assets that related parties own can play an important role in determining the allocation of consolidated income between them under the 1993 temporary and proposed Section 482 regulations. Somewhat similar intangibles valuation issues often arose (in connection with acquisitions of ongoing businesses) under Section 338 (before Congress added Section 197 to the Code with the Omnibus Budget Reconciliation Act of 1993). The composite valuation cases presented in Part II review the methodologies that tax practitioners traditionally used to value acquired intangible assets, the issues that the IRS raised in connection with these valuations, and, in very general terms, the ways in which such issues were resolved. (Again, these resolutions, while eminently plausible, are hypothetical.)

Chapter 2

Transfer Pricing and Valuation Regulations

In this chapter, I provide a brief history and overview of the statutes and regulations governing intra-company pricing (Sections 482 and 936(h)) and the valuation of acquired tangible and intangible assets (Section 338) for tax purposes. While there are numerous IRC sections, Sections 482 and, to a lesser extent, 936(h), are distinct in that they draw heavily on economic analysis and interpretation. Likewise, applications of Section 338 traditionally drew on broad economic and financial valuation principles, but will presumably do so to a lesser extent in the future, as a result of the new IRC Section 197 contained in the Omnibus Budget Reconciliation Act of 1993, as described below. Nonetheless, the history of Section 338 legislation, regulations, and issues remains of interest (in connection with intra-company pricing), in that the valuation of intangible assets will likely become increasingly important under the new Section 482 regulations.[1]

Readers familiar with these code sections and their evolving legislative and regulatory history may skip this chapter without loss of continuity.

---

[1]It is somewhat ironic that Section 482 regulations are moving in this direction just as Congress is attempting to simplify the law regarding the amortization of acquired intangibles.

2.1 Transfer Pricing Regulations: Internal Revenue Code Section 482

Section 482 of the IRC sets out guidelines that multinational firms and IRS technical specialists (principally economists and international examiners) are to follow in establishing and assessing intra-company transfer prices charged for tangible and intangible property exchanged, services provided, and loans extended among related parties, or members of a "controlled group." The way in which these guidelines are implemented determines how a multinational firm's consolidated income is apportioned among the countries in which it operates. In essence, Section 482 requires intra-company transfer prices to conform to those that would be charged if all parties to the intra-company transaction(s) at issue were unrelated. That is, extant guidelines are based on the *arm's length standard.*

Section 482 is intended to prevent multinational firms from artificially reducing their tax burdens by applying non-arm's length transfer prices to intra-company transactions, and lodging a disproportionate share of their consolidated income in low-tax countries. EC countries and Japan endorse similar legislation.[2] If applied consistently across countries, the arm's length standard should also prevent double taxation, and minimize tax-related distortions in foreign direct investment and intra-company trade thereby. At present, however, each separate taxing jurisdiction determines how the consolidated income earned by multinational firms operating in its borders should be allocated across jurisdictions (with particular emphasis on the share that should be reported in its own jurisdiction) essentially independently.[3] When these separate allocations differ across jurisdictions, either because the different taxing authorities apply a standard other than the arm's length principle in practice, or because they interpret and implement the arm's length standard differently under a given set of circumstances, multinational firms may

[2]See Lawlor, W.R., ed., *Cross-Border Transactions between Related Companies: A Summary of Tax Rules* (Deventer, The Netherlands: Kluwer, 1985).

[3]That is, there are very few simultaneous audits and relatively limited exchanges of information between taxing jurisdictions. Note that the Advance Pricing Agreement Program, described subsequently, is an exception to this general rule.

be double-taxed on that portion of their income that is allocated to more than one taxing jurisdiction.

The past seven years have witnessed very significant changes in the U.S. regulations governing intra-company pricing for tax purposes. At present, a set of temporary Section 482 regulations are in effect, having superseded another set of regulations, the "1968 regulations" that were in effect until April 21, 1993. The ongoing process of reformulating transfer pricing regulations began with an important legislative change in 1986, followed by a lengthy discussion draft (the "White Paper") comprised of proposed changes to the then-extant 1968 regulations, which was released jointly by the Treasury Department and Internal Revenue Service on October 18, 1988, again by a separate (and quite different) set of proposed transfer pricing regulations released on January 24, 1992, and, finally, by the temporary regulations released on January 21, 1993 and currently in effect.

Inasmuch as the (interim) end result, the temporary regulations, represents an amalgam of the various draft and proposed iterations that preceded it, and because part of my object in the subsequent case studies is to compare outcomes under the 1968 and temporary regulations, this chapter contains a brief history of these successive initiatives. Additionally, I briefly review the IRS's enforcement experience under the 1968 regulations, the institutional setting in which transfer pricing issues are resolved, and recent legislative and procedural developments that apply particularly to U.S. subsidiaries of foreign corporations.

2.1.1 The 1968 Regulations

The commissioner of the IRS has had the authority to reallocate income and expenses among related parties for over seventy years. However, it wasn't until the late 1950s and early 1960s, following the post-war period of reconstruction, that U.S. multinationals began to establish subsidiaries in low-tax countries on a significant scale and the U.S. Administration came to believe that these firms were manipulating transfer prices in large numbers, with a view to minimizing their U.S. tax burdens.[4] Congress and the Treasury Department, too, became increasingly concerned that U.S. multinationals were shifting large amounts of income "offshore" via transfer pricing manipulations.[5]

Hence, in 1961–62, Congress considered several specific amendments to Section 482 that would have increased the IRS's power in this area.[6] Interestingly, the formulary apportionment approach, whereby one allocates consolidated income to individual jurisdictions on the basis of a weighted factor formula intended to capture the related parties' relative contributions to profits, was one of the amendments considered.[7] Under this proposal, the formula to be applied was comprised of each entity's share of assets (excluding inventory), compensation of employees, and selling expenses. Ultimately, Congress concluded that the existing Statute provided the IRS with sufficient tools to police transfer pricing practices and minimize abuses. However, it directed the Treasury Department to develop more comprehensive regulations, or interpretive guidelines, to assist the IRS in implementing its broad statutory directives.[8,9]

---

[4] Federal Tax System–Message from the President of the United States, 107 Cong. Rec., 6456 (1961).

[5] *Hearings on the President's 1961 Tax Recommendations Before the Committee on Ways and Means*, 87th Cong., 1st Sess., Vol. 4, at 3549 (1961) (statement of M. Caplin, Commissioner of Internal Revenue, "Problems in the Administration of the Revenue Laws Relating to the Taxation of Foreign Income."

[6] Between 1943 and 1986, IRC Section 482 read as follows: "In any case of two or more organizations, trades or businesses (whether or not incorporated, whether or not organized in the United States, and whether or not affiliated) owned or controlled directly or indirectly by the same interests, the Secretary may distribute, apportion, or allocate gross income, deductions, credits, or allowances between or among such organizations, trades, or businesses, if he determines that such distribution, apportionment, or allocation is necessary in order to prevent evasion of taxes or clearly to reflect the income of any of such organizations, trades or businesses." Note that the Statute does not specify how the Secretary is to go about making this distribution, apportionment, or allocation.

[7] A number of states, lacking either confidence in, or the administrative and technical wherewithal necessary to apply, the separate accounting methodology and arm's length principle, currently utilize a formulary apportionment method to determine taxable income within their jurisdicitons. See Multistate Tax Compact, *All State Tax Guide* (P-H) 6310.

[8] Conf. Rep. No. 2508, 87th Cong., 2nd Sess., p. 19 (1962), reprinted in 1962–3 C.B. 1129, 1146.

[9] Note that regulations interpreting Section 45 of the 1928 Act, a forerunner

The Treasury Department's task was to develop a set of methodologies that both companies and IRS agents in the field—the former in a planning mode, the latter in an auditing capacity—could use to establish and evaluate arm's length prices.[10] The focus, at this point, was on U.S. multinationals' intra-company transactions in tangible property, loans, and services. Intangibles transfers within controlled groups and "inbound" cases involving foreign parent companies with U.S. subsidiaries were less common during this period.[11] The Treasury Department issued proposed regulations in 1965, and final regulations (the "1968 regulations") in 1968 and 1969. These regulations, described below, governed transfer pricing controversies, for better or worse, until the Tax Reform Act of 1986 introduced an important statutory change to Section 482, necessitating accompanying changes in the interpretive regulations.

Tangible Property Provisions

Under the 1968 regulations, arm's length prices for tangible property were to be determined under one of three methods, to be applied in the order of priority shown below:[12]

1. The Comparable Uncontrolled Price (CUP) Method;
2. The Resale Price Method; and,
3. The Cost-Plus Method.

The first of these methods, the comparable uncontrolled price or CUP method, looked to transactions between unrelated parties that involved tangible property very similar to that sold between the related parties at issue, and that took place under substantially similar terms and conditions. The genuinely arm's length prices charged in

of Section 482, had been issued in 1934. These regulations were "substantially identical to... Regs. 1.482-1(a), (b) and (c)" of the 1968 regulations issued subsequently. See McCawley, Harrison B., *Section 482: The Statute and the Regulations*, Tax Management, 115-3rd, 11/24/86.

[10]Stanley Surrey, Assistant Secretary of the Treasury for Tax Policy during this time and a pioneer in the field, spearheaded this effort.

[11]McLennan, B.N., "Responses to Section 482 Litigation: Advance Pricing Agreements or Arbitration?" 54 *Tax Notes* 4 (Jan. 27, 1992), p. 433.

[12]IRC Section 1.482-2(e)(2)(4).

these uncontrolled transactions were to be applied directly to the intra-company transactions in question. The CUP method took precedence over all other methods under the 1968 regulations.

The CUP method was clearly a reasonable procedure to use in determining arm's length transfer prices, if one was fortunate enough to find sufficiently comparable uncontrolled transactions. However, the standards to be applied—in terms of similarity of property and terms and conditions of the transaction—were not always clear under the 1968 regulations. Did the fact that a prospective CUP took place between unrelated parties as a one-time event, while the related party transactions were ongoing, indicate that adjustments to the CUP were necessary, or that the uncontrolled transaction was simply not sufficiently comparable? If the uncontrolled transactions involved much higher volumes than the controlled transaction, were adjustments for volume discounts indicated?[13] Such fine-tuning might sound like a relatively simple matter, but quantifying differences of these sorts with a reasonable degree of precision was often quite difficult, and, in the view of many, unduly burdensome to firms that had no need to make these calculations in the normal course of their business.[14] Further, whether and how these differences were quantified could translate into substantial differences in tax liabilities.

One turned to the resale price method[15] (assigned second priority under the 1968 regulations) to establish arm's length prices on intra-company sales of tangible property when sufficiently comparable uncontrolled transactions could not be found. The resale price method looked to comparable stand-alone *firms*, rather than *transactions*. Firm comparability was generally evaluated along three dimensions: functions performed by the controlled and uncontrolled parties, respectively; risks assumed by each; and intangible assets owned or licensed by each. The resale price method would typically be applied when one of the related parties functioned as a distributor, purchasing products from a related supplier for resale to third par-

[13]These are the sorts of issues raised in *U.S. Steel Corporation v. Commissioner*, 80-1 USTC P9307 (rev'g); 36 TCM 586.

[14]See, for example, Wickham, D.W., "The New U.S. Transfer Pricing Tax Penalty: A Solution, or a Symptom of the Cause, of the International Transfer Pricing Puzzle," 18 *International Tax Journal* 1 (Winter 1991).

[15]IRC Section 1.482-2(e)(2)(4).

ties. Under this method, the related distributor's transfer price was set such that it earned the same gross margin as uncontrolled distributors performing comparable functions, assuming similar risks, and, where relevant, contributing similarly valued intangible property. In recent years, the resale price method has been applied widely in inbound cases involving a foreign parent firm and a U.S. subsidiary, the latter purchasing products from its parent for resale in the U.S. market.[16]

Disputes over particular applications of the resale price method tended to revolve around issues of comparability under the 1968 regulations, both at the IRS Examination level and in litigated cases. More particularly, firms and the IRS often crossed swords as to whether prospective comparable uncontrolled firms were sufficiently similar to the related party at issue in terms of the below-the-line functions they performed and the extent of inventory risk they assumed. For example, the stand-alone distributor might provide more or less after-sales support; it might have greater or lesser responsibility for advertising in its local market, and so forth. With regard to inventory risks, stand-alone firms might receive price protection from their suppliers (in the form of retroactive price reductions on products held in inventory for a specified period of time in the event that their suppliers reduced product prices); unrelated distributors might enjoy generous return privileges, while the controlled distributor might not; and so forth. The salience of these differences and the quantification of their effects on arm's length returns were common points of contention between multinational firms and the IRS under the 1968 regulations.

If neither the comparable uncontrolled price nor the resale price method could be applied in a given instance, one would look to the cost-plus method to determine arm's length prices for tangible property under the 1968 regulations. This method was generally apropos

[16]General Accounting Office, Report to the Chairman, Committee on Ways and Means, *IRS Audit Coverage: Selection Procedures Same for Foreign and other U.S. Corporations* (1986). Also see Department of Treasury (Office of International Tax Counsel; Office of Tax Analysis) and Internal Revenue Service (Office of Assistant Commissioner-International; Office of Associate Chief Counsel-International), *A Study of Intercompany Pricing*, Discussion Draft, October 18, 1988 [hereinafter, the White Paper].

when one of the related parties at issue performed relatively simple manufacturing functions, and sold intermediate or finished products to other members of the same controlled group. It entailed applying comparable uncontrolled companies' markups over costs (gross profits divided by cost of goods sold) to the related manufacturing entity's cost base to determine arm's length incomes and, implicitly, arm's length selling prices.

Disputes over particular applications of the cost-plus method under the 1968 regulations also revolved around comparability issues, particularly the degree of risk assumed by controlled and stand-alone firms, respectively. The IRS frequently contended that the stand-alone companies which U.S. multinationals held up as comparable to their foreign manufacturing subsidiaries actually incurred far greater risks. Many (albeit not all) manufacturing subsidiaries examined sold most of their output—often an intermediate product—to their respective parents. If the latter routinely purchased all of their subsidiaries' output, regardless of the level of demand for their own final products, the subsidiaries' market risks were significantly diminished thereby, if not eliminated outright. An uncontrolled manufacturing operation, in contrast, typically produces a certain output based on projected demand, and sells only as much as its customers ultimately require.[17]

Finally, if none of the approved methods—CUP, resale price, and cost-plus—could be used to establish arm's length prices for tangible property, then one had recourse to a "fourth method" under the 1968 regulations.[18] In effect, this was a catch-all that allowed firms and the IRS to use any reasonable and defensible approach to setting arm's length prices.

Intangible Property Provisions

As with intra-company sales of tangible property, controlled transfers of intangible property—the license or sale of intangible assets to

[17]This issue of risk has figured prominently in a number of decided cases as well, notably *Bausch & Lomb, Inc. and Consolidated Subsidiaries v. Commissioner.*, 92 T.C. 525 (off'd 2nd Cir. May 14, 1991 D. No.89-415).

[18]IRC Section 1.482-2(e)(1)(iii).

a related party—were ideally to be priced by reference to comparable uncontrolled transactions. However, because comparable uncontrolled transactions in intangible property are exceedingly difficult to come by (in part because intangible property is unique to some degree virtually by definition and in part because controlled and uncontrolled intangibles licenses tend to differ systematically in several important respects),[19] the 1968 regulations included a list of twelve factors that one was to consider in establishing arm's length royalty rates:[20]

- Prevailing royalty rates in the same industry for similar property;
- Offers by competing transferors and bids by competing transferees;
- Terms of the transfer;
- Uniqueness of the property and the period during which the property is likely to remain unique;
- Degree and duration of protection of the property in the relevant countries;
- Value of services rendered by the transferor to the transferee;
- Prospective profits to be realized, or costs to be saved, through use or subsequent transfer of the property;
- Capital investment and start-up expenses required of the transferee;
- Availability of substitutes;
- Arm's length rates and prices paid by unrelated parties;
- Costs incurred by the transferor in developing the property; and,

[19] In fact, some economists argue that imperfections in the market for intangible property are the *raison d' être* for multinational firms. See, for example, Caves, Richard E., *Multinational Enterprise and Economic Analysis*, Cambridge Surveys of Economic Literature (Cambridge, U.K.: Cambridge University Press, 1982.)

[20] IRC Section 1.482-2(d)(2)(ii).

- Any other facts or circumstances that unrelated parties would have been likely to consider.

Clearly, some of these factors should play a role in establishing arm's length compensation for intangible property. However, the application of two different factors often yielded two distinct estimated arm's length royalty rates. Because the 1968 regulations did not prioritize among factors, they provided no basis for resolving disputes that arose when a firm established (or defended) its pricing of intangible property by reference to one factor, and the IRS assessed (and challenged) this pricing by reference to another—a very common state of affairs. Further, the data necessary to apply any one, much less all twelve, of these factors were often unavailable.

Cost-Sharing Provisions

The 1968 regulations sanctioned cost-sharing agreements among members of a controlled group.[21] Cost-sharing, an alternative to intracompany licensing, is another means of diffusing intangible property within a controlled group. Under a cost-sharing arrangement, participants share R&D expenses incurred in the course of developing the intangibles at issue, and are deemed to have joint ownership rights therein. Hence, an entity's cost-sharing contribution is in lieu of a royalty payment. Under the 1968 regulations, each participant's contribution was required to be proportionate, by some measure, to its anticipated benefits.

It often happened that individual group members participating in a cost-sharing agreement also manufactured (intermediate or final) products incorporating the jointly developed intangibles, and sold these products to other related entities within the controlled group. Under these circumstances, it became exceedingly difficult to determine arm's length transfer prices for property embodying the intangibles under the 1968 regulations. As discussed above, one would normally use the cost-plus method to establish arm's length prices for tangible property under these circumstances, absent cost-sharing. However, if the manufacturing affiliate(s) at issue partici-

[21] IRC Section 1.482-2(d)(4).

pated in a bona fide cost-sharing agreement, it was deemed to own potentially valuable intangible property and, as such, was entitled to a return thereon (in addition to a normal, risk-adjusted return on its investment in tangible assets). In principle, the combined arm's length return (on tangible and intangible assets) could be determined by reference to comparable uncontrolled transactions that involved similar property (that is, comparable tangible property that also embodied comparable intangible property), or comparable uncontrolled firms that performed similar manufacturing or assembly functions and had rights to intangible assets of comparable value. However, comparable uncontrolled transactions were exceedingly uncommon, and comparable hybrid firms, performing relatively routine manufacturing functions while claiming ownership rights in highly sophisticated, state-of-the-art intangible property, likewise rarely existed among the population of uncontrolled firms.

Services Provisions

To date, the 1968 regulations' services provisions have not been revised. Under some circumstances, extant services regulations provide for safe harbors, or deemed arm's length charges, when one entity performs services intended to benefit another member (or members) of the controlled group.[22] Specifically, where such services are not an integral part of either the renderer's or the recipient's business, the deemed arm's length charge is given by the costs (both direct and indirect) of rendering the services. If services are an integral part of either the renderer's or the recipient's business, the charge must include an arm's length markup over these costs.[23]

The services provisions set out fairly detailed tests to determine whether the integral business standard is met. Specifically, the safe harbor rules do not apply if:

- Either renderer or recipient is engaged in the trade or business of rendering similar services to unrelated parties;

[22]It should be noted that the benefit need not be realized to trigger a services allocation. See IRC Section 1.482-2(b).

[23]IRC Section 1.482-2(b)(1).

- The renderer performs similar services on behalf of one or more members of the controlled group as one of its principal activities;
- The renderer is peculiarly capable of performing the services, and the services are a principal element of the operations of the recipient; and,
- The recipient has received the benefit of a substantial amount of similar services from one or more members of the controlled group during the taxable year.

Note that services which benefit the recipient only indirectly and remotely will not give rise to an allocation under the services provisions.[24] Likewise, services that are duplicative (in that the recipient performs the same services) will not prompt a services allocation.[25] Stewardship (or supervisory) activities are deemed to benefit the parent firm cum investor in its subsidiaries; hence, it should properly incur these expenses.[26] Finally, services that are ancillary and subsidiary to the transfer of intangible property are to be dealt with under the intangibles provisions.

Loans Provisions

As with services provisions, the 1968 regulations' loans provisions have not been revised to date. Here, too, firms have recourse to a safe harbor in determining arm's length rates on intra-company loans under some circumstances.[27] This safe harbor takes the form of a range of deemed arm's length interest rates, with the lower bound equal to 100% of the "applicable Federal rate," or AFR, and the upper bound, 130% of the AFR.[28] The AFR is based on the average yield of actively traded U.S. Government securities in three maturity groups: short-term (three years or less), mid-term (between three

[24]IRC Section 1.482-2(b)(2)(i).

[25]IRC Section 1.482-2(b)(2)(ii).

[26]See *Columbian Rope Co. v. Commissioner*, 42 T.C. 800 (1964), acq. 1965 -1 C.B. 4, and *Young and Rubicam, Inc. v. United States*, 549 F.2nd 740 (Ct. Cl. 1977).

[27]IRC Section 1.482-2(a).

[28]IRC Section 1.482-2(a)(2)(iii).

and nine years) and long-term (more than nine years).[29] Firms can also defend a rate outside this range if they can demonstrate that the higher or lower rate is an actual arm's length amount.

The safe harbor applies only if the creditor entity is not in the trade or business of making loans or advances. If it is, it must charge a "true" arm's length rate.[30] In this event, all relevant factors are to be considered, including the amount and duration of the loan, the borrower's creditworthiness, the riskiness of the particular project to which the loan or advance will be applied, etc. Additionally, the safe harbor rules do not apply to loans or advances, the principal or interest of which is expressed in a foreign currency.[31]

Enforcement and Compliance

From the outset, the 1968 regulations proved very difficult to apply, principally because closely comparable uncontrolled transactions or firms were generally extremely hard to come by. Absent close comparables (or pricing methods that did not require finding comparable transactions or firms), both firms and the IRS necessarily resorted to inexact comparables. Hence, questions regarding the requisite degree, or standard, of comparability to be satisfied, and the desirability and feasibility of quantifying the effects of economically significant differences between comparables and related parties, almost invariably arose. This was true even in the seemingly straightforward cases involving only tangible property. However, the difficulties greatly were compounded when intangible property was transferred as well. Not only was it far more difficult to find defensible comparables, but the differences between them and the controlled transactions or firms at issue also tended to be both more substantial and intrinsically less quantifiable. Nor did the broad twelve-factor approach help matters much. As noted, the lack of prioritizing among them, and the dearth of data necessary to apply them, were fairly fatal flaws. This became increasingly evident as outbound intra-company transfers of

[29]IRC Sections 1274(d) and 1.482-2(a)(2)(iii).
[30]IRC Section 1.482-2(a)(2)(i).
[31]IRC Section 1.482-2(a)(2)(iii)(e).

intangible property (and, hence, Section 482 royalty issues) became increasingly common during the 1970s and 1980s.

At the same time, IRS representatives' access to company information and documentation was extremely restricted. Numerous companies were failing to comply with information document requests (IDRs), and benefiting thereby as a result of pressures on IRS agents to close out large cases on a timely basis. If firms were not sufficiently forthcoming with information in the limited time that IRS economists and international examiners had to put their cases together, Section 482 issues could not be developed adequately. If poorly developed adjustments were proposed, they would often be dropped posthaste at the Appeals level.

This problem of access to information was particularly acute vis-a-vis inbound transfer pricing issues (albeit by no means limited to them), because the foreign parents in these cases often maintained much of the documentation necessary to evaluate transfer pricing practices abroad. Thus, the IRS's ability to obtain the requisite company information via summons raised difficult jurisdictional issues.[32] As foreign direct investment in the United States increased dramatically throughout the 1980s, the volume of inbound cases rose sharply as well, and the attendent problem of obtaining company records maintained abroad became progressively more constraining.

In short, Section 482 was becoming exceedingly difficult to administer effectively at the Examination level. On the outbound side, the pervasive ambiguity in regulations governing controlled intangibles transfers and the lack of satisfactory comparables data enabled manufacturing affiliates operating in relatively low-tax countries to license intangible property from related developers (often their U.S.-based parent company), pay fairly minimal royalty rates therefor based loosely on "industry norms,"[33] and retain a very substantial share of the total income attributable to the licensed intangible. With one method of establishing arm's length royalty rates as good as another under the amorphous twelve-factor approach, the IRS had little basis for challenging the industry norm thesis effec-

[32]See *U.S. v. Toyota Motor Corp.*, 83-1 USTC 9302 (C.D. Cal. 1983.)

[33]Generally speaking, these norms reflect average rates for significantly less valuable intangible property.

tively at the Examination or Appeals level. On the inbound side, some foreign-based multinationals were very successfully exploiting the jurisdictional issues and logistical complexities that restricted IRS agents' access to confidential company information and documentation. Without such access, defensible transfer pricing cases simply could not be developed.

Nor was the IRS faring any better in the courts vis-a-vis litigated Section 482 cases. Its victories in this forum over the past decade have been very few and far between, and its setbacks increasingly numerous.[34] Here, too, intangibles transfers were often to blame. In a number of the cases it lost, the IRS argued (implicitly or explicitly) that the intra-company intangibles transfers at issue (generally from U.S. parent to foreign manufacturing affiliate) should not be recognized, in that unrelated parties would not enter into analogous agreements, and developed proposed adjustments along cost-plus lines (that is, by marking up the intangibles transferee's production costs by a proportionate amount determined by reference to functionally comparable uncontrolled firms that owned no intangibles and incurred very limited risks). The courts, unconvinced by the IRS's position and equally at sea with regard to the regulations, tended to make very extensive use of fourth methods (particularly profit splits) to resolve these cases.

Another common source of contention in litigated Section 482 cases involving intangibles transfers concerned the information that one should take into account in establishing arm's length compensation for the intangible assets transferred. The courts have tended to take the position that only information available at the time of the initial transfer—often as evidenced by firms' sales and profits projections—should be used to determine arm's length consideration to be paid by the transferee over the life of the agreement.[35] In

[34]See, for example, *Eli Lilly & Co. v. Commissioner*, 84 T.C. 996 (1985), *rev'd in part, aff'd in part and remanded*, Nos. 86-2911 and 86-3116 (7th Cir. August 31, 1988; *G.D. Searle and Co. v. Commissioner*, 88 T.C. 252, 376 (1987); *Bausch & Lomb, Inc. and Consolidated Subsidiaries v. Commissioner*, 92 T.C. 525 (off'd 2nd Cir. May 14, 1991 D. No. 89-4156); *Sundstrand v. Commissioner*, 96 T.C. 226 (1991); and, *Westreco, Inc. v. Commissioner*, No. 24078-88, T.C. Memor. 1992-561, 9/23/92, for example.

[35]See, for example, *Bausch & Lomb, Supra*, and *The R.T. French Company v. Commissioner*, 60 T.C. 836 (1973).

contrast, the IRS has sometimes taken the view that companies are able to predict the success of new products embodying the licensed intangibles (or the cost savings attributable thereto) more accurately than their projections might suggest, that projections can easily be manipulated to justify a desired intra-company royalty cross-charge, and that actual rather than projected results should therefore determine compensation on an ongoing basis. This position is also motivated by the fact that intra-company licenses often have much longer terms than license agreements between uncontrolled firms, without the escape or renegotiation clauses incorporated into the latter. As such, unanticipated changes in circumstances, which might prompt unrelated parties to renegotiate the terms of their (genuinely arm's length) license agreement, would have no effect on intra-company license terms based on projected, rather than actual, results.

2.1.2 The Tax Reform Act of 1986

Recognizing the difficulties that the IRS was encountering in its efforts to administer and enforce Section 482, the limited guidance provided (and problematic precedents established) by the courts, particularly with regard to the pricing of intangible assets, and the substantial sums of potentially taxable income being shifted offshore as a result, Congress amended Section 482 in 1986. Specifically, with the Tax Reform Act of 1986 (1986 Act), the following sentence was added to the Statute:

> In the case of any transfer (or license) of intangible property (within the meaning of section 936(h)(3)(B)), the income [paid to the related transferor] with respect to such transfer or license shall be commensurate with the income attributable to the intangible.

The Conference Committee Report accompanying the 1986 Act also introduced the concept of "periodic adjustments" in the consideration paid for transferred intangibles, whereby adjustments in the intracompany royalty charge may be warranted if the income attributable to the intangibles changes significantly after the initial transfer, due to events that were not foreseen at the time of the transfer. (It should be noted, however, that this clause did not find its way into the 1986 statutory change in Section 482.)

Additionally, the Committee Report directed the Treasury Department and the IRS to undertake a comprehensive study of extant intra-company pricing rules, with a view to implementing the *commensurate with income* requirement and modifying existing rules where otherwise necessary. In this connection, Congress provided a number of specific guidelines, among them:

- In determining the transfer prices of valuable intangible assets, primary weight should be given to the amount of income derived from the transferred intangible;
- The resultant allocation of income between licensor and related licensee should reflect each entity's relative economic contributions and the degree of risk it assumes;
- Substantial changes in the income stream attributable to the subject intangible should prompt corresponding changes in the associated transfer payments, even if the increase in income was not anticipated at the time of the transfer;[36] and,
- Bona fide cost-sharing agreements between related parties will continue to be permitted, albeit the agreement must be in writing and the participants must make a good faith effort to divvy up the costs of research and development in accordance with each party's relative benefits.[37]

The Treasury Department, with the cooperation and assistance of the IRS, has made several attempts to develop interpretive guidelines implementing this statutory change, one in the form of a discussion paper issued on October 18, 1988 (the aforementioned White Paper), the second incorporated into a set of proposed regulations released

[36]The authors of the White Paper attempted to reconcile the proposed periodic adjustments in transfer payments with the arm's length standard by suggesting that "...contractual arrangements between unrelated parties—particularly those involving high profit intangibles—are not entered into on a long term basis without some mechanism [formal or otherwise] for adjusting the arrangement if the profitability of the intangible is significantly higher or lower than anticipated." The White Paper, *Op. Cit.*, p. 63.

[37]Congress also proposed that these benefits be measured by profits, although the White Paper retreated from this position somewhat.

on January 24, 1992, and the third incorporated into the now-extant 1993 temporary regulations. These initiatives all contain specific adjustment methodologies to be applied when intangible property is transferred within a controlled group. All of them incorporate the periodic adjustment requirement discussed in the Committee Report to the 1986 Act (but ultimately omitted from the statutory changes). In addition, both the White Paper and the 1992 proposed regulations provide for changes to cost-sharing provisions, and the 1992 proposed regulations and the 1993 temporary regulations modify the rules applying to intra-company exchanges of tangible property as well. Finally, a separate set of proposed regulations released concurrently with the 1993 temporary regulations contains three profit split methodologies, to be applied only when both related parties to the controlled transactions at issue own "non-routine" intangibles that they either developed themselves (individually or in the context of a cost-sharing agreement) or acquired from third parties.

In the next three subsections, the White Paper, the 1992 proposed regulations, and the 1993 temporary regulations, respectively, are described.

2.1.3 The White Paper

A Study of Intercompany Pricing (the White Paper), drafted jointly by the IRS and the Treasury Department, represented a first attempt to flesh out the meaning of the "commensurate with income" terminology incorporated into the Statute with the 1986 Act. Additionally, the authors of the White Paper refined the concept of comparability as it applied to intangible property, proposed alternative intangibles pricing methods when very close comparable uncontrolled transactions could not be found, and modified the 1968 regulations' cost-sharing provisions.

General Comparability Standards

With respect to comparability, the authors of the White Paper proposed classifying prospective comparable uncontrolled transactions (in intangible property) into "exact" and "inexact" categories by reference to sets of "external" and "internal" standards. External standards consisted of those parameters that defined the economic environment in which the subject multinational operated. Internal standards, as the term suggests, referred to contractual features of the relationship between related entities (more specifically, to the terms of the technology transfer). Substantial differences between the subject controlled transaction and the proposed comparable uncontrolled transaction along either (or both) of these dimensions diminished the latter's evidentiary weight. Minor differences were tolerable, but then the comparable would be deemed inexact.

As under the 1968 regulations, the White Paper authors maintained that an exact comparable should always be given first priority in establishing and assessing intra-company royalty rates. With regard to the proper application of inexact comparables, the White Paper authors concluded that: "it is appropriate to make use of them, but...inappropriate to determine transfer prices [or royalty rates] solely on the basis of inexact comparables."[38]

Intangible Property Provisions

What to do, then, if comparable uncontrolled intangibles transactions were so inexact as to be useless, or sufficiently inexact as to require buttressing the case for a given royalty rate via an alternative methodology? A more precise and workable approach to determining deemed arm's length royalty rates was clearly in order, in lieu of the twelve factors that constituted the intangibles provisions under the 1968 regulations, but what specific fourth method was both feasible and reasonably consistent with the arm's length principle? The White Paper authors' answer to this methodological dilemma was to provide some economic justification for, and thereby sanction the wider use of, the courts' profit split approach. The White Paper's formalization also provided more guidance in determining a reasonable split in particular instances than case law had done to date.

In setting out their proposed methodology for determining arm's length royalty fees, the White Paper authors began with the simplest

[38]The White Paper, *Op. Cit.*, p. 91.

case: a situation in which only one related entity owned unique (as opposed to "routine") *self-developed* intangible assets, while the other entity utilized intangible property licensed exclusively from the related developer. In this event, the basic arm's length return method (BALRM) applied. In developing this methodology, the White Paper authors made use of an identity drawn from microeconomic theory: the combined payments that a firm makes to *all* factors of production (land, labor, materials, and tangible and intangible capital), both imputed and explicit, precisely exhaust its total revenues. Consider an affiliated entity that utilizes only factors that command normal returns, and licenses intangible property from a related entity. Under the BALRM method, this entity's total revenues should equal the sum of its competitively determined payments to all factors, *excluding* its licensed intangibles. Equivalently, the affiliate's operating profits should equal its (imputed and explicit) payments to, or before-tax returns on, the *tangible* capital it employs. This outcome is consistent with the *commensurate with income* requirement, in that the intangibles transferee—the related licensee—retains no intangible income.[39] It is effectively equivalent to giving no recognition to controlled transfers of intangible property via license.

Perhaps somewhat optimistically, the authors of the White Paper suggested that "the basic arm's length return method will probably be appropriate for most manufacturing affiliates."[40] However, if one encountered a manufacturing affiliate that owned non-routine self-developed intangible assets in its own right, a slightly more involved version of the arm's length return method would be required. Specifically, the combined income jointly attributable to all intangible assets used by both parties in the subject line(s) of business was to be determined by a process of elimination: applying the basic arm's length return method, one determined normal returns to productive factors other than intangibles; all income in excess of these normal returns constituted intangible income. This pooled intangible in-

[39]For this reason, the BALRM method has been likened to the cost-plus *cum* contract manufacturer approach (in which the uncontrolled comparable firms perform fairly simple functions and incur very limited risks) that the IRS attempted and lost in a number of decided court cases. See, for example, Tax Executives Institute, "Comments on the Section 482 White Paper: A Study of Intercompany Pricing," submitted to the IRS on May 19, 1989, p. 43.

[40]The White Paper, *Op. Cit.*

come, in turn, was to be split between the related parties at issue "...according to the relative value that the marketplace would put on each party's significant intangible assets had they been employed by unrelated parties operating at arm's length.... In splitting this residual amount between the related parties, it is not necessary to place a specific value on each party's intangible assets, but only a relative value."[41,42]

The Periodic Adjustment Requirement

In addition to proposing specific methodologies (the BALRM and BALRM with profit split) to determine arm's length consideration for transferred intangibles at the time of the initial transfer, the White Paper authors endorsed the periodic adjustment concept discussed in the Committee Report to the 1986 Act. In particular, an adjustment to the compensation paid for intangibles already transferred was warranted in light of:

- Substantial changes in income attributable to the intangible. This might be due to a change in the size and number of markets penetrated, the product's sales volume and revenue, the number of uses for the technology, improvements to the technology, etc.; or,

- Substantial changes in the relative economic activities performed and/or risks assumed by the parties to the transfer.

Cost-Sharing Provisions

On the subject of cost sharing, the White Paper contained several proposals that constituted clarifications of, more than departures

[41]The White Paper, *Op. Cit.*, p. 101.

[42]While the White Paper authors did not stipulate that this relative valuation of assets should be performed within individual classes of intangibles, this is necessary unless one is prepared to postulate that intangibles of all types yield uniform rates of return per annum, their different useful lives notwithstanding. However, if one determines relative asset values within asset classes, it is also necessary to determine relative asset values across asset classes for purposes of weighting the former.

from, the 1968 regulations. To prevent abuse, the authors maintained that cost-sharing regulations should specify the scope of research projects that could be undertaken jointly, define the types of costs to be shared (equivalently, the means by which research-related costs should be segmented from other costs), and clarify the bases on which the shared costs could be allocated. If it were left to firms to determine scope freely, they could in principle define cost-sharing agreements very narrowly, and require foreign subsidiaries operating in lower-tax countries to participate only in successful ventures, effectively shifting costs and risks to the U.S. participant thereby. Alternatively, if companies could define scope very broadly, subsidiaries might be deemed to own—and, hence, be entitled to a return on—intangibles that they did not actually use.

The White Paper authors proposed to limit the scope of joint research projects to three-digit Standard Industrial Classification (SIC) codes. That is, in general, a related entity could not *selectively* participate in research projects undertaken by one or more other members of the controlled group that fell within the same SIC code.[43] Nor could it participate in research from which it would not directly benefit, where "the benefit to be derived under a cost-sharing arrangement is the right to use a developed intangible in the manufacture of a product."[44] The authors also proposed that costs be defined to include both direct and indirect R&D expenses undertaken as part of the cost-sharing arrangement, and that these costs be allocated among participants so as to reflect each entity's "reasonably anticipated" relative benefits. In order to measure relative benefits, each party was to be assigned exclusive geographic rights to the technological products of the cost-sharing agreement. Benefits could be measured variously by units of production if the participants produced in uniform units, sales value if they did not, or estimated gross or net profits if the rights that each participant obtained in the jointly developed intangibles by virtue of its participation conferred significantly different profit potential. Finally, the White Paper condoned the use of "buy-ins" (whereby an entity joining a research venture in

[43]However, both corporations and the IRS were to be permitted some flexibility in this regard, if they could demonstrate that either a narrower or broader agreement was appropriate under a given set of circumstances.

[44]The White Paper, *Op. Cit.*, p. 118.

progress must compensate the original participants for pre-existing or partially developed intangible assets), and provided for periodic adjustments in individual participants' relative contributions if the economic environment, functions performed, and/or risks assumed by the parties changed significantly.

The White Paper's Reception

The White Paper stimulated considerable debate, part of its intended purpose. For the most part, firms were not favorably impressed with the basic arm's length return method, viewing it as another means of bringing an unjustifiably large portion of consolidated income back to the United States.[45]

Further, it had a number of methodological drawbacks. The simple BALRM method could only be applied in instances where the firm at issue operated in a single line of business, or where horizontally diversified firms could allocate assets and expenses to the particular line(s) of business at issue with a fair degree of precision. Moreover, the more complex version of the arm's length return method (the basic arm's length return method combined with a residual profit split) required that one determine the relative values of intangible assets owned by the two or more related parties at issue, as noted above. While relative valuations are an easier proposition than absolute valuations, they are generally far from simple and straightforward.

Foreign taxing authorities and practitioners also took strong issue with both the fairly crude split of intangible income under this methodology, and the periodic adjustment requirement. The former appeared to be inconsistent with the separate accounting framework, a cornerstone of bilateral tax treaties, and smacked of an arbitrary, overall apportionment methodology. The periodic adjustment requirement was viewed as a flagrant violation of the arm's length standard, a long-standing international norm.

[45]See, for example, Stoffregen et. al., "The BALRM Approach to Transfer Pricing: One Step Forward, Two Steps Back," *Tax Notes*, Vol. 42, No. 12 (March 6, 1989), p. 1257.

2.1.4 The 1992 Proposed Regulations

The White Paper was followed several years later by the 1992 proposed Section 482 regulations. Partly in response to growing concerns about foreign-based multinationals' perceived transfer pricing abuses, and partly because of the negative reactions to the White Paper proposals described above, the 1992 proposed Section 482 regulations parted company with the White Paper in a number of important ways. First, and most broadly, the proposed regulations elaborated on—in the view of some, redefined—the arm's length principle:

> ...[T]he general principle to be followed [in evaluating intra-company dealings] is whether uncontrolled taxpayers, each exercising sound business judgement on the basis of reasonable levels of experience (or, if greater, the actual level of experience of the controlled taxpayer) within the relevant industry and with full knowledge of the relevant facts, would have agreed to the same contractual terms under the same economic conditions and other circumstances.

Many private sector practitioners interpreted this passage to extend the IRS's powers in evaluating intra-company pricing practices. Related parties seldom deal with one another precisely as uncontrolled firms do; hence, some degree of ambiguity almost inevitably arises in ascertaining whether particular related party practices are arm's length. The "prudent businessman standard," as the above criterion came to be known, appeared to go a significant step further than the arm's length principle, in that it enabled the IRS to substitute subjective judgement as to what was and was not prudent behavior in lieu of exact parallels among uncontrolled firms.

The 1992 proposed Section 482 regulations also put forth some new methodological concepts, which differed from both the 1968 regulations and the White Paper. While the statutory amendments to Section 482 were driven chiefly by Congressional concerns about transfer pricing abuses by U.S.-based multinationals, the 1992 proposed regulations reflect a greater emphasis on perceived abuses by foreign-based firms with U.S. subsidiaries. They were at least partially an outgrowth of several IRS districts' attempts to deal with an enormous proliferation of inbound cases involving foreign parent suppliers and U.S. distributors.

The size of these cases did not always warrant assigning limited IRS economist resources to them. However, Section 482 cases raise issues that are fundamentally economic rather than legal, and the IRS stands a relatively better chance of resolving a transfer pricing case favorably—be it at the Examination, Appeals, or Tax Court levels—if it is developed by an economist. Hence, the IRS contemplated a new approach: if one could develop a large database of loosely comparable stand-alone distributors' operating results, these data could be used to form either an average or a range of arm's length profit ratios that could be applied across a number of cases, and the requisite economist input per case minimized. On smaller inbound cases (albeit not on large ones), several IRS districts reportedly attempted such an approach and negotiated settlements on this basis. It is a relatively short step from this focus on the operating results of large numbers of inexactly comparable companies to the centerpiece of the proposed regulations, the comparable profit method described below.

Intangible Property Provisions

The 1992 proposed regulations set out three methods of determining arm's length consideration for intangible property transferred between related parties (through license or sale), which were to be applied in the order of priority shown:

- The Matching Transactions Method;
- The Comparable Adjustable Transactions Method; and,
- The Comparable Profit Method.

The matching transactions method, or MTM, was simply the familiar comparable uncontrolled price method, applied to intangible property. If one was fortunate enough to find intangibles transactions between uncontrolled parties that were virtually identical to those at issue between the related parties, with regard to both property and terms, the consideration paid by the unrelated recipient of the intangible was to be applied to the controlled transaction as well.

No *ex post* test of reasonableness had to be satisfied if arm's length compensation was determined via the MTM.

The comparable adjustable transactions method (CAT), given second priority, allowed for some differences between controlled and arm's length transactions, respectively, in both the transferred intangible property itself and the terms and conditions of the transfer. Specifically, the property was not required to be identical, but only substantially similar. Differences in economic conditions and contractual terms were required to be quantifiable, or "adjustable," with reasonable accuracy. As with the MTM, the genuinely arm's length consideration paid by the uncontrolled licensee—with these adjustments—was to be applied to the controlled transfer. Unlike the MTM, the results produced via the comparable adjustable transactions method had to satisfy an *ex post* test of reasonableness. Specifically, the transferee's profits—which would reflect its payment for intangibles as determined under CAT—were required to fall within an allowable range of hypothetical arm's length incomes, termed a "comparable profit interval." This profit interval concept, and the way in which it was to be constructed, are described below in connection with the proposed regulations' comparable profit method.

In lieu of the White Paper's simple BALRM and BALRM with profit split, the authors of the 1992 proposed regulations advocated the comparable profit method, or CPM, to be applied when neither MTMs nor CATs could be found. In essence, the CPM approach (*a la* the 1992 proposed regulations) entailed calculating a range of profits ("constructive operating incomes") based on profitability measures (or "profit level indicators") drawn from broadly similar stand-alone firms, which were then applied to the related transferee's ("tested party's") financial data. Approved profit level indicators included rates of return on operating assets, Berry ratios (revenues relative to operating expenses), gross margins over revenues or cost of goods, etc. The drafters of these proposed regulations anticipated that a subset of constructive operating incomes would clearly cluster together, while other constructive operating incomes would be readily identifiable as outliers.[46] Those constructive operating incomes that

[46]In the 1992 proposed regulations' terminology, "[f]actors that must be considered in determining whether [a] constructive operating income diverges include

"converged," or grouped together, formed the arm's length range, or "comparable profit interval," while extreme values were eliminated.

Under the CPM, the tested party's pre- or post-adjustment operating income was required to fall within this comparable profit interval. If its reported operating income fell outside its comparable profit interval, the IRS would propose an adjustment that moved it within the interval. Under these circumstances, the distance between the relevant endpoint of the comparable profit interval and the tested party's reported income determined where in the interval its allowable income would fall, post-adjustment:

- If this distance was significant,[47] the tested party's operating income after adjustments would generally be equated to the "most appropriate point" in the interval (as determined by degrees of comparability between the tested party and individual firms used to construct the comparable profit interval, the adequacy and reliability of data, etc.);
- If this distance was not deemed to be significant, the tested party's adjusted operating income might be equated to a point short of, or exceeding, the most appropriate point, in effect a reward for relatively good behavior.[48]

Conversely, if the related transferee's reported operating income was contained in its comparable profit interval, then the consideration it paid for the rights to use the transferred intangibles would generally not be challenged.

---

the relative distance between the constructive operating income and the closest points in the interval compared to the distance between other points within the interval."

[47]That is, if the tested party's transfer pricing practices deviated significantly from the arm's length standard, by this measure.

[48]As the 1992 proposed regulations express this point, "[i]f the reported operating income of the tested party is not significantly outside the comparable profit interval, any adjustments made by the district director will take into account the amount of deviation between the comparable profit interval and the reported operating income. The closer the reported operating income is to the comparable profit interval, the smaller an adjustment may be. The adjustment must bring the operating income within the comparable profit interval but may be smaller than necessary to reach the most appropriate point in the interval."

Thus, the 1992 proposed regulations moved away from the intangibles profit split concept and the factor cost approach put forth in the White Paper. Instead, the drafters attempted to work within the framework of comparables-based methods, and to circumvent the "lack-of-comparables" problem by significantly broadening the concept of comparability. In effect, in lieu of an MTM or CAT, one was to make a good faith effort to find stand-alone firms that were comparable along all of the relevant dimensions (functions, risks, and intangibles ownership). If this proved impossible, however, the 1992 proposed regulations gave one license to scale back the standard of comparability: functions were not required to be identical, risks assumed did not have to be precisely analogous, and so forth.

The resulting division of intangible income between transferee and transferor under the comparable profit method depended on the particular comparables used to construct the comparable profit interval. If these uncontrolled entities owned non-routine intangible assets, their profits would incorporate a return thereon; likewise, the tested party's allowable profits, based on profitability measures drawn from these stand-alone comparables, would incorporate a return on intangibles. Alternatively, if the comparable stand-alone firms used to construct the tested party's profit interval did not own or license valuable intangible assets, their profits—and, hence, the tested party's allowable income—would embody a return only on tangible capital employed.

The Periodic Adjustment Requirement

The 1992 proposed regulations retained the periodic adjustment requirement first introduced in the Committee Report to the 1986 Act, and subsequently incorporated into the White Paper. Specifically, in determining arm's length compensation for transferred intangibles, the district director was expressly permitted to consider all relevant facts and circumstances throughout the period during which the intangible was used. However, unlike the White Paper, the proposed regulations were not specific as to the circumstances that warranted revisiting the compensation paid for intangible property.

Tangible Property Provisions

The 1992 proposed regulations also modified the 1968 regulations' tangible property provisions. Recall that the 1968 rules elevated the CUP method over the resale price method, and the resale price method over the cost-plus approach. The 1992 proposed regulations eliminated the prioritizing between resale price and cost plus-approaches. Under the 1992 proposed rules, the availability of data and the division of labor between the related parties determined which methodology applied in a given case. The comparable uncontrolled price method, however, retained first priority in the proposed regulations.

Additionally, and more significantly, the 1992 proposed regulations provided for an *ex post* test to evaluate the reasonableness of intra-company prices for tangible property established (by firms or the IRS) via the resale price or cost-plus methods—the same *ex post* test that applied when arm's length consideration for intangible property was determined via the CAT method. Specifically, related distributors whose transfer prices were established via the resale price method were required to earn incomes that fell within their comparable profit intervals. If the resale price methodology produced results (that is, income levels) that fell outside this interval, the candidate comparable(s) from which the resale margins were derived would be rejected, regardless of their suitability in terms of functions, risks, and intangibles owned or licensed.[49] Analogously, related manufacturing entities whose transfer prices were established via the cost-plus method were required to earn incomes that fell within their comparable profit intervals, as determined by stand-alone operations that were broadly similar. Thus, the 1992 proposed regulations could in principle have weighted a sample of potentially poor comparables' operating results more heavily than a smaller sample of very close comparables' results under some circumstances.

[49]Still more concretely, multinational firms could set transfer prices via the resale price method, only to find the IRS challenging these prices by reference to a comparable profit interval built up from less comparable stand-alone firms. Conversely, the IRS might develop a proposed adjustment using the resale price methodology, but if the tested party's post-adjustment operating income was not contained in its profit interval, the proposed adjustment would not stand.

Cost-Sharing Provisions

Finally, in keeping with both the 1968 regulations and the White Paper, the 1992 proposed regulations sanctioned cost-sharing agreements, albeit with some modifications. To qualify as bona fide, a cost-sharing agreement among related parties had to satisfy a number of requirements: it had to be set out in writing when the arrangement commenced; participants were required to maintain adequate records to verify the material provisions of the agreement and the cost shares borne by individual participants; they had to be able to use the intangibles ultimately developed under the cost-sharing agreement in the active conduct of their trade or business (albeit not necessarily in manufacturing, as the corresponding White Paper provisions stipulated); and, product areas were required to be "broad enough to encompass related intangible development," yet "narrow enough so that the costs shared are for the development of products or services that are of potential use to each eligible participant." (Thus, certain of the 1992 proposed regulations' cost-sharing provisions allowed firms more flexibility than the White Paper's cost-sharing proposals.)

As with both the 1968 regulations and the White Paper, the 1992 proposed regulations required cost shares (covering both the costs of successful and unsuccessful ventures) to be proportional to reasonably anticipated benefits. A cost allocation method that did not provide for adjustments in cost shares, in the event that economic conditions or the business operations and practices of the participants changed significantly, would not satisfy this requirement. Moreover, as in the White Paper, the drafters took the view that each party had to be assigned a specific interest in the prospective technology if benefits were to be accurately anticipated.

Finally, the 1992 proposed regulations provided an unambiguous, results-oriented (albeit rebuttable) means by which the district director could gauge whether participants were making a reasonable effort to share costs in proportion to anticipated benefits. Specifically, the regulations introduced the notion of a cost-to-income ratio, where the denominator, income, was given by the participant's average operating income attributable to intangibles developed under the arrangement over a specified period,[50] and the numerator, costs, included the average of intangibles development costs contributed by the participant over the same period. If the U.S. participant's cost-to-income ratio exceeded the other participants' collective cost-to-income ratio by more than two to one, the U.S. entity's contribution would be deemed "substantially disproportionate." In this event, the district director could deem that the U.S. entity had transferred intangible assets, and allocate income accordingly. Conversely, if the U.S. participant's cost-to-income ratio was not substantially disproportionate, the district director was to confine allocations to adjusted cost shares.

Response to the 1992 Proposed Regulations

Reaction to the 1992 proposed regulations' comparable profit methodology and *ex post* profit interval test was quite negative, both in the United States and abroad. The comparable profit methodology itself was viewed by many as a significant departure from the arm's length standard, in that it required profits, as distinct from prices, to fall within a specified range.[51] Numerous factors other than intracompany pricing influenced profitability, the argument went, including maturity of product and company, startup costs, operational efficiencies, market share decisions and strategies, management philosophies, financing decisions, etc. As such, unless the tested party and the comparables used to compute the profit range were identical in all relevant respects except pricing, an unlikely eventuality in light of the lax comparability standards that were to be applied under the CPM, differences in income could not be attributed solely to transfer pricing distortions.

Practitioners here and abroad also voiced concern about the primacy of the comparable profit method, which, as described, could

[50]Operating income attributable to intangibles developed under the cost-sharing arrangement was further defined as "all operating income that is directly or indirectly attributable to the intangible development area."

[51]The pronounced reaction to profits-based approaches to setting intra-company transfer prices *per se* is somewhat perplexing, inasmuch as profits-based pricing methods—resale price and cost plus—had been included in the 1968 tangible property provisions, and widely applied thereunder.

override results produced by the resale price or cost-plus methods even though the uncontrolled firms used to establish transfer prices under the latter methods might actually be more similar to the related party at issue than those used to construct the comparable profit interval. Additionally, the periodic adjustment continued to rankle, in that it was viewed as fundamentally inconsistent with the arm's length principle.

2.1.5 The 1993 Temporary Regulations

The 1993 temporary regulations meld elements of the 1968 regulations, the White Paper, and the 1992 proposed regulations. The cost-sharing provisions contained in the 1992 proposed regulations remain outstanding; with the release of the 1993 temporary regulations, all other previously proposed provisions were withdrawn.

In addition to proposing further changes in pricing methodologies, the 1993 temporary regulations incorporate a number of overarching changes:

- First, they weaken, but do not entirely eliminate, the 1992 proposed regulations' *ex post* comparable profit interval or "arm's length range" test (to be applied to arm's length cross-charges that are established via resale price, cost-plus, and comparable adjustable transactions methods). In particular, the 1993 temporary regulations provide that "an arm's length result of a controlled transaction is not necessarily a single amount, and a result from a controlled transaction will not be subject to allocation under Section 482 if it falls within the arm's length range established by two or more uncontrolled comparables." However, the district director is *not* required "to establish an arm's length range prior to making an allocation under Section 482." Hence, companies can use the arm's length range concept to fend off an adjustment, but, by the same token, the IRS is not required to "pre-test" its proposed allocations. Additionally, while this point is somewhat ambiguous, the IRS might still be able to challenge intra-company prices that firms establish via resale price or cost-plus methods by demonstrating that the tested party's pre-adjustment operating income is not contained in its arm's length range. (Stated differently, a result from a controlled transaction *may* be subject to an allocation under Section 482 if it does *not* fall within the arm's length range.)

- Additionally, the 1993 temporary regulations formally eliminate the fixed priority of methods contained in the 1968 regulations, already relaxed somewhat in the 1992 proposed regulations, and replace it with a "best methods" rule, whereby the method that will produce the most accurate arm's length result in a given situation should be used.[52] By the same token, the 1993 temporary regulations are far more specific as to (a) the circumstances in which each sanctioned pricing methodology should be applied (that is, when individual methods will produce the most accurate results), (b) the (general and method-specific) factors to be considered in evaluating comparability, (c) the (method-specific) standard of comparability to be satisfied, and (d) the adjustments required under each method when comparables are not exact.
- Finally, the 1993 temporary regulations clarify and elaborate on a number of important, albeit narrow, methodological issues that arose regularly at the Examination, Appeals, and Tax Court levels in the course of applying the 1968 regulations.

The 1993 temporary regulations' tangible and intangible property provisions are reviewed below, and the overarching changes and narrow methodological points they implement taken up in the subsequent subsections.

Tangible Property Provisions

The 1993 temporary regulations retain the three methods used to establish transfer prices for tangible property under the 1968 regula-

[52] However, the IRS's predilection for transactions-based methods over profit-based methods clearly remains, in that the 1993 temporary regulations stipulate that, "[f]or purposes of applying the best method rule of Section 1.482-1T(b)(2)(iii)(A), the comparable uncontrolled price method, when it can be reasonably applied on the basis of available data, ordinarily will provide the most accurate measure [of] an arm's length price for the transfer of tangible property."

tions (the CUP method, the resale price method, and the cost-plus method). Additionally, they add a fourth, the comparable profits method first introduced in the 1992 proposed regulations, albeit with some important modifications:

- The arm's length range is computed using only one of the approved profit level indicators, rather than a number of indicators concurrently, as the 1992 proposed regulations permitted.[53]
- The process of eliminating outlying values of constructive operating incomes is necessary only if the uncontrolled firms used to derive these incomes are significantly dissimilar from the tested party either in terms of functions or risks. In this event, the arm's length range will be comprised only of the interquartile range of constructive operating incomes.[54] Conversely, if one derives constructive operating incomes from reasonably comparable firms, the arm's length range (equivalently, the comparable profit interval) is coincident with the entire range of constructive operating incomes.
- The 1992 proposed regulations' "most appropriate point" concept is replaced by the midpoint of the arm's length range, and the punitive feature incorporated into the 1992 proposed regulations (whereby the more egregious a firm's perceived transfer pricing abuse, the larger its potential pricing adjustment[55]) is eliminated in the 1993 temporary regulations.

Additionally, the 1993 temporary regulations provide that one can apply "other [unspecified] methods" (termed "fourth methods" in the 1968 regulations) to determine arm's length prices for tangible property under limited circumstances. In particular, firms have recourse to other methods "[w]here none of the [other enumerated]

[53]Under the 1993 temporary regulations, such indicators, or approved profitability measures, again include rates of return on operating assets, gross profits over revenues or costs, revenues over operating expenses, operating income over sales, and gross income over operating expenses.

[54]Hence, the 1993 temporary regulations clarify the very ambiguous discussion of convergence in the 1992 proposed regulations.

[55]Recall that, under the 1992 proposed regulations, the distance between a tested party's reported operating income and the endpoint of its comparable profit interval factored into the magnitude of the IRS's proposed adjustment.

methods...can reasonably be applied under the facts and circumstances of a particular case."

While formally eliminating a fixed priority of methods (apart from "other" methods, clearly given a lower priority), the 1993 temporary regulations leave relatively little to the imagination vis-a-vis the process of selecting a methodology under the best methods rule. This determination depends chiefly on the availability of data, the division of labor between the controlled entities under consideration, and their respective ownership of intangible assets that were either self-developed or acquired from unrelated parties in a genuinely arm's length transaction.

Practically speaking, the comparable uncontrolled price method continues to take precedence over other, profits-based methods for purposes of determining arm's length intra-company prices for tangible property. Specifically, the former should be applied whenever uncontrolled transactions that involve very similar (tangible) property and take place under substantially the same terms and conditions can be found. If comparable uncontrolled transactions in tangible property cannot be found, one of the approved profits-based methods—resale price, cost-plus, or comparable profits—applies. In particular:

- The resale price approach will typically apply when the tested party purchases tangible property from a related supplier and resells it to unrelated parties, adding limited value thereto. It will be deemed to have added substantial value if it physically alters the good before resale or contributes non-routine intangible property, and conversely.
- The cost-plus method will apply if the tested party manufactures or assembles tangible goods and sells them to related parties.
- The comparable profits method appears to apply under the 1993 temporary regulations' tangible property provisions when:
  - The tested party neither owns intangible property that it developed itself nor licenses intangible property from third parties; and,

- The tested party does not function either as a distributor or as a manufacturer; or,
- The uncontrolled firms comprising the sample of prospective comparables fail to satisfy the significantly higher comparability standards applied under the resale price and cost-plus methods.

Intangible Property Provisions

Under their intangible property provisions, the 1993 temporary regulations combine the matching and comparable adjustable transactions methods introduced in the 1992 proposed regulations into a single comparable uncontrolled transactions (CUT) method. Where sufficiently comparable uncontrolled intangibles transactions cannot be found, and where only one of the controlled entities at issue utilizes intangibles that are either self-developed or acquired from unrelated parties, arm's length consideration is to be determined under the revised comparable profits method, in lieu of the 1968 regulations' twelve factors approach and the White Paper's BALRM and BALRM with profit split.[56] Finally, as under the tangible property provisions, firms have recourse to other methods when the comparable uncontrolled transactions and comparable profits methods cannot be applied.

The 1993 temporary regulations also retain the controversial periodic adjustment feature discussed in the Conference Committee Report to the 1986 Act and subsequently incorporated into both the White Paper and the 1992 proposed regulations:

> ...[T]he consideration charged [for a transferred intangible] in each year may be adjusted to ensure that it is commensurate with the income attributable to the intangible.... In determining whether to make such adjust-

[56]Note, however, that a version of the BALRM with profit split is incorporated into the set of 1993 proposed regulations released concurrently with the 1993 temporary regulations, to be applied only when both related parties to the controlled transaction at issue utilize intangible assets that they either developed themselves or acquired from third parties. These 1993 proposed regulations are subsequently discussed herein.

> ments in the taxable year under examination, the district director may consider all relevant facts and circumstances throughout the period the intangible is used. The determination in an earlier year that the amount charged for an intangible was arm's length will not preclude the district director in a subsequent taxable year from making an adjustment to the amount charged for the intangible in the subsequent year.

In short, the 1993 temporary regulations' answer to the dearth of comparable uncontrolled intangibles transactions is to endorse the comparable profits method and (consistent with the 1992 proposed regulations) relax the standard of comparability very considerably thereunder, rather than to move away from the comparables framework entirely (as the BALRM and BALRM with profit split did in one sense). While this expedient clearly enhances the regulations' "workability," it comes at the cost of some degree of accuracy and reliability, as several of the case studies reviewed in Part II herein will demonstrate.

Note also that, in restricting the comparable profits method to situations in which the tested party neither owns nor licenses intangible assets that it developed itself or acquired from third parties, the 1993 temporary regulations fail to address a fairly common fact pattern, in which both related parties to the controlled transaction(s) at issue use self-developed intangible property (often developed in the context of a cost-sharing agreement). Under these circumstances, and assuming no comparable uncontrolled transactions can be identified, the 1993 temporary regulations provide no basis for determining arm's length prices or royalties. (The set of 1993 proposed regulations released concurrently address situations of this sort. As such, they are a very important complement to the 1993 temporary regulations.)

Comparability Criteria and Standards of Comparability

The 1993 temporary regulations elaborate very substantially on the specific comparability criteria one should bring to bear in selecting uncontrolled transactions or firms, and on the standards of comparability that must be satisfied by them—both extremely common points of contention among firms and the IRS under the 1968 regulations. Under the new rules, comparability criteria consist of both general and method-specific elements, and comparability standards are method-specific.

In general, one is directed to consider functions, risks, contractual terms, economic conditions, and property or services in selecting comparables.[57] These considerations apply across methods, albeit the relative importance of particular elements varies by pricing method. Method-specific comparability standards and comparability criteria are discussed briefly below.

The Comparable Uncontrolled Price Method: As suggested above, transactions-based methods—comparable uncontrolled price (as applied to tangible property transfers) and comparable uncontrolled transactions (as applied to intangible property transfers)—impose the highest standard of comparability. Under the comparable uncontrolled price method, "minor" differences between controlled and uncontrolled transactions may be tolerable if they have no effect on the amount charged, or if the effects of such differences can be accounted for by a reasonable number of adjustments. If the differences between controlled and uncontrolled transactions or firms are "material," the comparable uncontrolled price method cannot be used.[58] The 1993 temporary regulations enumerate a number of specific potential differences in this regard, including:

- the quality of the products exchanged in controlled and uncontrolled contexts;
- sales volume;

[57]The broad rubric "economic conditions" is further broken down into the following elements: (a) the alternatives realistically available to a buyer and seller, respectively; (b) the similarity of geographic markets; (c) the relative size of each market, and the extent of overall economic development in each market; (d) the level of the market; (e) the relevant market shares for the products, properties or services transferred or provided; (f) the location-specific costs of the factors of production and distribution; and (g) the extent of competition in each market.

[58]This restriction would seem to apply even if the effects of material differences on price can be ascertained with reasonable accuracy, judging from an illustrative example in the 1993 temporary regulations.

- market level;
- geographic markets in which the controlled and uncontrolled transactions take place;
- dates of the transactions;
- alternative commercial arrangements realistically available to the buyer and seller; and,
- intangible property associated with the sale.

The 1993 temporary regulations do not classify all of these (and other unspecified) potential differences into "minor" and "material" categories.[59]

The Comparable Uncontrolled Transactions Method: The comparability standards that must be satisfied under the comparable uncontrolled transactions method are higher still. Both the intangible *property* involved in, and the *circumstances* of, the controlled and uncontrolled transactions must be comparable. Two items of intangible property will be considered comparable if they:

- are in the same class of intangibles;
- relate to the same type of products, processes, or know-how within the same general industry or market; and,
- have substantially the same profit potential.

Circumstances will be considered comparable if:

- the terms of the transfer are similar;[60]
- the transferred intangibles are at the same stage of development;

[59] For a discussion of whether these enumerated comparability dimensions suffice to ensure that the controlled and uncontrolled transactions should take place at the same price, see King, Elizabeth, "Economic Analysis in Transfer Pricing," in Gibbs, Briger, Lowell, Stark and Burge, eds., *International Transfer Pricing*, New York: Warren, Gorham & Lamont, forthcoming.

[60] Terms include rights granted, the exclusive or non-exclusive character of these rights, restrictions on use, and limitations on the geographic area where the rights may be exploited.

- rights to receive periodic updates or improvements in the transferred intangibles are comparable;
- the property involved in the controlled and uncontrolled transfers, respectively, is unique to the same degree;
- the licenses have similar terms, and similar termination and renegotiation clauses;
- risks assumed by the related and arm's length licensees are comparable; and,
- functions performed by related transferor and transferee and uncontrolled transferor and transferee, respectively, are similar.

While the temporary regulations' language to this point is somewhat ambiguous, it appears that one cannot adjust for differences in intangible property, although differences in circumstances may be acceptable if they have a definite and reasonably ascertainable effect on compensation.[61]

Profit-Based Methods—General: Product similarities per se are considered relatively less important for purposes of applying profits-based methods (resale price, cost-plus, and comparable profits) than transactions-based methods, on the (implicit) theory that: (a) the gross margins earned by distributors and manufacturers represent compensation for distribution services or manufacturing functions performed; (b) the same activities can be performed across a range of product markets; and (c) compensation for these activities would generally be uniform across product markets.

Stated differently, distributors and manufacturers must compensate their (below-the-line) productive factors—fixed, variable, and intangible—out of their gross margins. If one includes imputed as

[61]In particular, the 1993 temporary regulations state that "The intangible property involved in an uncontrolled transaction is comparable if [all of] the [enumerated comparability criteria]... are met. The circumstances involved in an uncontrolled transaction are comparable to those of a controlled transfer if any differences can be accounted for [with a reasonable number of adjustments, and where these differences have a definite and reasonably ascertainable effect on price.]"

well as explicit factor payments in this calculus,[62] total payments to below-the-line factors will exactly exhaust gross margins. Hence, abstracting from random variations in profitability, two unrelated distributors (or manufacturers) should earn the same resale (cost-plus) margins if their respective payments to all factors (including imputed costs in the form of a required return on equity and economic rent paid to scarce factors) per dollar of revenues (costs) are the same. The two entities' factor payments, in turn, should be the same if they perform the same productive activities, invest the same amount of capital per dollar of revenues (costs), incur comparable risks, and employ intangibles of similar value (if at all). Similarly, a controlled entity cum stand-alone distributor (or manufacturer) would earn the same margins as an uncontrolled firm if it employed the same productive factors and compensated them at the same rate. In line with this reasoning, the 1993 temporary regulations emphasize functional similarities and the nature and extent of risks in describing comparability criteria under profits-based methods. This emphasis is consistent with, but far more explicit than, the corresponding provisions under the 1968 regulations.

Resale Price and Cost-Plus Methods: The 1993 temporary regulations' profits-based methods also explicitly allow for the possibility that comparables—uncontrolled firms—will differ from the controlled tested party in terms of functions and (or) risks. However, to apply either resale price or cost-plus methods, adjustments for these differences *must* be made. (That is, their effects on profitability must be quantified.) Such adjustments are to be based on commercial practices, economic principles, and (or) statistical analysis. Relevant differences between controlled and uncontrolled firms under the resale price method may include (but are not limited to):

- inventory levels carried;
- scope and terms of warranties provided;
- sales, marketing, and advertising programs and services;
- sales volume;

[62]Imputed payments to factors include a required return on equity and economic rent (or opportunity costs) imputed to scarce factors.

- market level;
- foreign currency risks; and,
- extensions of credit and payment terms.

Under the cost-plus method, particularly relevant differences may include:

- the complexity of manufacturing or assembly;
- manufacturing, production, and process engineering capabilities and functions;
- procurement, purchasing, and inventory control activities; testing functions;
- selling, general, and administrative expenses;
- foreign currency risks; and,
- extension of credit and payment terms.

Comparable Profits Method: Comparability standards under the comparable profits method are significantly less stringent than other profits-based methods; the 1993 temporary regulations require comparable uncontrolled firms to be "only broadly similar, and significant product diversity and some functional diversity between the controlled and uncontrolled transactions is acceptable." Moreover, adjustments for differences in functions and (or) risks between the controlled tested party and comparable uncontrolled firms are not required under the comparable profits method, whether for purposes of determining arm's length prices for tangible property or arm's length consideration for intangible property. However, if they are not made, the arm's length range will be a subset of the constructed operating incomes, as described above.

Clarifications of Recurring Methodological Issues

Consider next the 1993 temporary regulations' clarifications of several important methodological issues that resurfaced repeatedly under the 1968 regulations' regime. A common point of contention between companies and the IRS under the 1968 rules concerned the relative weights to attach to written agreements between controlled parties and their actual conduct, respectively, where one supported and the other detracted from companies' claims that their pricing practices conformed to the arm's length standard. Further, while tax regulations apply on a year-by-year basis, extraordinary circumstances and imperfectly synchronized product cycles and industry-specific business cycles may warrant averaging multi-year data for purposes of comparing a controlled entity's results with those of uncontrolled comparables; the need for—and validity of—this relatively minor methodological twist was often hotly contested under the 1968 regulations, with the proponent—IRS or firms—often determined by whether the particular Section 482 adjustment contemplated was increased or reduced thereby. Additionally, firms regularly raised certain economic arguments to justify deviations from intra-company pricing based solely on comparables (e.g., the tested party cum distributor underpriced its competitors in order to penetrate the market), and, as frequently, the IRS contested them. The 1993 temporary regulations attempt to put many of these recurring points of contention to rest:

- They explicitly provide that the substance of a transaction takes precedence over its form, and give the district director express authority to disregard written agreements when the actual conduct of the related parties at issue is at odds with them.[63]
- They authorize the district director to (a) combine interrelated transactions for purposes of determining whether they are arm's length;[64] (b) use multiple-year data when adequate and reliable data for the taxable year under review are not available, when the company's business is sufficiently cyclical as to make analyses of a single year's data uninformative or when product life cycles necessitate a longer view; and (c) combine product

[63]This stipulation is presumably a direct response to several decided cases that elevated form over substance, notably *Bausch & Lomb. Supra.*

[64]For example, if a parent firm licenses intangible property to, and purchases tangible property embodying these intangibles from, its manufacturing affiliate, the district director may combine the results of these separate transactions in evaluating the arm's length character of the subsidiary's income.

lines and use statistical sampling techniques to determine the arm's length character of intra-company pricing.

- A "special circumstances" provision contained in the 1993 temporary regulations supports firms' claims that market penetration strategies may justify pricing below comparables for some (unspecified) period of time.[65] This argument has come up most often on inbound cases, involving captive U.S. distributors and their foreign suppliers, where the former earns exceptionally slim profit margins.[66]

- Under both the 1968 regulations and the 1993 temporary regulations, the resale price method calls for a comparison of the gross margins (normalized by revenues) earned by the controlled distributor and comparable uncontrolled entities, with no reference to the total consolidated profits jointly earned by parent/manufacturer and subsidiary/distributor. As such, it is entirely possible that a Section 482 allocation will allocate more income to the captive U.S. distributor than the parent and subsidiary jointly earned, thereby *creating* rather than simply *reallocating* income. To take an extreme example, if the two related entities—foreign parent firm and captive U.S. distributor—collectively report consolidated losses on the lines of business at issue, and uncontrolled distributors earn positive profits, then a Section 482 allocation based on these compara-

[65]Specifically, the "special circumstances" provision states that, "[i]n certain circumstances, the price for a controlled transfer of property may, for a limited time, be other than the amount charged in an otherwise comparable uncontrolled transaction because the controlled transfer is subject to a pricing strategy that is undertaken to enter new markets, to increase a product's share of an existing market, or to meet competition in an existing market (market share strategy). A controlled transaction may be priced in such a manner only if it can be shown that such price would have been charged in an uncontrolled transaction under comparable circumstances..." As regards time frame, the provision further states that "[t]he market share strategy [must be] pursued for a period of time [if pursued at all] that is reasonable, taking into consideration the industry and product in question.

[66]The IRS has frequently challenged both the market penetration premise, and the time frame during which such an argument should hold, at the Examination level. Further, it has raised the obviously important question of which entity—manufacturer or distributor—would bear the costs of market penetration in an arm's length situation.

bles will create income by an amount equal to the proposed adjustment.[67] As discussed in Chapter 4, the IRS has in practice been reluctant to create, as opposed to reallocate, income under the 1968 regulations. However, the 1993 temporary regulations provide a firmer foundation for doing so, by authorizing the district director to make allocations under Section 482 "even if two controlled taxpayers realize an overall loss that is attributable to a particular controlled transaction..."

- Cost differences between a controlled firm and a prospective uncontrolled comparable often arise if they operate in different geographic markets. Specifically, a manufacturing affiliate operating in a low-wage country incurs lower labor costs than a stand-alone manufacturing entity performing the same functions and incurring comparable risks in the United States. These cost differences between affiliate and comparable, referred to as "location savings," have to be allocated between the pair of controlled firms in some fashion for purposes of applying the cost-plus method, and this allocation has been a frequent point of contention in such cases in the past. The 1993 temporary regulations provide that the allocation of location savings should be determined by the "relative competitive positions of buyers and sellers in each location." (See Chapter 3 for a more detailed discussion of this location savings issue.)

2.1.6 The 1993 Proposed Regulations

All of the methods set forth in the 1993 temporary regulations for establishing or evaluating intra-company prices are based on comparables, whether transactions or firms. Hence, when both parties to the controlled transactions at issue own or license non-routine intangible property that they either developed themselves or acquired from unrelated parties, the temporary regulations' pricing methods will either be extremely difficult to apply (in the case of transactions-based methods and the cost-plus method), or explicitly cannot be

[67] In many instances, determining consolidated profits or losses on the pertinent lines of business is itself a difficult exercise, inasmuch as the parent firm may produce a range of diversified products, necessitating a potentially arbitrary allocation of costs across product lines.

applied (in the case of resale price and comparable profits methods). However, the 1993 proposed regulations released concurrently contain three profit split methodologies that can be applied only when both parties contribute non-routine intangible property.[68,69] These methods—the residual allocation rule, the capital employed method, and the comparable profit split method—are described briefly below.

Residual Allocation Rule

The first profit split methodology described in the 1993 proposed regulations, the residual allocation rule, is essentially the BALRM with profit split method first introduced in the White Paper. As a first step, one assigns market returns to the tangible and "routine" intangible capital that each controlled party uses in the productive activities at issue. The difference between combined operating profits and the combined market returns to these forms of capital constitutes combined intangible income. This residual, in turn, is allocated between the related parties based on their relative ownership of valuable, non-routine intangible assets. Under some circumstances,[70] the

[68]In addition, the intangible must contribute significantly to the combined income earned in the relevant business activity, and certain administrative procedures must be followed. The latter include a binding election to apply the profit split method.

[69]Note that the 1993 proposed regulations request comment as to the definition of valuable, non-routine intangibles. If the definition incorporated into final regulations (or if the *de facto* definition used in the interim) is sufficiently broad, these profit split methods may be used more widely than the discussion in the 1993 temporary regulations suggests. At present, the temporary regulations define the term "intangible" (of which "non-routine" intangibles are a subset) to mean "any commercially transferable interest in any item included in the following six classes of intangibles, that has substantial value independent of the services of any individual: (1) patents, inventions, formulae, processes, designs, patterns or know-how; (2) copyrights and literary, musical or artistic compositions; (3) trademarks, trade names or brand names; (4) franchises, licenses, or contracts; (5) methods, programs, systems, procedures, campaigns, surveys, studies, forecasts, estimates, customer lists, or technical data; and (6) other similar items." Comment is also requested as to whether this definition of intangibles should be expanded to include such items as work force in place, goodwill or going concern value. If so, and if "valuable, non-routine intangibles" encompass most or all of this broader (total) intangibles category, the profit split methods could be quite widely applicable.

[70]Specifically, when development expenditures are fairly constant over time.

relative values of intangible assets can be approximated by the entities' relative development expenditures; in others, it may be necessary to value the intangibles explicitly by capitalizing development expenditures and determining the resultant intangibles' useful lives.

Capital Employed Method

The second proposed profit split methodology, termed the capital employed method, applies only when each controlled entity incurs equal risks.[71,72] Under these quite restrictive conditions, the combined operating income earned by the controlled entities at issue is divided among them in proportion to their total operating assets, both tangible and intangible. Inasmuch as intangible asset values must be added to the value of tangible assets for purposes of this computation, the capital employed method necessitates valuing intangible assets explicitly rather than approximating relative values via development expenditures. Intangibles can be valued at fair market, or by capitalizing development expenditures and ascertaining the intangibles' useful lives.[73]

Comparable Profit Split

Finally, the 1993 proposed regulations contain a comparable profit split methodology. Under this method, one identifies a pair of uncon-

---

[71]The other restrictions that apply across profit split methods are apropos as well.

[72]Note that the 1993 proposed regulations request comment as to "the feasibility of measuring relative levels of risk" for purposes of applying the capital employed method, and do not contain an adequate definition or measure of risk. In fact, the 1993 proposed regulations state that "...risk is measured on the basis of the probability of success or failure rather than an absolute measure of the maximum potential gain or loss." Inasmuch as a probability distribution subsumes both potential gains or losses and probabilities of success and failure, a measure of risk based thereon would make considerably more sense than one based either on probability of success (or failure) or potential gains (or losses) alone.

[73]For purposes of this computation, intangibles acquired from a related party will be included in the asset base of the developer, rather than the related licensee's asset base, in keeping with the *commensurate with income* requirement.

trolled companies that divide functions, risks, and intangibles ownership between themselves in the same way as the pair of controlled entities at issue. The paired uncontrolled firms' respective shares of their combined operating income is used to divvy up the controlled entities' consolidated income. To apply this method, the combined return on assets earned by paired controlled and uncontrolled companies, respectively, must be reasonably similar. (As a practical matter, it is highly unlikely that one will find pairs of uncontrolled firms that resemble controlled entities so closely. Consequently, even if this approach is ultimately incorporated into final Section 482 regulations, it is likely to have very limited applicability.)

2.2 Transfer Pricing Regulations for Possessions Corporations: Internal Revenue Code Section 936(h)

IRC Section 936, a special set of transfer pricing regulations applying to a subset of U.S. corporations operating in U.S. possessions, was incorporated into the Code with the Tax Reform Act of 1976 (replacing its forerunner, Section 931). Congress enacted Section 936 (and its predecessor) with a view to stimulating investment in possessions territories through tax incentives, and, hence, to promote economic development therein. These incentives take the form of a credit against certain portions of the subject firm's taxable income. (Note that the Omnibus Budget Reconciliation Act of 1993, hereinafter, the "1993 Act," imposes a new cap on the amount of the Section 936 credit.) To qualify for this tax credit, corporations must meet certain specified conditions intended to measure the extent of their contributions to economic activity in the subject possession, described briefly below. Transfer pricing issues involving possessions corporations tend to be more clear-cut than Section 482 issues, and to draw more heavily on accounting and legal know-how than economic expertise. As such, IRS economists generally play a smaller role in developing them.

Because this legislation was motivated by Congress' desire to further economic development in U.S. possessions, tax avoidance concerns have been of secondary importance to some degree (although this is becoming less true). Consequently, the arm's length pricing rules that are to be applied strictly in other circumstances are relaxed somewhat vis-a-vis possessions corporations. Revenue Procedure 63-10 provides for one such deviation: under some circumstances, an entity located in a possessions territory may be permitted to retain the benefit of reduced labor costs in the latter area, relative to the United States proper. This provision is at odds with the arm's length standard if the market at issue is competitive. In such an industry, where all firms in the relevant geographic market face uniformly lower labor costs as compared with the United States, these "cost savings" would be bid away (that is, passed on to the firms' customers) through competition-induced adjustments in output or price.[74]

Section 936(h) sets out several ways in which parent firms and possessions corporations may divide their combined income. A particular company may either voluntarily opt to come under the *General Rule* or it may be precluded from electing out of this Rule (if it fails to meet the *Significant Business Presence Test*, Congress' means of ensuring that possessions territories benefit from investment in their regions in the intended ways). The *General Rule* requires that income attributable to intangible property be included in the gross income of the firm's U.S. shareholders.[75] Alternatively, if a possessions corporation meets the *Significant Business Presence Test* (and therefore has the option of electing out of the *General Rule*), it may divide intangible income in one of two ways: a simple profit split, or a more elaborate cost-sharing approach.[76,77]

[74]While some Appeals officers have mistakenly applied Revenue Procedure 63-10 more broadly, as a matter of law only subsidiaries operating in U.S. possessions are entitled to this benefit. The 1993 temporary Section 482 regulations' discussion of location savings is intended to clarify the scope of this Revenue Procedure.

[75]That is, a possessions corporation coming under the *General Rule* retains no intangible income.

[76]The *Significant Business Presence Test* must be satisfied with respect to each product or service for which the election out of the Section 936(h) *General Rule* is made. Additionally, to utilize the profit split methodology, the subject possessions corporation must be considered to manufacture the relevant product in the possession, as defined by Section 954(d)(1)(A).

[77]Note that, if firms with possessions corporations choose to elect out of the *General Rule* and divide intangible income via either the profit split or cost-

The profit split method entitles the possessions corporation to half of all profits[78] earned on the sale of the possession product(s) to third parties. Thus, under this election, intra-company transfer pricing becomes unnecessary. A cost-sharing election obligates the possessions corporation to contribute a specified amount to its U.S. parent's R&D effort, and to establish transfer prices on its intra-company sales of tangible property under Section 482 pricing rules. By virtue of its cost-sharing election, the possessions corporation is "treated as the owner of manufacturing intangibles previously developed by its U.S. affiliates."[79]

The amount of intangible income that the possessions corporation retains under a cost-sharing election depends on the magnitude of its cost-sharing payment relative to total intangible income associated with the possessions product(s). Before 1986, the required payment was calculated by multiplying worldwide product area research expenditures of the affiliated group by the share of the group's total sales in the product area accounted for by the possessions corporation. Product areas, in turn, were defined by three-digit SIC Codes. After 1986, a possessions corporation's cost-sharing contribution is required to be the *greater* of: (a) 110% of the pre-1986 statutory amount just described; or, (b) an amount commensurate with the income attributable to the intangibles at issue, per the 1986 Act's statutory amendment to Section 482. As such, after 1986, the possessions corporation will retain very little, if any, intangible income under a Section 936(h) cost-sharing election. In general, then, the profit split election has become more advantageous to firms.

Cost-sharing elections under Section 936 are not equivalent to cost-sharing agreements under Section 482, although the cost-sharing amounts under the two Sections are linked by the 1986 Act's statutory amendment. As alluded to above, possessions corporations' cost shares under Section 936(h) represent payment for intangibles already developed and currently in use. Thus, they are more akin to a recurrent buy-in payment than a contribution to an ongoing research

---

sharing method, the subject possessions corporations may no longer be entitled to labor savings.

[78]That is, income attributable to both tangible and intangible assets employed by both the possessions corporation and its U.S. parent.

[79]See the White Paper, *Op. Cit.*, p. 125.

joint venture. Note also that possessions corporations do not own any non-manufacturing intangibles by virtue of their cost-sharing contributions to R&D,[80] and are not entitled to any portion of income attributable to marketing intangible assets developed by their U.S. parents. (This caveat applies equally to possessions corporations' intra-company and third party sales.)

2.3 Concurrent and Subsequent Developments in Transfer Pricing

In addition to the statutory and regulatory developments outlined above, there have been a number of important parallel developments over the past several years, among them a series of hearings on perceived transfer pricing abuses by foreign-based multinational firms with U.S. subsidiaries, expanded access to foreign company information, transfer pricing penalty provisions, legislative initiatives intended to make IRS summons procedures more workable, proposed minimum taxes on the U.S. subsidiaries of foreign multinationals, and a relatively new "advance pricing agreement" option, whereby companies may enter into written agreements with the IRS that set out mutually agreeable pre-approved intra-company pricing policies (and thereby greatly reduce the scope of a transfer pricing audit and the magnitude of potential pricing adjustments).

Penalty Provisions

The Revenue Reconciliation Act of 1990 introduced significant new penalty provisions in the transfer pricing area,[81,82] which were elaborated on in proposed regulations released on January 13, 1993, and modified again with the Omnibus Budget Reconciliation Act of 1993.

[80] Such as trademarks and trade names.

[81] These penalties had antecedents in both the White Paper and the aforementioned 1990 hearings on alleged tax underpayments by foreign-based multinationals with U.S. subsidiaries (discussed in more detail subsequently).

[82] See "Penalties and Pricing Issues," in *International Transfer Pricing, Op. Cit.*, for a more detailed discussion of Section 482 penalties.

IRC Section 6662(a) imposes a penalty of 20% for underpayment of taxes due to (a) negligence or disregard of rules or regulations, (b) substantial understatement of income tax, (c) substantial valuation overstatement, (d) substantial overstatement of pension liabilities, and (e) substantial estate or gift tax valuation understatement. With the 1990 Revenue Reconciliation Act, Congress expressly extended the "substantial valuation misstatement" penalty provision to underpayments of tax resulting from non-arm's length pricing (over a given threshold level), as determined under Section 482. The Omnibus Budget Reconciliation Act of 1993, in turn, reduced the threshold net Section 482 transfer price adjustment (given in dollars) that triggers penalties under this provision, and added an additional threshold that is cast in terms of percentage of gross receipts.

Under the new rules (which apply to taxable years beginning after December 31, 1992), a substantial valuation misstatement exists if the transfer price for (intra-company exchanges of) property or services claimed on a return is 200% or more, or 50% or less, of the amount determined (under Section 482) to be arm's length. Similarly, a net transfer price adjustment that exceeds the lesser of $5 million[83] or 10% of the taxpayer's gross receipts constitutes a substantial valuation misstatement.

Additionally, Section 6662(h) provides for increased penalties of 40% in the event of "gross valuation misstatements," which may likewise apply to transfer pricing adjustments after 1990. Per the new rules, a gross valuation misstatement exists if the transfer price for intra-company exchanges of property or services claimed on a return is 400% or more (or 25% or less) of the arm's length amount, as determined under Section 482. Moreover, a net transfer pricing adjustment that exceeds the lesser of $20 million or 20% of the taxpayer's gross receipts constitutes a gross valuation misstatement.

Section 482 adjustments are exempted from the penalty determinations if firms can demonstrate that they acted in good faith, and had reasonable cause, in charging the intra-company prices at issue. The penalty-related statutory changes incorporated into the Omnibus Budget Reconciliation Act of 1993 further specify that transfer pricing adjustments will be excluded in determining the threshold if

[83]This figure was previously $10 million.

(i) the taxpayer establishes intra-company prices in accordance with the methods set forth in the Section 482 regulations, or, alternatively, establishes that none of these pricing methods would result in a price that would clearly reflect income (and, in this event, establishes transfer prices under an alternative method that is likely to result in a price that would clearly reflect income); (ii) prior to filing its return, the taxpayer has documented the way in which it determined intra-company prices, and established the reasonableness of this method; and (iii) the taxpayer produces this documentation within 30 days of a request by the IRS to do so. Note also that a taxpayer will not be considered to have had reasonable cause in charging intra-company prices that the IRS successfully challenges unless it satisfies conditions (i)-(iii).

Designated Summons

With the 1990 Revenue Reconciliation Act, Congress also provided the IRS with a new, and potentially very effective, tool to induce multinational firms to comply with the IRS's requests for confidential company documentation and information,[84] termed a "designated summons." This procedure suspends the statute of limitations that generally applies to transfer pricing issues for the period that the summons is the subject of judicial enforcement proceedings. The IRS has historically found the (standard) summons procedure to be of very limited practical utility because of the delays that it entails, an unworkable state of affairs if the statute of limitations continues to run while the summons is being enforced (as it does unless the summons is "designated").

Hence, the designated summons measure was intended to facilitate more effective use of the summons option, and enhance the IRS's ability to obtain the information necessary to evalute intra-company pricing practices, particularly vis-a-vis foreign-based corporations. However, "the designated summons is an extraordinary procedure that the IRS invokes judiciously, only following high level

[84] More specifically, the designated summons procedure eliminates an incentive to withhold information: the certainty that the statute of limitations will expire if one delays long enough.

review within Examination and the Office of Chief Counsel."[85] As one might expect, this review process restricts the use of the designated summons severely, and as of April 1992, only three such summonses relating to transfer pricing matters had been issued.[86] Further, Congress has taken the IRS to task for attempting to use the designated summons procedure to obtain information from U.S.-based multinational firms.[87]

Efforts to Improve Foreign Multinational Firms' Compliance with U.S. Tax Laws

Perceived transfer pricing abuses by foreign multinationals with U.S. subsidiaries in particular has been a very highly charged issue for several years. Congressman Pickle (D-Texas), Chairman of the Subcommittee on Oversight of the Committee on Ways and Means, held two rounds of hearings on the subject, the first on July 10–12, 1990, and the second on April 9, 1992. The first round of hearings was intended to clarify the extent of tax underpayments by foreign-based multinationals with U.S. subsidiaries,[88] identify the causes thereof, and

[85] See the Statement of Shirley D. Peterson, Commissioner of Internal Revenue, before the Subcommittee on Oversight, House Committee on Ways and Means, *International Tax Administration Issues*, April 9, 1992.

[86] *Ibid.*

[87] As reported in *Tax Management Transfer Pricing Report*, Vol. 1, No. 5, July 8, 1992, "At a June congressional hearing, Rep. Richard Schulze (R-Pa.) strongly criticized the IRS's use of the designated summons procedure against the Chevron Corp. (*U.S. v. Chevron Corp.*, No. C-91-2782-EFL, N.D. Cal., 11/15/91.)"

[88] As reported by Congressman Kanjorski (D-Pa.) in his remarks before the Subcommittee on Oversight of the House Ways and Means Committee, April 9, 1992, "IRS data released at [the] subcommittee's 1990 hearings revealed that foreign corporations controlled over a trillion dollars in assets in the United States, and made over $687 billion in sales in the U.S., yet paid only $4.6 billion in taxes in the U.S. The hearings also revealed that while U.S. corporations report an average profit on their overseas sales of 9%, foreign corporations report an average profit on their sales in the U.S. of only two-tenths of one percent (0.2%)." Estimates of the tax underpayments by U.S. subsidiaries of foreign-based multinationals vary widely. By Congressman Pickle's estimates, foreign companies have collectively understated their tax burdens by approximately $30 billion annually through transfer pricing manipulations. (Japanese firms are widely believed to violate U.S. transfer pricing regulations most egregiously.) This is a considerably larger estimate than the $45 billion in additional taxes that President-elect Clinton be-

develop legislative and administrative remedies. The second round was intended to evaluate how effective the remedies introduced in 1989 and 1990 were in curbing foreign firms' alleged transfer pricing abuses. These measures included the penalties and designated summons procedure described above, considerably expanded IRS resources, more streamlined procedures for hiring outside experts, and substantially enhanced record-keeping requirements applying to inbound investors contained in Section 6038(A) of the IRC.

While then-Commissioner Peterson maintained that these measures had already had some effect in encouraging greater compliance by foreign-based multinationals, that additional legislative measures were unnecessary, and that the IRS had taken a number of other important steps to improve compliance and enforcement, Congressman Pickle strongly expressed his concern that the alleged tax abuses he had identified in 1990 had continued unabated, suggesting that the legislative remedies already provided were not sufficient. Mr. Patrick Heck, assistant counsel to the House Ways and Means Oversight Committee, expressed this view in very stark terms in a public forum on June 11, 1992, suggesting that changes in the Internal Revenue Code—potentially including a move away from the arm's length standard—would be forthcoming if foreign-based corporations' compliance with U.S. tax laws were not significantly improved over the next two years.[89]

---

lieved could be collected from U.S. subsidiaries of foreign-based multinationals over a four-year period if Section 482 regulations were enforced more effectively (and many observers have questioned the basis for both estimates). Estimates at the low end range from $3 billion to $6 billion. Bear in mind also that these estimates relate only to underpayments of taxes by foreign-based multinationals operating in the U.S.; if one added underpayments by U.S.-based multinationals, the figures would be substantially higher. Interestingly, this dimension of compliance with Section 482 regulations has garnered vastly less attention.

[89] As reported in *Tax Management Transfer Pricing Report*, "Heck told a transfer pricing seminar sponsored by the American Tax Institute in Europe that 'the Treasury and IRS have been given everything they need to make [the regulations] work.' If the U.S. Treasury does not begin collecting more tax dollars from foreign-owned businesses, Congress is likely to move on changes in the tax code that would facilitate collections from these firms... If the results from the next two years do not show signs of improved taxpayer compliance, the arm's length standard of transfer pricing may be abolished in the United States, Heck warned." See *Tax Management Transfer Pricing Report*, Vol. 1, No. 4, June 24, 1992.

Similarly motivated by the ineffective enforcement of Section 482 as it applies to foreign-based firms, other members of Congress have already proposed more radical departures from current practices. For example, in H.R. 4304, introduced in 1992, Congressman Kanjorski (D-Pa.) called for a 5% alternative minimum tax to be applied to multinational firms' net business proceeds. This tax was to be structured in such a way that "only very large corporations, which have little or no expenses in the United States (and thus no deductions), and which pay little or no taxes under current law (and thus receive little or no tax credits), will pay the new alternative minimum tax."[90] Similarly, Representative Richard Schulze (R-Pa.) proposed a border tax. House Ways and Means Committee Chairman Rostenkowski (D-Ill.) and Representative Gradison (R-Ohio) introduced H.R. 5270, the Foreign Income Tax Rationalization and Simplification Act of 1992, on May 19, 1992. This bill—which was not enacted in 1992—contained proposed tax legislation aimed squarely at the U.S. operations of foreign-based multinationals. Specifically, the bill set forth a special rule that applied to foreign-controlled U.S. corporations, or branches of foreign corporations. Such subsidiaries or branches operating in the United States would have been deemed to earn a specified minimum level of U.S. taxable income, and been taxed accordingly.[91]

Nor has the pressure on foreign-based multinational firms with U.S. affiliates abated in 1993. On March 25, 1993, following up on the House Ways and Means Oversight Committee's 1990 hearings, the Senate Committee on Governmental Affairs also held hearings on the compliance and enforcement problems engendered by Section 482, particularly as regards inbound companies, and the associated costs—forgone revenues, excessive litigation, and U.S. firms' competitive disadvantages. During these hearings, the Chairman, Senator Byron L. Dorgan (D-N.D.), unambiguously expressed his view that a formulary apportionment method had distinct advantages over the separate accounting framework.

---

[90]Remarks by Paul Kanjorski (D-Pa.) before the Subcommittee on Oversight of the House Ways and Means Committee, April 9, 1992.

[91]This minimum income was to be computed as 75% of an amount equal to their gross receipts in the United States, multiplied by an average profit rate for domestic companies engaged in the same line of business.

Advance Pricing Agreements

Among its efforts to improve voluntary tax compliance, the IRS initiated a new program whereby companies could request pre-approval of their transfer pricing polices in March 1991. This pre-approval consists of company-specific Advance Pricing Agreements, or APAs, between firms and the IRS. As of late May, 1993, 9 APAs had been completed,[92] 15 were in the final drafting stages, between 36 and 48 companies were in the pre-filing stage, and another 45 were in various intermediate points in this process.

Advance Pricing Agreements require interested companies to submit proposed transfer pricing procedures to the IRS, along with the requisite supporting documentation.[93] This proposal is evaluated by the IRS, disagreements between the IRS and firms regarding proposed pricing policies are resolved through a series of discussions, and, hopefully, a satisfactory compromise agreement is worked out. "Critical assumptions" constitute an important part of this agreement. In essence, these assumptions lay out certain initial conditions that must remain in effect for the life of the agreement (generally three years). Provided these conditions continue to hold and companies adhere to the terms of their individual agreements, the IRS refrains from a full-fledged Section 482 audit for the duration of the agreement. (The extent of its more limited review and oversight, for purposes of evaluating compliance with the APA and ascertaining whether the critical assumptions remain valid, is somewhat unclear at this stage.) U.S. taxing authorities have not made, and will not make, the terms of individual advance pricing agreements public, due to confidentiality concerns.[94] However, as of late May 1993, the

[92]These nine include Apple Computer's pioneering APA with U.S. and Australian tax authorities; Sumitomo Capital Markets' accord with U.S., British, and Hong Kong tax authorities; Barclay's APA with U.S. and British authorities; and Matsushita's APA with U.S. and Japanese tax authorities.

[93]Section 10 of Revenue Procedure 91-22, 91-1 C.B. 526 sets forth the provisions to be included in Advance Pricing Agreements (including the filing of annual reports, the scope of examinations thereunder, revocation, cancellation, revision and renewal of the APA, record retention policies, changes in critical assumptions, and so forth).

[94]In a public forum held on May 21, 1993, Mr. Robert E. Ackerman, Director of the APA Program, noted that the IRS has decided against making public redacted versions of completed APAs, because of concerns about confidentiality.

IRS was readying a document containing broad guidelines on APAs covering financial products for release later in the summer.

At the outset, a number of individuals within the IRS expressed reservations about the feasibility and desirability of APAs, arguing that the more abusive firms would have no incentive to incur the expense associated with the process and supply the extensive information required. Such companies' anticipated benefits were limited, the argument went, in that they actually paid very little in taxes in any event. Moreover, providing the IRS sufficient information to evaluate their pricing proposals could have put them at a distinct disadvantage if they ultimately failed to reach an agreement, and, thus, had to submit to a full-scale Section 482 audit. While there may be some merit to these concerns, a significant subset of companies clearly believe that the benefits outweigh the costs.

Predictability in tax burdens and the probable avoidance of potential pricing penalties[95] are clearly the APA's strongest selling points, with the attendant savings in time and money that would otherwise be expended in contending with a full-blown transfer pricing audit a significant added benefit. Methodological flexibility is another important virtue from the standpoint of firms (although it is potentially concerning from a policy perspective). The IRS can and does entertain a much broader range of pricing methods in the context of an APA, sometimes bypassing the approved transactions and profits-based methods altogether. Some companies, whose operations do not readily "fit" the prototypes on which the 1968 and temporary regulations are based, find this a very compelling motivation. Trading companies and financial institutions have been among

---

(Note, however, that "details about Matsushita's APA were leaked by top Tokyo tax administration officials to Japanese newspapers. The speculation is that the tax authorities, which have publicly supported the APA concept, want to educate Japanese companies in the U.S. about the scheme and impress on the U.S. Congress and the public that the Japanese companies are cooperating with the IRS." See Susumu, Awanohara and Burton, Jonathan, "Clinton's Tax Take," *Far Eastern Economic Review*, Nov. 26, 1992.)

[95]The preamble to the proposed penalty regulations states that, "[i]f a transfer pricing methodology is developed and applied pursuant to an Advance Pricing Agreement in any tax year, then the use of such methodology to establish intercompany prices for a different year may be considered evidence of reasonable cause and good faith."

the first to take advantage of the APA option. In the current environment, foreign-based multinationals may also find the certainty associated with APAs very appealing.

2.4 Institutional Dispute Resolution Procedures and Competent Authority Proceedings

As the above discussion of 1968, 1988 draft, 1992 and 1993 proposed, and 1993 temporary Section 482 regulations illustrates, and as the case studies in Part II following will make far more clear, transfer pricing guidelines cannot be reduced to hard-and-fast rules that are invariant to the facts and circumstances of individual cases. Rather, they must be interpreted and adapted to the often highly idiosyncratic set of facts that individual cases present. Consequently, both the IRS and corporations turn to economists to apply these regulations in particular instances (the former to evaluate firms' compliance after the fact, and the latter both to assess exposure to potential pricing adjustments given their prevailing transfer pricing practices, and, among the more far-sighted firms, to develop arm's length prices in the first instance). Economists, for their part, rely on a combination of observed results among uncontrolled parties and microeconomic theory in developing such cases.[96] Observed results take precedence when comparables can be identified. Microeconomic theory potentially plays an important role when comparable firms or transactions

[96]To date, statistical analysis has been used very sparingly in Section 482 cases, in part because these techniques are not necessarily widely known and accepted by (IRS and private sector) attorneys and accountants working on transfer pricing issues, and in part because the data necessary to apply them may be difficult to obtain. I would argue that wider use of such methods is potentially a very fruitful middle ground between the often futile search for comparable uncontrolled transactions or firms that are, individually, virtually identical to the controlled transaction or firm at issue, and the profit split or formulary apportionment methods that effectively abandon comparables-based methods. With a sufficiently large sample of inexactly comparable transactions or firms, statistical analysis essentially enables one to construct a very close composite comparable. See discussion in Chapter 8.

don't exist.[97] (Inasmuch as commercial practices, and, hence, observed results, don't always conform to theoretical predictions, this would seem to be a reasonable ordering of priorities.)

Needless to say, economists on either side of a transfer pricing issue do not always see eye to eye, and the parties they represent may have very different objectives. However, a workable tax system necessitates resolving the vast majority of tax disputes well before Tax Court. Accordingly, the IRS is structured in such a way as to resolve contentious issues through one-on-one negotiations with companies, if possible, at various levels.

Examination: *Examination* teams are responsible for carrying out the transfer pricing audit and developing the IRS's preliminary position, as set forth in the *Revenue Agent's Report*, or RAR. IRS economists and international examiners collaborate closely in this case development process. If the Examination Team proposes a pricing adjustment, companies and the IRS will often attempt to resolve their differences (regarding the amount of income that should be reported in the United States) at this level through a first round of direct negotiations.

Appeals: Failing a resolution at the Examination level, companies can have their cases heard by *Appeals*. In order to avail themselves of this stage of the appeals process, firms must file a formal protest to the issues (contained in the RAR) that they are contesting.

Appeals officers operate largely autonomously, answerable neither to Examination nor to IRS trial attorneys. They act as intermediaries between firms and IRS Examination, and attempt to work out a compromise in light of the merits of each party's position, limitations in IRS legal resources, and *hazards of litigation*.[98] The term

[97]See King, Elizabeth, "Economic Analysis in Transfer Pricing," in *International Transfer Pricing, Op. Cit.* for a discussion of the potential role for economic theory in the absence of comparables.

[98]Note that Appeals officers typically rise through the ranks within the IRS. They may or may not be attorneys, and they may or may not have an expertise in international tax issues, but they are virtually never economists. Responsibility for resolving cases at the level of Appeals is not segmented by type of issue, and

"hazards of litigation" refers to the likelihood that the courts will uphold the IRS's position on a given case. If an Appeals officer believes that the government may not be sustained in Tax Court, he or she may decide to settle on terms that are relatively more favorable to the firm than the Examination Team's preliminary position. These settlements—often arrived at by splitting the difference between each party's initial position in some proportion[99]—may bear little relationship to the arm's length standard,[100] and frequently become precedent-setting for the individual firms to which they relate. Alternatively, Appeals officers may uphold the Examination Team's findings, and forward the case to IRS District Counsel, which may or may not decide to litigate it. (If District Counsel does not litigate a case forwarded by Appeals, the case is returned to the latter for settlement.)

Reasonably enough, Appeals officers have revised their assessment of litigation hazards upward very substantially in the face of the IRS's string of reversals in Tax Court over the past twenty-odd years, and, consequently, tend to offer settlement terms that Examination views as overly generous.[101] Moreover, IRS trial attorneys have become understandably pessimistic about the prospects of prevailing in Section 482 cases that progress to the courts, and commensurately more reluctant to take an aggressive stance in identifying "litigation vehicles." Multinational firms, in turn, are much more resistant to settling at the Examination level, because the IRS's setbacks in court,

---

a relatively small portion of Appeals officers' workloads involves transfer pricing (or valuation) issues. Hence, formal economic training is not necessary in the majority of Appeals cases; rather, a broad background in accounting and tax law is far more important. However, the lack of economic training *is* undeniably a problem vis-a-vis the types of issues discussed herein. See Chapter 8 herein.

[99]The Appeals officer might simply multiply the Examination Team's proposed pricing adjustment by his or her estimate of the (numerical) probability that the adjustment would be sustained if the case were litigated.

[100]Negotiations with Appeals often cover a range of bundled issues, and one set (e.g., a proposed pricing adjustment) may be traded off against another in the process of working out an overall settlement. This practice also accounts for some portion of the negotiated settlements of pricing issues that bear little relationship to the arm's length principle.

[101]In fact, the rate at which Appeals sustains transfer pricing adjustments (the "sustension rate") declined markedly between 1987 and 1992. See United States General Accounting Office, *International Taxation—Updated Information on Transfer Pricing*, March 25, 1993.

combined with Appeals officers' tendency to negotiate relatively favorable settlements and IRS trial attorneys' reluctance to litigate, have created a very rational expectation that they will fare better in these forums. (It remains to be seen whether Tax Court judges and, hence, Appeals officers, will evaluate the relative merits of firm and IRS positions on pricing issues differently under the 1993 temporary regulations. If not, one can expect this dynamic to continue.)

Competent Authority: Firms also have the option of initiating *Competent Authority* proceedings. As discussed above, a firm that operates across jurisdictional boundaries may be double-taxed if taxing authorities in different countries, acting independently, allocate overlapping portions of its consolidated income to their respective jurisdictions. Given that the United States, OECD countries, and Japan all endorse legislation based on the arm's length standard for purposes of regulating intra-company transfer prices, multinational firms will not be double-taxed provided that taxing authorities in each jurisdiction agree as to the particular allocation of income implied by this standard (or, less ambitiously, a consistent allocation) in specific instances.[102] While this agreement on broad principle undoubtedly reduces the incidence of double taxation, it does not eliminate the potential therefor, inasmuch as the arm's length principle, applied to the same set of facts and circumstances, can and does yield very different interpretations and results. Bilateral tax treaties are designed principally to prevent double taxation, and Competent Authority is charged with interpreting, applying, and administering the provisions of such treaties. More specifically, "...Competent Authority has exclusive jurisdiction to grant or deny adjustments relating to international double taxation, to negotiate correlative foreign tax adjustments, and to determine whether the period of limitations on refunds or credits with respect to the issue has expired."[103] In the United States, the Assistant Commissioner (International) of the IRS performs this function.[104]

[102] This is something of an oversimplification; sourcing rules and other features of tax laws must be comparable as well.

[103] See Abrutyn and Halphen, 402-2nd T.M., *Income Tax Treaties—Administrative and Competent Authority Aspects, p. A-19.*

[104] Note that, if the issue under consideration is interpretative, the Associate Chief Counsel (International) must be consulted.

Competent Authority proceedings have procedural and substantive consequences for both companies and taxing authorities,[105] the specific nature of which depends partly on when a firm requests Competent Authority assistance. A company may file a request for Competent Authority Assistance immediately following an examination in lieu of a protest to Appeals (if it agrees to the proposed adjustment), and bypass the latter entirely. When this occurs, the Competent Authority representative may uphold, reduce, or withdraw the proposed reallocations altogether in the course of negotiating with his or her opposite number in the foreign jurisdiction.

Alternatively, a company may request Competent Authority assistance after it has negotiated a mutually satisfactory agreement with Appeals, or when it has failed to arrive at a compromise and the case is docketed for Tax Court.[106] However, if Competent Authority becomes involved after an Appeals settlement has been concluded, and this settlement is based on an assessment of hazards, Competent Authority will not reduce it further, as a matter of policy. Rather, its involvement will be limited to seeking relief in the foreign jurisdiction(s). Similarly, if the case is docketed for Tax Court, the IRS may or may not agree to involve Competent Authority.[107]

Once Competent Authority has accepted a case, the issues covered therein are transferred to it from Examination or Appeals. Administrative proceedings on the covered issues at the latter levels are suspended until the *Mutual Agreement Procedure* (the treaty provision empowering Competent Authority to negotiate with its counterparts in other countries) has run its course. Note that U.S. Competent Authority is *not* obligated to resolve a disputed tax issue, but merely to attempt such a resolution. Moreover, in doing so, it has a somewhat freer hand than Examination (in practice) and Appeals (in theory). It may consider the treaty partner's transfer pricing

[105] See Abrutyn and Halphen, *Op. Cit.*

[106] See, for example, "Docketing Case Does Not Block Use of Competent Authority, ACI Says," in *Tax Management Transfer Pricing Report*, Vol. 1, No. 3, June 10, 1992.

[107] More specifically, once a case has been docketed for Tax Court, it comes under the jurisdiction of the Office of Chief Counsel, which may or may not release jurisdiction back to the Assistant Commissioner (International), a necessary step before Competent Authority can become involved. See Rev. Proc. 91-23.

guidelines, the *OECD Report on Transfer Pricing*, prior Competent Authority settlements with the treaty partner concerning the subject and other firms, etc.[108] Ultimately, as noted above, Competent Authority's primary goal is to prevent double taxation.

Finally, companies have recourse to the courts, or, as of very recently, to an arbitration procedure.[109] Thus far, the latter option is largely untested,[110] and relatively few major transfer pricing cases have been heard in a court of law,[111] although close to 100 such cases were pending as of late 1992.[112] As noted above, in a number

[108]See Article 25 of the U.S. Model Treaty.

[109]With the adoption of Tax Court Rule 124, the Tax Court endorsed the use of arbitration under some circumstances.

[110]Apple Computer was the first to enter into an agreement with the IRS to arbitrate a Section 482 case. Arbitration hearings were scheduled to begin in July 1993. While there is a good deal of flexibility as to how a negotiated arbitration agreement is structured, the Apple stipulation calls for a binding resolution, to be decided by a three-member panel comprised of a retired judge, an economist, and an industry expert. As the attorneys representing Apple explain the process, "[t]he stipulation provides for 'baseball' type arbitration. The parties will each pick a separate amount of income for each of the three years at issue. Each party is precluded from changing the amount it submits, and must prove that its proposed amount is correct, or at least more correct than the amount submitted by the other party. Although the panel may well form its own view of the appropriate adjustment, if any, for each year at issue, its choices will be limited to the amounts proposed by the parties. There can be no 'baby-splitting' between the numbers offered by the parties for a given year." See Clark, Kenneth B., et. al., "A Different Approach to Resolving Section 482 Disputes," *Tax Notes*, June 29, 1992.

[111]In 1990, the then-Commissioner of Internal Revenue put this number at a meagre twenty since 1964, a significant underestimate of the total number of decided cases, but reasonably accurate as regards the very large and influential Section 482 cases. See Statement of Fred T. Goldberg, Jr., Commissioner of Internal Revenue, before the Subcommittee on Oversight, House Committee on Ways and Means, July 10, 1990. Among the most notable decided Section 482 cases are *The R.T. French Company v. Commissioner*, 60 T.C. 836 (1973); *E.I. dupont de Nemours Co. v. Commissioner.*, 608 F.2d 445 (Ct. Cl. 1979), cert. denied, 100 S. Ct. 1648 (1980); *U.S. Steel Corporation v. Commissioner*, 80-1 USTC P9307 (rev'g); 36 TCM 586; *Hospital Corporation of America v. Commissioner*, 81 T.C. 520 (1983); *Eli Lilly & Co. v. Commissioner*, 84 T.C. 996 (1985), *rev'd in part, aff'd in part* and *remanded*, Nos. 86-2911 and 86-3116 (7th Cir., August 31, 1988); *G.D. Searle and Co. v. Commissioner*, 88 T.C. 252, 376 (1987); *Bausch & Lomb Inc.*, 92 T.C. 33 (1990); *Sundstrand v. Commissioner*, 96 T.C. 226 (1991); and *Westreco, Inc. v. Commissioner*, No. 24078-88, T.C. Memo. 1992-561, 9/23/92.

[112]See *Tax Management Transfer Pricing Report*, Vol. 1, No. 11, Oct. 7, 1992.

of decided Section 482 cases, judges departed from both IRS and firm positions, utilizing a variety of fourth methods (predominantly profit splits) to arrive at a settlement.[113,114]

Thus, when all is said and done, resolutions of transfer pricing disputes, whether at the Examination, Appeals, Tax Court or Competent Authority levels, often bear little relationship to the arm's length standard. The potential for resolving transfer pricing disputes through arbitration could represent an improvement in this regard, but it may prove to be a very cumbersome process, and is largely untested to date.

2.5 Valuation of Acquired Assets for Tax Purposes: Internal Revenue Code Section 338

Corporations acquiring business enterprises can elect to treat a qualified stock purchase[115] as a purchase of the acquired company's underlying assets under Section 338 of the IRC. After January 29, 1986, and before the addition of IRC Section 197 (with the 1993 Act), companies making such an election were required to allocate the deemed

Further, transfer pricing cases represented more than 20% of the 400 largest cases docketed in Tax Court.

[113] See the White Paper, *Op. Cit.*, Chapters 4 and 5, for a discussion of notable decided pricing cases, the Service's unsuccessful attempts to identify comparables, and the fourth methods on which specific outcomes have been based.

[114] Unfortunately, these resolutions provide virtually no intelligible precedents from a case development perspective, because judges, with expertise in the law rather than microeconomic theory, are not best suited to justify a particular methodology—such as a given split of profits—on convincing theoretical grounds. Nor is this necessarily their goal. Thus, from an economic perspective, decided cases often appear quite arbitrary. Further, under the 1968 regulations, the profit split methods routinely used by the courts to resolve litigated cases could not be applied at the Examination level, unless one could justify the use of "fourth" methods by demonstrating that none of the higher-ranking pricing methods applied.

[115] Under a qualified stock purchase, the acquiring corporation must have acquired by purchase within a twelve-month period at least 80% of the total voting stock and 80% of the total value of stock of the acquired corporation.

purchase price (or adjusted grossed-up basis) sequentially across four distinct asset classes:

1. Cash and cash equivalents ("Class I" assets);
2. Certificates of deposit, U.S. government securities, readily marketable stock, and similar items ("Class II" assets);
3. Property, plant and equipment, land, other tangible property, accounts receivables, and amortizable assets ("Class III" assets); and,
4. Goodwill and going concern value ("Class IV" assets).

This approach was termed the "residual method," in that goodwill and going concern value (neither of which could be amortized before the 1993 Act's statutory changes[116]) were determined as a residual, after deducting the collective value of assets in Classes I–III from the total deemed purchase price. Further, because depreciation and amortization lives differed for different types of (tangible and intangible) assets included in Class III, these assets generally had to be valued, and their useful lives determined, individually.

Thus, under pre-1993 law, the tax consequences of a given merger were very sensitive to the relative values that acquiring companies assigned to individual assets—particularly intangible assets—and the IRS regularly reviewed, and often challenged, these valuations. As with Section 482 cases, valuation issues often involved many millions of dollars. IRS economists and engineers were assigned the task of evaluating companies' valuation submissions, correcting methodological flaws, and proposing alternative valuations where necessary. Valuation issues were resolved along the same procedural lines as Section 482 transfer pricing issues.

2.5.1 The Key Controversy Before 1993: Where Goodwill Begins and Ends

As the above description suggests, companies electing Section 338 had an incentive to maximize the value of assets with the shortest

[116]Treas. Reg. 1.167(a)-3.

useful lives (in order to realize depreciation and amortization benefits up front), and minimize the value of assets that were deemed (under pre-1993 law) to have indeterminate or infinite lives (i.e., goodwill and going concern value). Inasmuch as the latter were calculated as a residual, as described above, this amounted to carving out as many intangibles as possible from what would otherwise fall into the Class IV residual category, and arguing that they properly belonged in the Class III category of depreciable and amortizable assets. Assembled workforce intangibles, employment contracts, customer and advertiser lists, core deposits, premium population bases, computer software, favorable location, policy and procedure manuals, and many others were among those that taxpayers often distinguished from goodwill and going concern, and attempted to amortize.[117]

However, before the 1993 Act, these intangible assets could only be amortized if they satisfied a two-prong test that had evolved out of case law.[118] Specifically, if the subject intangible had a value separate and distinct from goodwill, and a limited useful life that could be ascertained with reasonable accuracy, it could be amortized accordingly. Conversely, if the intangible at issue failed either of these "prongs," it could not be amortized. Goodwill, in turn, has been defined by case law to consist in part of the "expectancy of continued patronage, for whatever reason" (*Boe v. Commissioner*, 307 F.2d 339 (9th Cir. 1962), *aff'g* 35 T.C. 720 (1961)). Going concern has variously been defined as "the additional element of value which attaches to property by reason of its existence as an integral part of a going concern" (*VGS Corp. v. Commissioner*, 68 T.C. 5563 (1977)) and "the ability of a business to continue to operate and produce income without interruption as a result of a takeover."[119]

Predictably, then, under pre-1993 law, companies and the IRS came to blows principally over which intangible assets were genuinely

[117]See *Intangibles Digest* prepared by Ms. Patti Burquest-Fultz and Joan Rood, Large Case Program, National Office, December 1990.

[118]While one finds the general outlines of this test in numerous prior cases, *Houston Chronicle Publishing Company v. United States*, 481 F.2d 1240 (5th Cir. 1973), *cert. denied*, 414 U.S. 1129 (1974) is generally cited in connection with it.

[119] *Winn-Dixie Montgomery, Inc., v. U.S.*, 444 F2d 677, 685, n. 12 (5th Cir. 1971); *Solitron Devices, Inc. v. Commissioner*, 80 T.C. 1, 19-20 (1983). Also see *Meredith Broadcasting Co. v. United States*, 405 F.2d 1214 (Ct. Cl. 1969); *Fong v. Commissioner*, T.C. Memo. 1984-402.

separate and distinct from goodwill and had finite and reasonably ascertainable lives (and, thus, could legitimately be amortized), and which did not. Companies often interpreted the two-prong test described above to mean that intangible assets were depreciable if they could be shown to have a useful life and a reasonably determinable value. The IRS, in contrast, tended to stress that taxpayers also had to demonstrate that the subject assets were separate and distinct from goodwill, or the "expectancy of continued patronage;" assigning a value and a finite life to a given asset per se did not suffice.

More proactively, the IRS also prepared a number of position (or "coordinated issue") papers on specific intangible assets (assembled workforce, customer-based intangibles, market-based intangibles, employment contracts, order backlog, and covenants not to compete) prior to the 1993 Act, arguing essentially that many of these intangibles were indistinguishable from goodwill and/or going concern value essentially by definition.[120] (See Appendix A at the end of this chapter for a brief summary of these position papers.) As the IRS described it, coordinated issue papers "...set forth the IRS's current 'thinking.' The papers, however, [were] clearly not revenue rulings or regulations, and therefore [were] not official pronouncements of Service Position."[121]

Official pronouncements or not, coordinated issue papers were intended to provide "unofficial guidance for the field." IRS agents had to raise coordinated issues if they were identified in the course of an audit (the issue papers were intended in part to facilitate this identification), and the development of these issues had to follow the reasoning laid out in the position papers. In order to develop a case along other lines, or to settle a case via negotiations at the Examination level, one was theoretically required to request a "variance"

---

[120]These position papers were published in full in *Tax Related Documents, Special Supplement: Complete Text of the Internal Revenue Service's Industry Specialization Program Coordinated Issue Papers, Tax Analysts*, February 1, 1993.

[121]Remarks by Mr. John J. Monaco, Executive Director of the IRS's Coordinated Examination Programs, before the Tax Executives Institute, March 30, 1992; published in an article entitled: "Position Paper on Industry Specialization Program," *Tax Related Documents, Special Supplement: Complete Text of the Internal Revenue Service's Industry Specialization Program Coordinated Issue Papers, Op. Cit.*

from the Industry Specialist coordinating the valuation issue, which might or might not have been approved.[122,123]

The precise nature of these differences between taxpayers and the IRS regarding the correct interpretation of the two-prong test in particular, and the scope of goodwill in general, is articulated exceptionally clearly in *Newark Morning Ledger Company v. U.S.*[124] In this case, the intangibles at issue were "paid subscribers," for which the Morning Ledger claimed depreciation deductions. While the IRS did not contest the Morning Ledger's estimate of paid subscribers' useful lives, it argued that this evidence was largely irrelevant, inasmuch as the intangible itself constituted goodwill essentially by definition. The Morning Ledger, for its part, took the position that goodwill was simply the residual value after one has deducted all identifiable intangibles with limited useful lives and reasonably ascertainable values from the value of the ongoing business overall, not only as a computational matter but by definition as well.

The alternating decisions at different legal stages in this case (and many others) also attest clearly to the persistent ambiguities and complexities surrounding the nature and boundaries of goodwill: the

[122] In practice, some settlements were negotiated between Examination-level IRS representatives and taxpayers "off the record," along lines that were not entirely consistent with positions laid out in the National Office position papers.

[123] Interestingly, Appeals was not bound by the IRS's coordinated issue positions on specific intangible assets. Further, a number of position papers were at odds with several significant decided cases. For these reasons, companies often rejected out of hand the IRS's attempts to establish per se rules to the effect that specific intangible assets were non-amortizable by their very nature (a position espoused in several coordinated issue papers), and routinely contested proposed adjustments based on this reasoning. Thus, settlements of valuation issues worked out in Appeals often bore little resemblance to the position that Examination was essentially required to put forth. Anticipating this result, the Examination team on a given valuation issue often developed both a primary position based on the relevant coordinated issue paper, and an alternative position that addressed the specific methodological points that a given taxpayer raised (which the coordinated issue position almost invariably failed—and, in fact, was not intended—to do). The alternative position was intended to provide the Appeals officer with a means of evaluating the taxpayer's arguments, and, hence, some basis for negotiating a compromise short of complete capitulation.

[124] Supreme Court of the United States, 91-1135, 4/20/93. Rev'd and remanded U.S. Court of Appeals, 3rd Cir.; 90-5637, 9/12/91, 945 F2d 555. Rev'd and remanded District Court decision, 90-1 USTC 50, 193, 734 F.Suppl. 176.

District Court held for the Morning Ledger, but the Appeals Court reversed this decision, noting that, "...under the proper definition of goodwill, the $67 million amount established by Morning Ledger [to be the estimated value of the 'paid subscriber' asset] is quite clearly comprised largely, if not exclusively, of amounts properly attributable to goodwill." The case was ultimately heard before the Supreme Court, which reversed the Appeals Court's decision and held for the petitioner, maintaining that "a taxpayer able to prove that a particular asset can be valued and that it has a limited useful life may depreciate its value over its useful life regardless of how much the asset appears to reflect the expectancy of continued patronage."[125]

With a view to simplifying the law regarding the amortization of intangible assets, and putting an end to the endlessly recurring controversies over the scope of goodwill and going concern value, Congress incorporated a new code section (Section 197) into the IRC with the 1993 Act. Section 197 provides for the straight line amortization of "amortizable Section 197 intangibles" over a fifteen-year period.[126] An amortizable Section 197 intangible, in turn, is defined as "any Section 197 intangible which is acquired by the taxpayer after the date of enactment of this section, and which is held in connection with the conduct of a trade or business or an activity described in Section 212."[127] Section 197 intangibles, in turn, are defined to include numerous previously controversial intangible as-

[125] More generally, under pre-1993 law, the courts, like companies, tended to view the issue of whether customer-based intangibles were part of goodwill as primarily factual. In a number of instances, judges decided cases in ways that were entirely consistent with the IRS's substantive position (as enunciated in its coordinated issue paper on customer-based intangibles). There have also been several notable exceptions (among them, *Citizens & Southern Corporation and Subsidiaries v. Commissioner*, 91 T.C. No. 35, September 6, 1988, as well as the Supreme Court's decision in *Newark Morning Ledger Co. v. U.S.*), where the judge determined that the acquiring companies at issue had established a reasonable basis for distinguishing customer-based intangibles from goodwill even when both elements were acquired and the seller's business was carried on by the buyer substantially unchanged.

[126] While proposed legislative changes to prohibit the amortization of certain types of intangible assets—specifically, customer-based intangibles—were jockeyed about for some time in the mid-1980s, they did not come to pass. See the November 5, 1987 version of the Omnibus Budget Reconciliation Act of 1987–H.R. 3545.

[127] The legislation includes an exclusion for "self-created" intangibles.

sets, among them goodwill; going concern value; workforce in place; business books and records, operating systems, or any other information base (including lists or other information with regard to current or prospective customers); any customer-based intangible; any supplier-based intangible; other similar items; and any covenant not to compete (or other arrangement that serves the same purpose) entered into in connection with an acquisition of an interest in a trade or business or substantial portion thereof.[128]

These new provisions should quell the often-heated controversies over where goodwill and going concern leave off and amortizable intangible assets begin, in that the new law eliminates the tax incentives to distinguish between them. (The present Section 338 regulations will have to be amended to incorporate the statutory changes. As expressed in the House Committee Report: "[i]t is anticipated that the residual method specified in the regulations will be modified to treat all amortizable Section 197 intangibles as Class IV assets....")

2.5.2 Areas of Broad Consensus: Valuation and Lifing Methodologies

From the standpoint of transfer pricing, the specific methodologies that taxpayers employed to value individual acquired intangible assets under Section 338 (before the addition of Section 197), and the IRS's assessment of them, are perhaps of greater interest than the definitional "goodwill and going concern value vs. other intangibles" issue described above. While the specific tax incentives at work under Section 338 pointed to maximizing the value of short-lived assets and minimizing the value of goodwill and going concern, the 1993 proposed profit split regulations under Section 482 create analogous incentives to maximize the value of intangible assets held in relatively

[128]Other Section 197 intangibles include any patent, copyright, formula, process, design, pattern, knowhow, format or similar item; any license, permit or other right granted by a governmental unit or an agency or instrumentality thereof; and, any franchise, trademark or trade name.

low-tax jurisdictions.[129] Hence, broad methodological questions regarding the valuation of intangible assets, long familiar territory to valuation practitioners, are increasingly of interest to transfer pricing practitioners.

Most valuation practitioners, both in and outside the IRS (and, more broadly, both in and outside the subfield of valuation for tax purposes), agree on broad methodological principles: how to value an asset, and how to ascertain its useful life. While reasonable people can and do differ as to how these methods should be applied in particular instances,[130] basic valuation and lifing principles, founded on an established body of economic, financial, and statistical theories, are firmly in place.

In general, both tangible and intangible assets are valued in one of three ways: the *income approach*, the *market comparison* method, or the *replacement cost* approach. The income approach to valuing assets amounts to projecting the income stream that the assets are expected to generate, and discounting this stream at the acquiror's risk-adjusted opportunity cost of capital. The cost of capital used to discount projected income is typically calculated as a weighted average of the cost of debt (on an after-tax basis, to reflect the net cost to the borrower after associated tax benefits are taken into account) and the cost of equity, respectively.[131] Practitioners generally rely on the Capital Asset Pricing Model (CAPM) to determine required returns on equity investments.[132] (While not uniformly endorsed by

---

[129] Note, however, that these purely tax-related incentives may well be offset by the multitude of other considerations that enter into multinational firms' intracompany pricing decisions in a given instance.

[130] The last case study reviewed in chapter 5 touches on some of these differences.

[131] Weights are often calculated based on industry-wide rather than company-specific averages.

[132] Briefly stated, the CAPM holds that the risk associated with an investment in equity (or any other asset, for that matter) is a composite of "diversifiable" and "non-diversifiable" (or "market") risk elements. Diversifiable risk can be eliminated by investing in a portfolio of stocks with returns that are not perfectly correlated. Market risk, in contrast, cannot be eliminated through diversification. All firms are subject to some degree of market risk. Investors, for their part, are rewarded only for bearing non-diversifiable risk (that is, risk that is not unique to a specific company). Under the CAPM, required returns to a given equity investment are comprised of two distinct components: a "risk-free" rate, compensating the investor for the time value of his or her money, and a measurable

financial economists, it is by far the most widely accepted approach.) The market comparison method looks to actual market values of comparable assets that are traded individually to value individual assets that were purchased en masse. Finally, the replacement cost approach, which approximates an asset's value as the cost of reproducing it, as the terminology suggests, is also a widely used valuation technique. It can also be used to value both tangible and intangible assets, provided that they are reproducible. Iowa Curve analyses are generally used to determine the expected useful life of both tangible and intangible assets.[133]

The choice of valuation methods is generally dictated by the availability of data. If an asset is not freely traded, the market comparison approach generally won't be apropos. Consequently, it is used very sparingly to value intangible property. If an asset cannot be reproduced, the replacement cost approach is clearly not suitable. If the income stream associated with a given asset cannot be predicted with reasonable accuracy, the margin of error one builds into a valuation computed via the income approach may be unduly high. As a general proposition, the fewer assumptions and projections one has to make in applying a particular valuation methodology, the more plausible one's asset valuations.

Despite these broad areas of consensus regarding valuation methodologies in general, taxpayers and the IRS often differed as to how they should be applied in a given instance under Section 338. Stated differently, the IRS often challenged specific applications of the in-

---

return to risk-bearing. The latter component, in turn, is a composite of (a) the market-determined price of a "unit" of risk; and (b) a parameter ("beta") that measures the covariance of the asset's return with the market return, divided by the variance of the market return. Each of these elements can be determined with a fair degree of accuracy (and used to compute the required return on an equity investment). Financial economists have written a great deal on the subject of the CAPM. See Brealey, Richard A. and Stewart C. Myers, *Principles of Corporate Finance*, New York: McGraw-Hill Book Company, 3rd Edition, 1988, Chapters 8 and 9, for an introductory discussion. This text also contains a bibliography of more advanced material on the CAPM.

[133]See Smith, Gordon V. and Russell L. Par, *The Valuation of Intellectual Property and Intangible Assets*, New York: John Wiley & Sons, 1989, Appendix B, "The Use and Abuse of Iowa Curves When Quantifying Appraisal Depreciation," for a synopsis of Iowa Curve techniques.

come, market comparison, and replacement cost approaches on fairly narrow methodological grounds.

For example, the projections of revenues and costs that the income approach entails might not have accorded with the acquired company's earnings history, or, if it did, there may have been compelling reasons to expect past and future performance to differ. The discount rate might have incorporated an unrealistic measure of risk (in the form of a "beta" that was too high or too low). An income stream jointly attributable to a group of assets used in concert may have been disaggregated into separate income streams attributable to individual assets in an arbitrary or inconsistent fashion. Similarly, applications of the market comparison approach may have been based on traded assets that were dissimilar from the acquired assets in some important respects. An application of the replacement cost approach may have been based on an under- or overestimate of all of the costs that one would incur in replacing the subject asset, or on historical rather than current costs, and so forth. (A number of these methodological issues, and their resolutions, are illustrated in the valuation case studies reviewed in Chapter 7.)

Appendix A: Summary of Coordinated Issue Papers

This appendix briefly summarizes the IRS's industry-wide coordinated issue papers relating to valuation issues.

Assembled Workforce: Under pre-1993 law, companies electing Section 338 often argued that an assembled workforce was an intangible asset because there was a "value inherent in having a trained staff of employees in place [excluding those that had separate employment contracts] when a business [was] acquired," and the benefits therefrom extended beyond the period in which the expenditures necessary to create the workforce were made.[134] (Hence, these expenditures constituted an investment, and the product thereof—an

[134] See *Intangibles Digest, Ibid.*

up-and-running workforce—an asset.) Companies generally valued this intangible by the replacement cost method, and determined its useful life in accordance with turnover rates. In its position paper on this intangible, the IRS held that an assembled workforce was part and parcel of going concern value and, as such, was non-amortizable.

Customer-Based Intangibles: According to the IRS's definition, customer-based intangibles, such as core deposits, subscriber lists, and patient relationships, consist of intangibles that are "closely associated with continuing the customer relationships developed by the acquired business."[135] Under pre-1993 law, companies electing Section 338 often took the position that these types of intangibles could be valued with reasonable accuracy by the replacement cost or income approach, had a finite life that could be estimated via statistically determined survival rates and, hence, were separable from goodwill and going concern. In its position paper on this intangible, the IRS held that when customer-based intangibles were acquired as part of an ongoing business, and "the purchaser merely steps into the shoes of the seller," these assets were indistinguishable from goodwill, and, as such, were non-amortizable.

Market-Based Intangibles: All market-based intangibles derive from a favorable market position. In its coordinated issue paper thereon, the IRS broke down this class of intangibles into two distinct categories: *existing market share intangibles*, representing "the present value of the increased revenues from lack of competition in the market area [at issue];" and *future market share intangibles*, representing the present value of projected increases in revenues attributable to future growth in the market area. The IRS's position paper on market share intangibles held that both types were inextricably bound up with either goodwill or going concern, in that both were "bottomed upon the expectation of the company's ability to attract as well as retain business." Further, in the IRS's view, "future market share" intangibles represented the future growth of the business, rather than a wasting asset.

---

[135] See ISP Coordinated Issue Paper, *Customer Based Intangibles*, January 1990.

Employment Contracts: Employment contracts designed to ensure that a target company's key employees will remain with the firm after it is acquired can obviously be very valuable to the acquiror. The IRS's coordinated issue paper on employment contracts relates to such contracts entered into by a target company in the course, and in consequence, of acquisition negotiations. Per this position paper, the IRS did not generally consider an employment contract entered into by a target company to be an asset of the target unless the following three-prong test (first enunciated in *Barnes Group, Inc. v. United States*)[136] was satisfied:

- The employment contract was entered into prior to the sale of the acquired company;
- The employment contract was not conditioned upon the sale of the acquired company; and,
- The acquired company had a substantial business purpose independent of the proposed sale of the company for entering into the employment contract.

The court, and, hence, the IRS, reasoned that an employment contract entered into as part of an acquisition, which would have no effect until the target company's stock was acquired and could be vitiated if the acquisition did not take place, could serve no business purpose of the acquired company. (By the same token, the three-prong test also suggested that employment contracts which were independent of acquisition negotiations, and had a substantial business purpose, may have been considered an amortizable intangible asset under pre-1993 law.)

Order Backlog: A target company often possesses a backlog of unfilled customer orders that passes into the hands of the acquiror when the acquisition is consummated. Under pre-1993 law, companies electing Section 338 sometimes argued that this order backlog was an amortizable intangible, in that it satisfied the two-prong

[136]872 F2d 528 (2d Cir. 1989).

test.[137] In its coordinated issue paper on this intangible, the IRS maintained that an order backlog was inextricably bound up with goodwill, in that it was "an important factor that contributes to, if not itself constitutes, the expectancy of continued customer patronage." As an alternative position, the IRS held that order backlog intangibles represented the going concern value of an acquired company: "[o]rder backlog allows the buyer to step into the shoes of the seller and represents the ability of a business to continue to function and generate operating revenues without interruption as a result of a change in ownership." Accordingly, in the IRS's pre-1993 thinking, an order backlog was inseparable from goodwill and going concern and, as such, was not amortizable.

Covenants Not to Compete: In the course of acquisition negotiations, a seller may enter into a covenant not to compete with the acquiring company. Rather than espousing a per se rule of non-amortizability regarding this type of intangible before 1993, the IRS would look to the facts and circumstances of particular cases to determine whether a covenant not to compete was an amortizable asset. Most importantly, the covenant had to "comport with economic reality" and be separable from goodwill. In determining whether a particular covenant had economic substance, the IRS would consider whether the seller could in fact compete with the buyer, and whether the seller policed the agreement to ensure that the buyer conformed to its written commitments (in keeping with a number of court cases). The value assigned to covenants was also an important element in determining their validity (and, hence, their amortizability). The IRS position paper provided that, in general, the amount of the purchase price allocated to a covenant not to compete should compensate the seller for its projected earnings losses absent the covenant.[138]

---

[137] Recall that this test required taxpayers to demonstrate that the intangible had a value separate and distinct from goodwill, and a limited useful life that could be ascertained with reasonable accuracy.

[138] See also *Dixie Finance*, 474 F.2d at 504-05.

Part II

Transfer Pricing and Valuation Regulations in Practice

Part II of this book is composed of ten case studies and a concluding chapter containing policy recommendations. I construct composite transfer pricing cases with a view to representing all of the methods explicitly sanctioned by Section 482—both 1968 and 1993 temporary versions—for establishing and evaluating intra-company transfer prices. Additionally, one of the transfer pricing cases is based on the capital employed method contained in the 1993 proposed regulations. The three valuation case studies included in Part II are similarly representative of a range of recurring methodological issues.

My overarching objective in reviewing these composite case studies is to consider:

- Why Section 482 transfer pricing regulations (both 1968 and 1993 temporary versions) will often fail to produce arm's length results, and may in fact produce results that are inconsistent across similarly situated firms;
- How these problems are compounded by the institutional context in which transfer pricing disputes are resolved;
- What insights the history of Section 338 issues provides as to the relative merits of different approaches to valuing intangible property, and the potential sources of controversy over such issues in connection with intra-company pricing; and,
- How statutory legislation and administrative practice can be made more consistent.

Hence, in the final chapter of Part II (Chapter 8), I pull together the method-specific critiques developed in the preceding case studies, and argue that intra-company pricing disputes arise as frequently as they do, and administrative practice diverges from statutory tax legislation as much as it does in this area, largely for two reasons: Section 482 regulations are highly ambiguous on a number of key points,[139] and disputed issues are resolved via administrative procedures that are extremely ad hoc. This state of affairs lends itself to

[139] This statement applies with very nearly equal force to both 1968 regulations and 1993 temporary regulations.

the unequal tax treatment of similarly situated firms, and to corporate tax liabilities that are often less, and occasionally more, than existing statutes mandate. Chapter 8 summarizes a number of policy recommendations that would narrow the gap between statutory legislation and administrative practice.

As noted in the introduction to this book, I assume, for purposes of discussion, that existing tax legislation remains in place. The arm's length standard is embodied in an extensive network of bilateral tax treaties to which the United States is a party, and it is unambiguously the international norm. Consequently, the U.S. Congress will probably not deviate from it unilaterally. For this reason, my policy recommendations go to how both regulations and dispute resolution procedures should be modified so that they are applied more uniformly and conform more closely to the statutory arm's length standard. However, in principle, the direction of change could also be reversed: Congress could modify tax laws to accord more closely with actual practice.

Stated differently, I do not advocate higher or lower corporate tax burdens per se, as an end in itself.[140] However, similarly situated firms should be treated uniformly for tax purposes. Tax burdens should be predictable. The distortions introduced into economic decision-making by virtue of the existing lacunae between tax legislation and administrative practice should be reduced. On a more ideological level, administrative practice should be subordinate to, and consistent with, statutory legislation in a democracy. To bring these salutory changes about, either laws or regulations and dispute resolution processes need to be changed. At present, the latter appear more malleable than the former.

[140] In this connection, it should be noted that, on purely economic grounds, one can make a compelling case that corporations should not be taxed.

Chapter 3

The Cost-Plus Method

3.1 Background

Recall that the cost-plus method of determining intra-company prices typically applies when one member of a controlled group performs assembly and/or manufacturing functions, and sells the fruits of these labors—intermediate or final products—to another member. If the manufacturing affiliate at issue in such cases operates in a relatively low-tax country, and sells its output to its U.S. parent, intra-company pricing designed solely to minimize effective global tax burdens—which may or may not be the only consideration that enters into transfer pricing decisions in a given instance—would lead the offshore affiliate to charge its parent as high a price as possible (potentially an excessively high price, relative to an arm's length price). If the parent is overcharged in this way, an unduly large share of the multinational firm's consolidated income will remain lodged in the manufacturing subsidiary.

In testing the reasonableness of manufacturing affiliates' transfer pricing practices under the cost-plus method, IRS economists typically look both to the markup over costs that the subsidiary charges, and the set of costs included in the base to which this markup is applied. The latter issue arises principally because parent firms may sell inputs to their manufacturing affiliates that they would generally consign to uncontrolled entities performing comparable functions. Arm's length markups over costs and industry practices regarding the composition of the cost base are ascertained by reference to stand-alone firms that are functionally comparable to the affiliate, and incur similar risks.

Under the 1968 regulations, IRS economists often drew comparable uncontrolled firms from the ranks of "contract manufacturers" for purposes of applying the cost-plus method. In essence, such firms perform manufacturing services under contract. They generally produce according to specifications—and in volumes—prescribed by the hiring firm. Their payment is based on services rendered, rather than the market price of the products they manufacture or assemble. As such, they incur limited (albeit some) market risks.[1] In these respects, some (albeit not all) manufacturing affiliates are close cousins.

In recent years, however, judges—and, consequently, IRS attorneys and Appeals officers—have widely rejected cost-plus analyses. Companies argue against the IRS's applications of the cost-plus method on the grounds that its "comparable" contract manufacturers are in fact not comparable to their manufacturing affiliates at all. Specifically, they argue that the skills their subsidiaries bring to bear, the intangible assets they utilize, the risks they incur, etc., clearly differentiate them from contract manufacturers. Because these arguments have carried weight in court and at the Appeals level, they have influenced IRS decisions over pricing methodologies early on in the audit process.

Consulting economists have levelled a more general—and more damning—critique of the cost-plus method *per se* over the years. The cost-plus approach measures income relative to costs, and equates this measure of profitability across firms. However, microeconomic theory predicts a systematic relationship between income and assets invested, rather than current costs.[2] Hence, unless the ratio of com-

---

[1] Contract manufacturers are common in a variety of industries, such as electronic components, where end-user demand for products fluctuates widely and suppliers do not maintain sufficient capacity in-house to satisfy peaks therein. Because contract manufacturers charge for services, they typically utilize a cost-plus method of pricing.

[2] More precisely, microeconomic theory predicts that, in markets with free entry and exit, firms' economic rates of return should be equalized across industries of equal risk. An economic rate of return, in turn, is defined as the interest rate

parable firms' assets to their cost of goods happens to be the same as a given manufacturing affiliate's assets to its cost of goods, there is no reason to expect them to earn uniform cost-plus margins, even if they would earn comparable returns on operating assets.

These criticisms of the cost-plus method notwithstanding, it survived the reformulation of transfer pricing regulations over the past several years and remains part of the interpretive guidelines. In this chapter, I review two composite cost-plus cases. The discussion of these two cases is intended to:

- Clarify the means by which IRS economists assess potential abuse under this method;
- Suggest how the development of such cases will differ under old and new regimes;
- Underscore several problems that regularly arose in attempting to apply the cost-plus method under the 1968 regulations;
- Demonstrate that some of these issues are not resolved in the 1993 temporary regulations; and, lastly,
- Suggest some further refinements thereto.

3.2 Cost-Plus Case 1: Leather Goods

The first of these cost-plus cases involves a parent firm located in the southwestern United States and a subsidiary operating in a U.S. posessions territory. Together, they produced a variety of leather goods (handbags, belts, and briefcases) for both men and women.

3.2.1 Summary Functional Analysis

The division of labor between parent (P) and subsidiary (S) was as follows: S manufactured briefcases according to P's specifications,

that equates the present value of the benefits flowing from a given undertaking with the initial investment required.

purchased all of its raw materials requirements as well as some managerial services from P, and sold all of its output to P. P designed, manufactured, and distributed handbags and belts, and designed and distributed the briefcases that it purchased from S. P's sales of leather goods imported from S consistently constituted approximately a third of its total sales in value terms.

P also contributed valuable marketing intangibles vis-a-vis its distribution efforts, selling both the leather products that it manufactured and those that it imported from S under its own label to retail and wholesale distributors, and directly to end-user customers through factory outlets and mail order catalogs. S did not underwrite any of P's marketing or selling expenses.

3.2.2 Intra-Company Transfer Pricing Policy

The company established its transfer prices for the briefcases that S sold to P by means of a set formula that began with P's wholesale price and worked backwards, in modified resale price fashion. Transactions between P and unrelated wholesale distributors were genuinely arm's length (with the wholesale price set at two-thirds of the retail price). Distributors received a 2% discount if payment was made within thirty days; this discount cost was borne solely by P.

P's per-unit gross profit on sales of products manufactured by S was equal to the difference between the wholesale price it charged independent distributors (net of the 2% discount) and the transfer price it paid S for the product. This transfer price, in turn, was arrived at by deducting a nominal 5% sales commission, along with certain transport-related expenses that P bore ($0.50 freight charges per unit of product shipped, and a 10% handling fee), from its revenues. Hence, revenues on products manufactured by S were divided approximately (15:85) between P and S (with S claiming the larger portion). The division of profits on these sales was slightly less heavily skewed towards S.

3.2.3 Potential Issues

The first order of business in this case was to determine whether P should have been cast in the role of sales branch in relation to S—as the company effectively did—in light of the range of functions it performed vis-a-vis products that it imported from S. If so, one would then determine whether it earned a sufficient return as such. If not, one would characterize the firm more accurately, select a "tested party" (either P or S) based on the likelihood of finding defensible comparables, identify a set of comparable uncontrolled firms, derive cost-plus margins therefrom, and, lastly, adjust the tested party's operating results accordingly (by applying the arm's length markup(s) over costs to the tested party's cost base).

Recall that P designed and distributed the leather goods that it imported from S; it developed the trade name it attached to these goods; it supplied S with detailed product specifications, volume requirements and raw materials; it projected demand; it purchased all of the product that it ordered from S outright (regardless of intervening changes in the level of end-user demand therefor) and, as such, incurred significant inventory risks. Clearly, this list of functions performed and risks assumed does not conjure up the image of a simple selling agent.

S, for its part, performed relatively simple manufacturing functions, incurred virtually no marketing expenses, and assumed minimal risks. Given that S's operations were substantially more limited than P's, we were far more likely to find uncontrolled firms that were comparable to S than to P; hence, we selected S as the tested party in this case.

As discussed in Part I, under both 1968 and temporary Section 482 regulations, prospective comparables are selected based on the functional similarities between them and the tested party, and similarities in the form and extent of risks that they assume. An outbound pricing issue exists if comparables earn significantly less than the tested party (after incorporating all necessary adjustments to "correct for" economically significant differences between them), and not otherwise.

3.2.4 Adjustment Methodology under the 1968 Regulations

Two alternative cost-plus adjustments were developed in this case:

- The first adjustment was based on virtually the only uncontrolled firm that operated in the same product market as S and performed broadly similar functions;
- The second adjustment was based on comparables that were similar both in terms of functions and risks, but operated in distinct product markets.

Cost-Plus Application 1: Private Label Manufacturer Comparable: Under the first cost-plus application, our proposed comparable was a U.S. private label manufacturer, somewhat different from a contract manufacturer, albeit in ways that benefitted the taxpayer. As with contract manufacturers, private label manufacturers produce largely to customer orders, and according to specifications that customers provide. As such, they do minimal design work and incur limited finished product inventory risk. However, private label manufacturing is a more substantial business than contract manufacturing in several regards. It may demand more sophisticated skills and equipment, generally requires suppliers to maintain larger stocks of purchased (as opposed to consigned) inventory, and often necessitates dealing with a substantially broader customer base.

The particular private label manufacturer we used as a comparable for purposes of this application was much larger than S. It performed some marketing, although this activity was limited to the wholesale level. It obtained its materials requirements from independent suppliers, and paid the going arm's length markup. When timely supplies of materials could not be assured, it maintained substantial inventories.

Inasmuch as this comparable performed a broader range of support functions than S and incurred somewhat greater risks, it would generally command a somewhat higher gross profit markup over above-the-line costs than S cum stand-alone manufacturer.[3] In theory one could—and in practice one should—quantify this incremental gross profit, and net it out of the comparable's total gross profits before calculating its (residual) arm's length markup over costs, to be applied to S. Practically speaking, however, this level of refinement is often not feasible, due to time, data and resource constraints.[4] Moreover, because a proposed pricing adjustment at the Examination level typically serves as a starting point in negotiations with the taxpayer under audit, rather than the end result, many have felt that this degree of precision is not necessarily called for, particularly when the profit differential (that is, the gross profits attributable to activities that only the comparable performs) is not believed to be very significant and the differences work to the taxpayer's advantage, as they did in the instant case. For all of these reasons, we did not quantify the difference in profits attributable to differences in functions and risks, but only suggested whether profits would be increased or decreased as a result of each.

Our first adjustment was calculated in two steps. In the first step, we adjusted S's cost of goods in two ways:

- First, we deducted the raw materials that S purchased from

[3] As discussed in Part I, gross profit margins are comprised of the sum of payments, both imputed and explicit, to below-the-line productive factors. If two entities employ essentially the same factors (in the same proportions) per dollar of above-the-line costs (as is reasonably likely if they perform the same functions), and compensate them at the same rate (as is highly likely if they operate in the same factor markets and incur comparable risks), their gross margins relative to above-the-line costs should therefore be comparable (leaving aside random variability in earnings). Analogously, if two entities perform different functions and/or incur different levels of risk, the productive factors that they utilize per dollar of above-the-line costs, and/or their imputed cost of capital, should likewise differ. More particularly, the entity performing additional support functions will likely employ additional below-the-line factors, and its gross margin should be sufficiently high to compensate these incremental factors.

[4] IRS case managers effectively determine how much time should be allotted to developing individual issues on their cases. Further, case managers' personnel reviews—and, hence, their prospects for promotion and performance awards—depend in part on whether they close cases promptly and keep current on audit cycles. For this reason, pressures to close cases can be quite strong, even if it means cutting short the development of a potentially strong issue. Resource limitations—access to computers, software, on-line databases, and so forth—are no minor matter either.

P from S's cost of goods sold, because firms employing the services of private label manufacturers generally consign such materials to them. Further, private label manufacturers dealing at arm's length generally do not mark up consigned materials in determining payment (on a cost-plus basis) for manufacturing services rendered.

- Second, we estimated the labor savings that S realized by virtue of operating in a possessions territory rather than the U.S. proper, and added this amount directly to its cost base preliminary to applying an arm's length markup thereto. (Recall that S was entitled to these labor savings under Section 936(h), in that it operated in a U.S. possession.)

As a second step in calculating our first adjustment, we applied the private label comparable's gross markup over its cost of goods (derived from its 10-K reports filed with the Securities and Exchange Commission) to S's adjusted cost of goods to obtain its arm's length gross profits, before taking its labor savings directly into account. We then added S's labor cost savings to this arm's length gross profit amount to obtain its allowable gross profits under Section 936(h).[5] The differential between S's allowable and reported gross profits constituted our first proposed cost-plus adjustment.

Cost-Plus Application 2: Footwear Contract Manufacturing Comparable: Because there were so few prospective comparables in the leather accessories industry, and because they were significantly inexact in any event, we developed an alternative cost-plus adjustment as well. In calculating this second adjustment, we drew comparables from the leather footwear contract manufacturing industry in the U.S. proper. Production processes in leather accessories utilize similar equipment (exceptionally powerful sewing machines), involve many of the same tasks, and use some of the same

[5]In effect, the labor savings approach sanctioned by Section 936(h) is equivalent to assuming that the manufacturing affiliate enjoys a unique process technology relative to U.S. competitors that permits it to produce at a lower unit cost by the amount of labor savings. As such, while it charges the same price (if the industry is competitive), it earns higher profits by the amount of the cost savings it enjoys by virtue of its superior "technology."

raw materials as leather footwear manufacturing. Accordingly, the fixed and variable factors of production required in these endeavors are fairly similar. Adjusting for labor savings, then, S and our proposed contract manufacturer comparables presumably incurred similar explicit factor costs. Further, in our judgment, they incurred comparably limited risks, and, hence, faced comparable costs of capital. Putting these observations together, leather footwear contract manufacturers' gross markups should have been fairly similar to that which S would have earned (after adjusting for labor savings) on a stand-alone basis.

To obtain financial information on these comparables, we turned to the *Census of Manufacturers* published by the U.S. Department of Commerce.[6] Using non-rubber footwear contractors' value of shipments and their cost of materials and wages, as published in the *Census*, coupled with S's proportionate overhead costs,[7] we derived an approximate gross markup on costs. This markup, in turn, was applied to S's adjusted cost of goods sold[8] to determine arm's length profits before directly accounting for cost savings. Again, as a final step, S's labor savings were added to this arm's length profit computation. Our proposed transfer pricing adjustment was given by the difference between S's allowable and reported profits.

3.2.5 Possible Adjustment Methodology under the 1993 Temporary Regulations

This case comes under Section 936(h) rather than Section 482. As such, the 1993 temporary regulations would not come into play unless the company had made a cost-sharing election.[9] However, consider

[6] Approximately every five years, the Commerce Department publishes fairly detailed financial data on contractors producing non-rubber footwear, among other things.

[7] Data on contractors' overhead costs are not published by the *Census*; however, as a percentage of cost of goods, we assumed they would be roughly comparable to those incurred by the tested party, S.

[8] Again, S's cost base was adjusted downward by netting out raw materials that would have been consigned on an arm's length basis, and upward by the amount of its labor savings.

[9] See discussion in Chapter 2.

how the case might be analyzed under the 1993 temporary regulations if S did not operate in a U.S. possessions.

The logical choice of pricing methods under the "best methods" rule remains cost-plus. However, as noted, the 1993 temporary regulations are far more explicit than their predecessor as regards both comparability criteria and the standards of comparability to be satisfied under the cost-plus (and other) methods. In comparing pricing and adjustment methodologies under the 1968 and temporary regulations, then, the first order of business is to determine whether the same firms would satisfy these more stringent comparability criteria and standards. Further, adjustments for differences in functions and risks between the tested party and comparable uncontrolled firms *must* be made under the 1993 temporary regulations. If the effects of such differences on the uncontrolled firms' profitability cannot be ascertained with reasonable accuracy (or if no stand-alone firms that satisfy the new comparability standards can be found), the comparable profits method may be used in lieu of the cost-plus approach.[10] Finally, the 1993 temporary regulations contain a provision which may preclude IRS economists from treating purchased raw materials as if they were consigned. These issues are taken up below.

Comparability Criteria

As discussed in Chapter 2, one is directed to consider a number of specific factors in selecting comparables under the 1993 temporary regulations. A subset of these factors apply across methods; the remainder are specific to the cost-plus method. (Recall that the listed method-specific criteria are not necessarily intended to be comprehensive.) The basic comparability criteria that apply across methods include:

- Functions;
- Risks;

[10] As discussed in Chapter 2, this methodology imposes a much less exacting standard of comparability and does not require adjustments for differences. Recall, however, that the extent of the arm's length range depends on how similar one's comparables are, and whether adjustments for differences have been made.

- Contractual terms;
- Economic conditions; and,
- Property or services.

Functions and risks weigh more heavily under profits-based methods (such as cost-plus), while property or services and contractual terms carry the day under transactions-based methods. Economic conditions, broadly defined to encompass a number of facets (alternatives reasonably available to buyers and sellers, the extent of competition in each market, the similarity of distinct geographic markets, the relative size of each market, the level of each market, relative market shares, and location-specific factor costs), will generally be relevant for both profits- and price-based methods.

Differences between prospective uncontrolled comparables and the controlled tested party that may be "particularly relevant" under the cost-plus method include:

- The complexity of manufacturing or assembly operations;
- Manufacturing, production, and process engineering capabilities;
- Procurement, purchasing, and inventory control activities;
- Testing functions;
- Selling, general, and administrative expenses;
- Foreign currency risks; and,
- Extension of credit and payment terms.

Recall that, under the 1968 regulations, we utilized an inexact comparable drawn from the leather accessories industry (a private label manufacturer) to determine one arm's length markup in this case, and another set of comparables (contract manufacturers that were more similar in terms of functions and risks than the private label comparable) drawn from the leather footwear industry. Would these comparables be screened out by the 1993 temporary regulations' more detailed comparability criteria (assuming that the effects of remaining differences on profitability could be quantified with reasonable accuracy)? Consider the private label comparable first.

The Private Label Comparable: The private label manufacturer's core functions—producing leather accessories according to specifications provided by its customers on an order-by-order basis—were quite similar to S's activities. However, it also performed limited marketing functions, while S did not; it maintained much larger materials inventories than S, and incurred commensurately greater risks; it performed a number of support functions associated with maintaining a large network of suppliers and customers that S did not have to undertake; and so forth. While these differences in functions and risks are potentially significant, such dissimilarities are acceptable under the new regime, provided that one adjusts the uncontrolled entities' profits accordingly before deriving arm's length markups to apply to the tested party's cost base.

Likewise, the requisite similarity in economic conditions would probably be satisfied, albeit some adjustments for differences would be necessary here as well:

- Both the private label manufacturer and S operated in the same product market, and at the same levels therein.
- The private label manufacturer's (actual) market share was considerably larger than S's (hypothetical) market share, but neither would have exercised market power in any event (entry into the industry was not restricted). Hence, all other things equal, they should have charged the same price or fees for manufacturing services on a genuinely arm's length basis, despite differences in their respective scale of operations. (Adjustments for differences in scale may be necessary nonetheless, however, because unit costs and, hence, profitability may differ if there are scale economies in the manufacturing activities at issue.)
- While S and the independent private label manufacturer operated in different geographic areas (the former in a U.S. possessions and the latter in the United States proper), these geographic areas effectively comprised a single economic market (albeit with different cost conditions).

- While S enjoyed location-specific labor (or wage) savings by virtue of operating in a possessions territory, these lower wage rates were available to all firms that located in its geographic market, and "entry" into this geographic area was not restricted. As such, one would expect the savings attributable thereto to be passed along to customers (i.e., P) on an arm's length basis, through competition-induced fee reductions.[11] (Stated differently, S would generally not retain wage savings.) Note, however, that this line of argument presupposes that firms are efficient, and always act immediately on an opportunity to reduce costs or otherwise increase profits, which may not be entirely accurate. If in fact location-specific wage savings were not fully offset by location-specific dissavings[12] and/or the transportation costs incurred by locating "offshore," (and U.S.-based firms' failure to do so was explained by inertia or some other form of inefficiency), the U.S. private label manufacturer's costs would be higher than S's, and its profits (and return on assets) commensurately lower. Presumably, this state of affairs would not be sustainable, in that investors in the private label firm would not be content with lower-than-normal returns for extended periods, but it might prevail for a short time (and, therefore, necessitate adjustments for purposes of calculating S's arm's length income).[13]

In short, provided that one could determine (a) how much of the private label manufacturer's gross profits were attributable to the additional marketing and support functions, incremental inventory risks and scale economies that distinguished it from S; and (b) the precise amount by which the private label manufacturer's costs were higher

[11] Recall that, under the 1993 temporary regulations, location savings are to be allocated to either S or P based on "the relative competitive positions of buyers and sellers in each location."

[12] These dissavings included (a) the more generous benefits packages that employees in the possessions territory received, (b) the generally lower levels of labor productivity (output per worker), and (c) the higher location-specific costs of electricity.

[13] On the other hand, the fact that the private label firm had not relocated its manufacturing activities in the possessions territory may simply indicate that there were no net location savings to be had. In this event, no location-specific cost adjustments would be called for.

by virtue of operating in the United States proper rather than the possessions territory (if net location savings, less incremental transportation costs, were positive), this comparable would probably pass muster for purposes of applying the cost-plus method under the 1993 temporary regulations. (Methods of quantifying these differences are discussed below.)

The Leather Footwear Contract Manufacturer Comparables: Consider next the comparables drawn from the leather footwear contract manufacturing industry. As discussed above, these comparables were functionally very similar to S, and incurred analogous inventory and market risks. However, because they operated in different product markets, one must also demonstrate that economic returns on these activities (in this case, gross margins over costs) in the separate markets would be similar.[14] If such a case can be made, then the leather footwear contract manufacturers used as comparables under the 1968 regulations should also pass muster as comparables under the 1993 temporary regulations.

In justifying the use of contract manufacturer comparables under the 1968 regulations, we argued essentially this case.[15] Thus, the 1993 temporary regulations' comparability standards may not alter the choice of comparables in this instance.

Required Adjustments

The leather footwear contract manufacturing comparables require very few adjustments under the 1993 temporary regulations. How-

[14] In this regard, the extent of competition in each market—one of the elements of "economic conditions" enumerated in the 1993 temporary regulations—is particularly important.

[15] Recall the basic elements of this argument: there were virtually no barriers to entry into the business of manufacturing leather products to order; additionally, both S and leather footwear contract manufacturers incurred limited risks. Hence, both should have had (the same) normal risk-adjusted cost of capital. Moreover, they utilized very similar production processes and drew on comparable skills. As such, their payments to other productive factors (per dollar of above-the-line costs) should likewise have been similar. For these reasons, one could reasonably expect S and the contract manufacturer comparables to earn similar gross markups on costs.

ever, the private label manufacturer differed from S in a number of economically significant ways.

Statistical analysis is one means of quantifying the effects of these differences on the private label manufacturer's profits. That is, given a sample of stand-alone firms that perform varying combinations of broadly similar marketing and manufacturing functions, preferably in the same industry (and invest in the combination of assets that relate to these functions), operate at different scales, and incur different forms and levels of risk, one can use regression analysis to disaggregate profits (the "dependent variable") into returns on different forms of risk-bearing and investment, scale effects (collectively, the "explanatory variables"), and random variability. This general attribution of profits to different forms of risk, investment, and scale effects could then be applied to the private label manufacturer, and its profits segmented accordingly.[16]

Realistically speaking, however, IRS resources and the time allotted to developing individual pricing issues are likely to remain limited. For this reason, a more rough-and-ready approach to quantifying the effects of differences in functions and risks between comparables and tested party will probably be more common. One such approach amounts to segmenting the comparable into two distinct "divisions," and allocating its total realized gross margin to each hypothetical division in a more approximate way. One division should correspond to the set of activities that both comparable and affiliate perform, and the other, to those that the comparable alone performs.

In the instant case, the first step in this more approximate approach to quantifying differences would entail identifying all below-the-line factors of production (including tangible and, perhaps, intangible capital) that the private label manufacturer utilizes in the marketing, support, and inventory-carrying activities that it alone performs. The costs associated with these below-the-line inputs, including an imputed risk-adjusted return on tangible and intangible

[16]As noted in Chapter 2, and as discussed at greater length in Chapter 8, statistical analysis is useful not only as a means of quantifying the effects of differences between individual inexact comparables and the tested party; it also obviates the need for this "case study" approach. Stated differently, one can use statistical techniques to build up a composite comparable, rather than rely on individual flesh-and-blood inexact comparables.

capital employed,[17] should be netted out of its total gross profits. The residual gross profits are attributable to the common activities that both S and the private label comparable perform. Absent scale economies, one can compute S's arm's length markup over costs by dividing the private label comparable's residual gross profits by its cost of goods associated with the common activities. To adjust for scale effects, one should start by determining the source of the scale economies, and quantifying the resulting cost savings. For purposes of computing arm's length markups, the private label manufacturer's cost advantages relative to S should be eliminated. (That is, one should determine how much higher the private label manufacturer's costs would be if it operated at S's smaller scale, and reduce its margin accordingly.)

Composition of the Cost Base

Recall that both applications of the cost-plus method under the 1968 regulations entailed netting out materials from S's cost base that it actually purchased from P, but which P would likely have consigned to an unrelated party performing comparable manufacturing services (judging from standard industry practice). A passage in the 1993 temporary regulations may bear directly on this consignment issue:

> ...[T]he district director will test the arm's length character of the results of a taxpayer's transaction *as actually structured* by the taxpayer [my *emph.*], and ordinarily will not treat the transaction as if it had been structured in a different manner. Pursuant to the comparability analysis of section 1.482-1T(c)(3), however, the district director may consider the alternatives available to the taxpayer in determining whether the terms of the controlled transaction would be acceptable to an uncontrolled taxpayer faced with the same alternatives and operating under the same circumstances. In such cases the district director may adjust the consideration charged in the controlled transaction based on the cost of an alternative, but will

[17]The CAPM can be used to determine a required return on equity capital.

not restructure the transaction as if the alternative had been adopted by the taxpayer.

This clause (more particularly, the "as actually structured" terminology) suggests that IRS economists may no longer be able to treat materials that controlled affiliates purchase from related parties as if they had been consigned, for purposes of applying the cost-plus method. At first blush, this interpretation seems to suggest (and may in fact mean) that all of S's raw materials should be included in its cost base for purposes of determining arm's length gross profits, and the method described above applied otherwise unchanged. However, the further stipulation that the district director may take into account the "alternatives available" to the taxpayer suggests a different approach.

P had the option of consigning materials to S cum stand-alone manufacturer. By selling rather than consigning them, it obtained the use of funds that would otherwise have been tied up in materials inventory.[18] Beyond this, there was no real advantage to selling over consigning (other than potentially justifying a higher transfer price). Applying the "alternatives available" framework described in the 1993 temporary regulations, P should have been willing to pay a slightly higher price for the manufacturing services (or tangible property) that it purchased from S by virtue of the fact that it sold materials to S outright. However, this differential should not exceed the value of the economic benefit that P derived thereby—the arm's length inventory financing costs that it saved.

In summary, the IRS's proposed adjustment under the 1993 temporary regulations might differ from that under the 1968 regulations in the following ways:

- The economically significant differences between the private label manufacturer and S would have to be quantified;
- The materials that P actually sold to S, but which the IRS treated as consigned under the 1968 regulations, would likely

[18]If there was some prospect that P would not have purchased all of S's output, P would also have reduced its own inventory risk somewhat by selling rather than consigning materials, but this consideration is not relevant in the instant case, because P routinely purchased all of S's output.

> be treated differently under the 1993 temporary regulations. If the IRS attaches more weight to the regulations' "as actually structured" terminology than the "alternatives available" clause in applying them, S's cost base should be increased by the amount of materials it purchased from P. Conversely, if it weights the "alternatives available" stipulation more heavily, P's transfer price to S might only be increased by the amount of the financing costs P saved by virtue of selling materials to S rather than consigning them.

The quantification of differences between our comparables and S would likely work to the taxpayer's disadvantage in this case, in that it would reduce the arm's length markup applied to S's cost base, reduce S's arm's length profits, and, hence, increase the IRS's proposed adjustment. Either alternative treatment of S's materials would benefit the taxpayer.

3.2.6 Taxpayer's Position

The taxpayers in this composite case study objected principally to our treatment of their subsidiaries' materials. In particular, several firms argued that their subsidiary/parent relationships were structured in such a way that the subsidiaries purchased their materials requirements outright, and that the IRS could not simply disregard this structure. Moreover, the parent firms did not repurchase unused materials, nor did they formally contract to purchase all of the output that they had their respective offshore affiliates produce. Thus, in form (if not necessarily in substance), the subsidiaries incurred greater risks than functionally comparable contract manufacturers.

3.2.7 Resolution

The cases that make up this composite case study were resolved on terms that were far more favorable to the taxpayers at issue than the IRS Examination teams' proposed pricing adjustments. Specifically, the Appeals officers, generally citing "hazards of litigation," worked out a series of compromises whereby the taxpayers paid the government approximately one-fifth of the proposed Section 482 adjustments, on average.[19]

Would Appeals have resolved cases of this sort differently under the new regime (leaving aside the arm's length range defense described below)? If Appeals officers based their settlements solely on the 1993 temporary regulations themselves, this composite case, and similar cases, would probably be resolved on terms more favorable to the government. In particular, *S*'s inventory risk would be evaluated in terms of its potential for inventory losses, and the magnitude thereof. Similarly, the lack of a written agreement between *S* and *P* per se, obligating the latter to purchase all of *S*'s output, would not demonstrate that *S* actually assumed significant demand-related risks. On the other hand, Appeals officers might read the 1993 temporary regulations to support the taxpayer's argument that *S*'s cost base should include the materials it purchased from *P*.

However, Appeals officers weight their assessments of litigation hazards very heavily in negotiating settlements of pricing issues. Hence, if they do not anticipate a change in Tax Court decisions on similar issues (before a body of case law has built up), Appeals settlements may well be similar (in their reasoning and, more concretely, in proportionate terms[20]) under the 1993 temporary regulations, at least in the short run. In the longer term, if judges base their future decisions on the 1993 temporary regulations, and interpret them in ways consistent with IRS economists' interpretations—both very big "ifs"—Appeals officers' assessments of litigation hazards in cases of this sort should follow suit, and gradually diminish over time.

In addition to arguing methodological fine points, however, taxpayers can also refute a proposed cost-plus adjustment by demonstrating that the affiliate's reported operating profits are within an "arm's length range," developed from a sample of (potentially very inexact) "comparable" firms.[21] Hence, in evaluating the relative mer-

[19] Appeals officers are instructed to settle a very large percentage of the cases they review. This partially accounts for the generous settlements they tend to negotiate.

[20] As described in Chapter 2, Appeals officers sometimes simply apply their subjective estimate of the probability that the Government would be sustained in court to the total proposed adjustment to arrive at a settlement figure.

[21] As discussed in Chapter 2, where the term "comparable" is interpreted very

its of a proposed Section 482 adjustment and the taxpayers' rebuttal, Appeals officers have essentially been instructed (by the terms of the 1993 temporary regulations) to give greater evidentiary weight to an amalgam of potentially poor comparables' operating results than to the operating results of an uncontrolled firm (or firms) that satisfy a much higher standard of comparability. This sizeable loophole should work very much to taxpayers' advantage, and may in fact undo whatever gains there were to be had (from the IRS's perspective) by adding the "alternatives available" terminology, elevating substance over form explicitly, and clarifying the comparability criteria and standards to be applied under the cost-plus method. Within reason, it is often a simple matter to select comparables (that need not be very comparable) with a view to justifying a given result.

3.3 Cost-Plus Case 2: Consumer Electronics

The second cost-plus case reviewed in this chapter concerns a parent firm that produced a range of electronic kitchen equipment for use in private households, and its captive supplier of electronic components and assemblies, located in the Far East.

3.3.1 Summary Functional Analysis

During the audit period, the U.S. parent in this case (P) designed, manufactured and sold several models of automatic coffee-makers, toasters, and blenders. Its Far Eastern subsidiary (S) assembled a variety of electronic components for use in P's product lines.

At its inception, S purchased virtually all of the subcomponents it used in its assembly operations from P at cost. It gradually expanded its local sourcing, and the proportion of subcomponents it purchased from P for use in its assemblies declined significantly during the audit period. Additionally, P provided engineering assistance and

liberally for this purpose—as it may be—the 1993 temporary regulations stipulate that the arm's length range must be based on at least four uncontrolled firms.

purchasing services (e.g., visiting and qualifying local vendors), the former at cost and the latter free of charge. S sold all of its output to P.

3.3.2 Intra-Company Transfer Pricing Policy

P's move offshore was prompted by a precipitous decline in its market share in the late 1970s. The company attributed this decline to the fact that its major competitors were all availing themselves of much cheaper foreign labor; consequently, they were able to undercut P's prices and draw customers away. P was essentially forced offshore in an effort to cut its labor costs and thus regain its cost-competitiveness.

P implemented a transfer pricing policy that enabled S to capture the bulk of cost savings attributable to offshore assembly. Specifically, P stipulated that it would pay no more for electronic assemblies and parts that it purchased from S than it had previously cost to produce the same assemblies and parts in its U.S. facilities, net of freight (and in fact set intra-company prices at this level). Hence, S's revenues were approximately equal to production costs in the United States; these revenues, less S's actual costs, comprised both P's cost savings and S's profits.

During the period in question, the differential in labor costs between the United States and the Far East was enormous. For example, in 1983, an electronics assembly worker in South Korea earned roughly one-seventh of his or her American counterpart's salary.[22] In 1974, workers employed in Singapore's semiconductor manufacturing industry earned $0.57 per hour on average, a small fraction of U.S. wages for comparable work.[23] Consequently, S's profits were very substantial.

[22]Deiter, Ernst, "Automation and the Worldwide Restructuring of the Electronics Industry: Implications for Developing Countriess," *World Development*, Vol. 13, No. 3, March 1985.

[23]Yuen-Ching Lim, Linda, *Multinational Firms and Manufacturing for Export in Less Developed Countries: the Case of the Electronics Industry in Malaysia and Singapore*, Vol. I, unpublished Ph.D. Dissertation, University of Michigan, 1978.

3.3.3 Potential Issues

Both 1968 and 1993 temporary Section 482 regulations require that S's arm's length income be determined by valuing the functions and services that it performed and the risks that it assumed in the specific geographic market in which it operated. Hence, U.S. production costs should not be a factor in this calculation. (As distinct from the first cost-plus case reviewed, S is not located in a possessions territory.) Stated differently (and as discussed briefly in the prior cost-plus case), S should retain the cost savings attributable to operating in the Far East only if an uncontrolled company operating in the same market would do so.[24]

The Asian market for electronics assembly services was intensely competitive during the 1970s. Fixed costs and required skill levels were relatively low, the requisite technology limited and widely available, and entry virtually unrestricted. Independent Asian companies earned margins of between 5%–20% over their costs for comparable electronic assembly services, where this cost base was generally net of consigned materials and reflected the substantially lower wage rates paid in the Far East.

Had P paid an unrelated vendor of comparable assemblies an amount equal to its own in-house costs, this fortunate vendor would have earned gross margins of between double and quadruple its competitors' margins. In so doing, P would have eliminated all benefits of foreign sourcing and, with it, its hopes of recouping its diminishing share of the consumer products market segments in which it operated. In short, this taxpayer's transfer pricing policy was not consistent with arm's length practices.

[24]Note that, in the prior cost-plus case study, we compared the offshore affiliate at issue with a U.S.-based comparable. For purposes of analyzing the case under the 1993 temporary regulations, it was important to consider the possibility that the U.S.-based comparable had not acted on a freely available opportunity to reduce its costs (by relocating its production facilities) and, hence, earned below-normal returns. If so, the offshore affiliate—which was operating in the lower-cost area—should have earned a normal return (and, therefore, a higher return than the particular comparable we had selected). In the instant case, this issue doesn't arise, because we are comparing S with stand-alone comparables operating in the same geographic market.

3.3.4 Adjustment Methodology under the 1968 Regulations

As with the first cost-plus case reviewed, we computed the Section 482 adjustment to S's reported income by multiplying its (actual) cost of goods sold by comparable companies' gross margins relative to costs, and compared this magnitude—"allowable income"—with its reported income. Again, the composition of the cost base was an issue. As noted (and unlike the previous case), S began procuring some materials locally after its first several years of operation. Accordingly, we deducted only specialized materials from S's cost base, the bulk which continued to be provided by P throughout the audit period.

3.3.5 Possible Adjustment Methodology under the 1993 Temporary Regulations

This case would probably be developed in essentially the same way under the 1993 temporary regulations, albeit with the different treatment of materials purchased from related parties described above.[25] That is, the IRS might not deduct a portion of S's materials from its cost base on the theory that P would have consigned them on an arm's length basis, if they were in fact sold. Rather, the materials issue might be dealt with in one of two different ways: under the 1993 temporary regulations, S's cost base might include materials purchased from P, and its transfer price increased by the markup on these incremental costs (potentially a very considerable increase); alternatively, the transfer price calculated under the 1993 temporary regulations might only differ from that calculated under the 1968 regulations by the amount of P's inventory financing cost savings.

3.3.6 Taxpayer's Position

The issues that the taxpayers in this composite case raised generally related to the reasonableness of our claims that labor savings should accrue to their respective U.S. parents. One firm maintained

[25]See the discussion of this issue in the first cost-plus case reviewed.

that several other taxpayers had been allowed labor savings in separate Appeals settlements involving manufacturing affiliates located in Asia, entitling it to the same treatment. Another disputed our characterization of the Asian assembly services market as competitive, and a third argued that its offshore affiliate possessed exceptional skills that uniquely suited it to perform the assembly functions at issue. As such, the argument went, the affiliate, wielding a measure of market power, would have retained labor savings on an arm's length basis.

3.3.7 Resolution

Most of the cases that make up this composite case study were resolved at the Examination or Appeals levels through negotiations between taxpayers and IRS representatives. By and large, taxpayers and the government "split the difference" as in the first composite cost-plus case, albeit on terms that were relatively more favorable to the government, on balance.

In light of the fact that the 1993 temporary regulations explicitly address the question of cost savings, Appeals might take a harder line in these types of cases under the new regime. (Again, this presupposes that the regulations will factor directly in Appeals settlements and/or that Appeals officers will assess litigation hazards more optimistically because of the change in regulations.) Similarly, the taxpayers at issue might conclude that litigation poses greater hazards under this regime, and therefore settle (at the Examination or Appeals level) on terms closer to the IRS's proposed adjustments. While taxpayers in cases of this sort can resort to the arm's length defense described above under the temporary regulations, the very large differential in margins reported by S and functionally comparable unrelated companies operating in the Far East, respectively, would nonetheless have been difficult to justify. That is, one would have to venture fairly far afield to find companies operating in the Far East that earned the much higher margins reported by S, and somehow rule out those that were more closely comparable. In short, cost-plus cases in which labor savings is the principal point of contention may well be resolved on terms significantly less favorable to taxpayers under the 1993 temporary regulations.

3.4 Critique of the Cost-Plus Method: 1968 Regulations and 1993 Temporary Regulations

As the two composite cases reviewed in this chapter indicate, applications of the cost-plus method amount to characterizing one of the controlled entities (preferably the one that performs fewer functions and owns no, or more limited, intangible assets) in terms of the range of functions it performs and the substantive risks it assumes, identifying a set of companies that are comparable in these regards, and applying the comparable firms' arm's length markups to the controlled entity's cost base. This sounds straightforward. Historically, the difficulties have arisen in (a) convincing all concerned that the uncontrolled firms used to develop arm's length markups over costs were in fact sufficiently comparable (the IRS's choice of comparables was not a major point of contention in either of the cases discussed above, but it frequently is); (b) determining the proper cost base to which the arm's length markup should be applied; and (c) making adjustments for the inevitable differences between one's proposed comparables and the controlled tested party, including cost differences arising from the geographic locus of productive activities. The 1993 temporary regulations will likely alleviate some of these sources of controversy, but certainly not all. Further, the "arm's length range" defense available to companies under these regulations will create some new issues.

3.4.1 Comparability Issues

For purposes of arguing comparability under the cost-plus method, a common source of disagreement between companies and the IRS under the 1968 regulations concerned the definition and measurement of risks. In particular, distinguishing form from substance with regard to the affiliate's risks was frequently a highly contentious issue.

While economists typically inclined more towards substance, judges, Appeals officers, and attorneys often placed considerable weight on the content of intra-company agreements (or the lack thereof).

The 1993 temporary regulations are far more specific as to the set of criteria and the overall standard of comparability that must be satisfied by prospective comparable stand-alone firms. Similarly, they define risk somewhat more clearly (although specific measures are not proposed), and state unambiguously that substance takes precedence over form with regard to evaluating risk:

> In determining the extent to which a controlled taxpayer actually bears a risk and in determining whether the income earned by the controlled taxpayer over a reasonable period of time is commensurate with the risk assumed, the district director will evaluate the economic substance of the controlled transactions.

Hence, the 1993 temporary regulations may well reduce controversies surrounding comparables selection (and the attendant inconsistencies in cost-plus applications across firms) for purposes of applying the cost-plus method. However, this salutory change may be tempered, if not entirely eclipsed, by the "arm's length range" defense, and the fact that some cases that would have been developed along cost-plus lines under the 1968 regulations may be relegated to the comparable profits method under the 1993 temporary regulations.[26]

For purposes of constructing an arm's length range, whether for defensive purposes or to apply the comparable profits method, the standard of comparability is extremely loose.[27] Consequently, controversies over comparables will likely be at least as common, and as contentious, as they were under the 1968 regulations when these segments of the 1993 temporary regulations are brought to bear. Similarly, negotiated settlements of cases that draw on these provisions are unlikely to be consistent, either across firms or with the arm's length standard.

---

[26]That is, when the standard of comparability applied under the cost-plus method cannot be satisfied.

[27]See discussion in Chapter 2.

3.4.2 The Cost Base Question

The issue of whether IRS economists should, or even could, legitimately treat materials that one member of a controlled group sold to another as if they had been consigned arose in both of the cost-plus cases reviewed above. While IRS representatives interpreted the 1968 regulations to give them the authority to do so, taxpayers routinely took issue with this procedure. As noted in the discussion of these cases, the 1993 temporary regulations will probably not eliminate this source of controversy. In fact, the combined "as actually structured" and "alternatives available" provisions contained therein will likely perpetuate, and possibly exacerbate, disputes regarding the proper treatment of materials purchased from related parties.[28]

The opportunity cost framework implicit in the "alternatives available" terminology is very familiar territory to economists. Profit-maximizing firms will undertake a particular venture (or, more narrowly, accept a given set of terms vis-a-vis this venture) only if it leaves them at least as well off (measured in terms of profits) as the next best feasible alternative. Against this backdrop, the form of a particular transaction becomes rather unimportant. However, the "alternatives available" approach is far less familiar—and less persuasive—to judges and attorneys, a fact of life that is demonstrated plainly in a passage from the Tax Court's *Bausch & Lomb* decision.

In this case, the IRS (respondent) argued that B&L (the U.S. parent) had the capability to produce the product at issue (contact lenses) in-house at a cost of approximately $1.50, and would not have paid a stand-alone lens manufacturer more for the product than this amount.[29] Inasmuch as B&L actually paid its Irish manufacturing

[28]In general, this set of directives is salient whenever the intra-company transactions at issue are structured differently than inter-company transactions, a common state of affairs. As such, the ambiguities noted apply across a fairly broad range of issues.

[29]Note that the IRS's expert considered in-house costs to be pertinent in this instance because in-house production was one of the alternatives available to the U.S. parent, B&L. Hence, in-house production costs established an upper bound on the price that B&L should have been willing to pay. However, this does not necessarily mean that in-house production costs constituted an arm's length price. If a lower-cost alternative were available, it should establish arm's length

subsidiary $7.50 per lens, this make/buy comparison (a straightforward application of the alternatives available or opportunity cost framework) implied a very substantial proposed pricing adjustment. However, Judge Korner was decidedly less than receptive to the logic underlying it:

> [R]espondent argues that B&L *could have* produced the contact lenses purchased from B&L Ireland itself at a lesser cost. However, B&L *did not* produce the lenses itself.... B&L Ireland was the entity which actually produced the contact lenses. Respondent is limited to determining how the sales to B&L by B&L Ireland would have been priced had the parties been unrelated... We have determined that the $7.50 charged was a market price.

Hence, in Judge Korner's view, determining compensation in a given transaction by reference to the alternatives available to the parties is tantamount to disregarding the actual structure of the relationship. This type of misunderstanding is likely to pervade Section 482 issues—both cost-plus and others—for a long time to come, given the seemingly conflictual nature of the 1993 temporary regulations' "as actually structured" and "alternatives available" provisions.

3.4.3 Adjustments for Differences between Comparables and Controlled Manufacturing Affiliate

Exact comparables will naturally remain a rarity under the new regime. As such, IRS economists and company representatives will continue to be faced with the need to adjust for economically significant differences between comparable firms and controlled manufacturing affiliates. The 1993 temporary regulations expressly require these adjustments, while providing minimal guidance as to precisely

prices. (Hence, the IRS also argued that "B&L Ireland was little more than a contract manufacturer the sale of whose total production was assured... " and whose income should be determined accordingly.) More generally, the "alternatives available" or "opportunity cost" approach relates arm's length consideration in a given transaction to the *best* (e.g., the least-cost or highest-profit) alternative.

how they should be computed (with the exception of cost differentials arising from the respective locations of comparables and affiliates). Specifically, the temporary regulations state that adjustments for differences should be based on commercial practices, economic principles, or statistical methods, without weighting one approach more heavily than another. By failing to prioritize among these alternative means of quantifying differences, while making such adjustments more salient, the 1993 temporary regulations may actually exacerbate controversies over this issue.

The exception to this very sparing guidance—the basis for allocating location savings—is a very important one, however. In the second composite cost-plus case study discussed above, and, more generally, in many cost-plus cases under the 1968 regulations, the allocation of location savings between affiliated companies was the central issue. Basing this allocation on the relative competitive positions of (related) buyer and seller makes good economic sense, and should ameliorate disputes about the issue considerably.

3.4.4 Summary

In summary, the 1993 temporary regulations will likely rein in disputes about appropriate comparables under the cost-plus method, by clarifying comparability standards and unambiguously elevating substance over form in the evaluation of risk. However, the proper treatment of materials purchased from related parties remains ambiguous. A fuller description of the opportunity cost approach to determining arm's length compensation, and a more unambiguous endorsement thereof, would help to reduce controversies over this issue. Further, the various approaches to quantifying the effects of differences between comparables and a given tested party should be prioritized, perhaps in the fairly innocuous form of a simple "if-then" statement as to when the different approaches are apropos. Moreover, the "reasonable accuracy" standard to be applied to these quantifications is altogether too nebulous, with the unfortunate result that Appeals officers will flesh it out over time through successive incremental (and potentially inconsistent) judgments. To forestall this process, the final Section 482 regulations (to be issued within three years after the release of the 1993 temporary regulations) should elaborate on the requisite degree of precision in adjusting for differences between comparable firms and controlled tested parties.

3.5 The Broader Setting

The outcomes in the composite cost-plus cases reviewed in this chapter begin to illustrate how and why some multinational corporations pay very minimal taxes, and why similarly situated firms are not necessarily treated uniformly under the Section 482 regulations. Broadly speaking, these trends are the outgrowth of a number of interrelated factors, including:

- A host of perplexing precedents in many of the major decided Section 482 cases;
- Appeals officers' attendent assessments of litigation hazards;
- Very limited IRS resources;
- Ambiguities that are intrinsic to the arm's length standard (and, as such, perhaps unavoidable);
- Ambiguities in the interpretive regulations (many of which are avoidable); and,
- Very limited coordination within and across IRS districts.

Several of the same factors collectively create the potential for unreasonable and unsubstantiated proposed Section 482 adjustments, to which firms that are complying fully with tax laws must respond.

The subsequent case studies illustrate in more detail how the regulations themselves (both 1968 and 1993 temporary versions) contribute to these results. As such, it is useful to flesh out their remaining root causes, and the complexities they create for the IRS and taxpayers alike, briefly here.

Judges' decisions on a number of litigated Section 482 cases, many of which involved the cost-plus method, are based on very flawed economic reasoning. (The *Bausch & Lomb* decision is a clear case in point.) In light of these decisions, Appeals officers have scaled up their assessments of litigation hazards very considerably over the last decade. Further, Appeals officers tend to take very narrow decisions that apply to a highly specific fact pattern, and generalize them very broadly, compounding the problems posed by peculiar precedents.[30] In a short-term sense, companies have benefitted from this state of affairs, inasmuch as the Examination team's proposed adjustments typically exceed the settlements negotiated by Appeals by a very wide margin. However, the arbitrariness of Appeals settlements (and Tax Court decisions) presents problems for taxpayers as well as the IRS, in that it greatly complicates their tax (and possibly business) planning efforts. Moreover, with the prospect of new (and potentially very hefty) Section 482 penalties looming, this uncertainty has recently become considerably more costly.

Limited resources and time pressures at various levels in the IRS also go some way towards explaining why some multinational firms have quite small tax burdens (relative to arm's length tax burdens), and why others, whose pricing practices broadly conform to the regulations, may nevertheless bear an additional, and potentially quite substantial, compliance cost. Appeals officers are forced to settle the vast majority of cases they are assigned, and companies, cognizant of this pressure, often use it to their advantage by adopting a very unyielding stance. Hence, even proposed adjustments that are carefully developed and documented are very often settled at a fraction of their initial level.

By the same token, pressures to close cases promptly at the Examination level—the product of efforts to remain current in terms of tax years—has sometimes meant that IRS technical specialists are unable to develop potential pricing issues adequately.[31] Further,

[30]Having Appeals officers evaluate the litigation hazards posed by Section 482 pricing issues in particular is inherently problemmatic. Relatively few Appeals officers are attorneys, and none are economists. As such, they are not best suited to evaluate litigation-related risks, or the economic merits of a proposed pricing adjustment and a taxpayer's rebuttal. Moreover, they are not required to, nor do they, consult IRS litigating attorneys or economists on a regular basis in making this assessment.

[31]For example, IRS representatives have traditionally made very limited use of the legal remedies available to extract information from companies that are not complying with information requests, because of the delays that they entail. (The

the number of experienced IRS economists is quite limited, relative to the number of potential pricing issues. This imbalance has led some IRS districts to develop short-cut approaches to building Section 482 cases that are not wholly supportable on economic grounds. While Appeals rarely supports pricing adjustments based on incomplete or inadequate analyses, the IRS Examination team may nevertheless propose them. Inasmuch as some subset of these issues will have no foundation on closer examination, the IRS's resource constraints may impose an unnecessary cost—that of mounting a defense against unwarranted proposed pricing adjustments that will ultimately be dropped—on multinational corporations that are complying fully with Section 482 regulations.

The lack of effective coordinating mechanisms within and across IRS districts, coupled with the open-ended nature of the Section 482 regulations (and the ambiguities intrinsic to the arm's length standard), create an environment in which similarly situated firms are bound to be treated inconsistently. To the extent that the statute and accompanying regulations are ambiguous, particularly on fundamental points, they cannot be applied without a large dose of interpretation. Without effective coordinating mechanisms within and across IRS districts (and assuming that some portion of proposed pricing adjustments are sustained in whole or in part), inconsistencies in interpretation and, hence, in tax treatment, will be allowed to stand. By and large, there are very limited institutional mechanisms that facilitate communication and coordination among IRS economists (and, to a lesser extent, other technical specialists), and similarly situated taxpayers *are* treated differently on a fairly regular basis. This unfortunate fact of life has become increasingly apparent to firms—and increasingly embarrassing to the IRS—with the growing number of brother-sister corporations audited by separate IRS Examination teams.

---

designated summons procedure described in Chapter 2 was designed to ameliorate this particular problem somewhat, although, as noted, Congress' intent appears to have been that foreign companies should bear the brunt of this legal resource, rather than domestic firms.) Without the information requested, IRS economists and international examiners often have no hope of developing the potential issues adequately.

Chapter 4

The Resale Price Method

4.1 Background

Early on, transfer pricing adjustments proposed by U.S. tax authorities typically involved U.S. parent firms importing manufactured products from related manufacturing affiliates in low-tax, low-wage jurisdictions—the prototypical cost-plus case. However, a growing share of intra-company trade takes place between related entities operating in industrialized countries with roughly comparable tax rates, and so-called "inbound" issues, involving foreign parents with U.S. subsidiaries, are becoming increasingly common. In such cases, U.S. tax authorities tend to focus on the transfer price that subsidiaries pay their related suppliers for imported product, their below-the-line costs, and, relatedly, the range of services they perform on their parents' behalf, in the belief that foreign-based multinationals seek to pay as large a share of their total tax burden in their home countries as possible.[1] Various explanations have been proffered for this

[1] In fact, as discussed in Chapter 2, many individuals in U.S. tax administration and enforcement believe that abuses are rife in inbound pricing cases, and tax revenues foregone annually as a result amount to billions of dollars. This belief is founded in part on comparisons of trends in foreign-owned assets and taxes collected from said owners over time: despite a tripling of foreign-owned assets, and a doubling of foreign-owned companies' gross income earned in the U.S., total taxes collected from these companies remained nearly constant over a ten-year period. See Pear, Robert, "I.R.S. Investigating Foreign Companies over Units in

preference, including "'patriotic duty,' the need to compensate the country's government for non-tax subsidies, or the fact that effective tax rates may be lower than nominal rates."[2]

Many inbound pricing cases encompass multiple issues, none of which amount to enormous sums individually, whereas classic "outbound" cases tend to be more single-issue. Such a diversified approach disguises individual abuses more effectively, and greatly increases the resources necessary to develop all of the issues properly. As such, inbound issues are often more involved, from a purely practical standpoint.

In this chapter, I review a composite inbound case, involving a foreign parent and a captive U.S. distributor, developed along modified resale price lines. The case clarifies the ways in which IRS economists evaluate whether an adjustment is warranted in a particular instance (beyond mechanically applying resale margins), and illustrates some of the complexities that arise in putting together such a case under both 1968 and 1993 temporary regimes.

There are several important differences between the 1968 and 1993 temporary regulations as regards when and how one would apply the resale price method. As discussed in Chapter 2, the 1993 temporary regulations provide a firmer footing for transfer pricing adjustments in circumstances where both related parties report losses individually (and, hence, on a consolidated basis) than the 1968 regulations. (This scenario may be more likely in inbound contexts than elsewhere, for a variety of reasons.) By the same token, they lend credence to inbound taxpayers' frequent argument that market penetration strategies justify a differential between their prices and those charged by uncontrolled competitors. Additionally, the set of circumstances in which the resale price method would apply under the 1993 temporary regulations is somewhat narrower as compared to the 1968 regulations, in that one is expressly precluded from utilizing it

---

U.S.," *New York Times*, February 18, 1990. Concurrent decreases in corporate tax rates do not fully explain this pattern.

[2]See Testimony by Mr. Frederick T. Goldberg, Jr., Commissioner of Internal Revenue, before the Subcommittee on Oversight, House Committee on Ways and Means, July 10, 1990, p. 85.

when the captive distributor adds substantial value by contributing non-routine intangible assets.[3]

4.2 A Resale Price Issue: Electronic Home Entertainment Products

This (composite) inbound case involves a foreign parent headquartered in Europe (P), and a U.S.-based subsidiary (S). The latter distributed P's high-end electronic home entertainment products in the U.S. market.

4.2.1 Summary Functional Analysis

S sold to dealers, distributors, and OEM customers. S's sales of products to OEM customers were invariably unbranded (that is, the products did not contain the company's trademarks or names). The products it sold to all other customers bore the trademarks and names originally developed by P in its domestic market. S conducted comprehensive market research, projected demand, defined product requirements, positioned new products, advertised extensively, and repaired products to the component level.

With very few exceptions, P manufactured all of the products that S sold in the United States. Moreover, while P distributed products in its home market and elsewhere (in addition to manufacturing), all U.S.-bound products were sold through S. In the event that customers required customization of products, or the products required extensive repairs beyond the component level, P was prepared to provide technical assistance. However, such support was very rarely called for.

[3]Unfortunately, the 1993 temporary regulations do not provide an alternative methodology, in lieu of the resale price method, under these circumstances. (In particular, the comparable profits method does not fill this void: as discussed in Chapter 2, the comparable profits method does not apply when the tested party utilizes non-routine intangibles that it developed itself or acquired from third parties.)

4.2.2 Intra-Company Transfer Pricing Policy

Despite repeated questions on this point, the taxpayer never informed the IRS how it formulated its intra-company transfer prices. The U.S.-based subsidiary purported to know nothing of the factors that its parent considered in establishing transfer prices; while S maintained that it attempted to negotiate a reduced transfer price intermittently, P had the final say, and was generally unresponsive to S's requests for price reductions.

4.2.3 Potential Issues

S earned gross margins that were somewhat lower than those reported by unrelated U.S. distributors selling similar product lines. However, its bottom-line results were markedly lower, ranging from *de minimis* to negative. In and of itself, this poor showing did not necessarily indicate that S violated the arm's length standard in its dealings with P. Closely comparable stand-alone distributors may have fared equally badly as a result of industry-wide influences; alternatively, S may have underperformed relative to comparables for reasons that had nothing to do with its intra-company pricing practices.

Comparisons of comparables' net margins with S's bottom line results can confirm or eliminate the possibility that S's poor results were the rule rather than the exception, but not the alternative possibility that, while S earned lower-than-normal returns, this was not the result of its transfer pricing practices per se. To ascertain whether S's slim-to-negative net margins were explained by factors other than unduly high transfer prices, we considered the underlying causes thereof. Finally, to determine whether these causes constituted violations of the arm's length standard, we considered whether an unrelated entity in S's position would have entered into a similar relationship with its suppliers (that is, whether it would have accepted comparable terms in negotiating with its suppliers, confronted the same obstacles in obtaining the kinds of products customers demanded, incurred comparable below-the-line expenses, and so forth).

The analysis below begins with a discussion of exchange rate risks. Following this, we consider the distribution of excess shipping costs between S and P, the frequency of transfer price negotiations, S's lack of price protection, P's unresponsiveness to S's product requirements, and, finally, the wide range of support functions that S performed (and, consequently, the substantial below-the-line expenses that it incurred) in comparison with proposed comparables.

Exchange Rate Fluctuations

Distributors sometimes pay their foreign suppliers in their own (the distributors') currency, with the result that the suppliers incur the associated exchange risks. This is by no means a hard-and-fast rule, however, and one observes a variety of arrangements for the sharing of such risks on an arm's length basis. However, it is virtually always the case in genuinely arm's length dealings that the arrangement for shifting or sharing exchange risks is consistently applied over time. In the instant case, P determined whether S paid for product at a fixed price quoted in dollars, or at a fixed price quoted in P's currency, on an order-by-order basis. If P's currency appreciated relative to the dollar, S would pay the fixed price quoted in P's currency. Conversely, if P's currency depreciated, S would pay the fixed price quoted in dollars. This arrangement had the effect of shifting all exchange risks (and losses) to S, while eliminating the upside potential for exchange gains.

Incremental Costs of Shipping by Air Due to Delayed Production

By the terms of its intra-company contract, S was required to place orders with P four months in advance of the required delivery date. While S abided by these terms religiously, P often experienced delays in production and, as a consequence, ended up shipping product by air rather than by sea, a considerably more costly option. To the extent that P was solely responsible for such delays, it would seem reasonable to expect it to bear some part, if not all, of the incremental costs. On an arm's length basis, such incremental shipping costs are sometimes shared by the distributor and manufacturer (although the fault may lie exclusively with the latter). In the instant case, S bore all incremental shipping costs.

Frequency of Transfer Price Negotiations; Price Protection

P generally negotiated transfer prices with S annually. (These transfer prices consisted of fixed quotes in both dollars and P's currency.) Yet, the prices of a number of products that S imported for resale declined continuously during the audit period, because of ongoing product improvements and new product introductions at frequent intervals. Thus, unless S accurately anticipated the timing of new product introductions (and the magnitude of the associated price declines) at the beginning of the year, and factored them into the transfer prices it negotiated with P, it could not hope to earn a reasonable return. Absent such perfect foresight, annual negotiations were inadequate to contend with these unstable market conditions. Nor did stand-alone distributors enter into agreements with their suppliers that provided for prices to remain fixed for a full year under these market conditions. Moreover, while S provided price protection to its intermediate customers (dealers and distributors), it did not receive price protection from its (related) supplier.

Thus, S bore all of the risks associated with potential price variability in the U.S. market. While unrelated distributors of similar products generally assumed some risk associated with price variability, the degree of risk was bounded by a combination of more frequent adjustments in purchase prices and a measure of price protection.

P's Slow Response to U.S. Market Trends

Despite the fact that P maintained very high product quality standards, its sluggish and often inadequate response to S's evolving product requirements contributed significantly to the latter's poor performance as well. The tax years at issue in this case witnessed very substantial improvements across a number of key product lines. Certain technical features were absolutely *de rigueur*, by virtue of evolving product safety guidelines, product compatibility issues, and pronounced consumer preferences; without them, the products simply could not be sold in the U.S. market. *S* was fully aware of these requisites—in many instances, anticipating the necessary product innovations long in advance—and communicated its requirements to *P* in considerable detail. However, *P* was exceedingly slow to respond. In one instance, it labored for two years to develop a state-of-the-art product after receiving detailed specifications from *S*, and worked for fully nine months to develop relatively minor modifications of an existing product line. During these lapses, *S* saw its market share decline markedly. Its related status vis-a-vis *P* precluded it from bridging to other, more accomodating suppliers with more competitive products to offer, as a stand-alone distributor would have done.

Support Functions and Associated Below-the-Line Expenses

S performed substantial support functions (notably advertising and field service), and incurred the associated expenses directly. Some prospective comparables performed analogous functions on behalf of their (unrelated) suppliers, but were compensated in the form of product price discounts or dollar-for-dollar reimbursements; many other prospective comparables performed no such support functions, and a very small number performed similar support functions and incurred the associated costs.

Summary

In short, judging from preliminary gross margin comparisons, *S* paid *P* a somewhat lower (intra-company) purchase price for the electronic home entertainment products that it distributed than stand-alone distributors paid their unrelated suppliers for broadly similar products. However, *S* also incurred substantially more below-the-line expenses than most stand-alone distributors, bore all of the incremental costs of shipping products by air rather than by sea in the event of delays in *P*'s production runs, assumed all of the costs and risks associated with exchange rate fluctuations (without the upside potential for exchange gains), assumed all of the risks of successive declines in its selling price (with virtually no possibility of negotiating reductions in its purchase price), and labored under the added disadvantage that its supplier was highly unresponsive to its product requirements. Taken together, these factors explained S's narrow-to-negative net margins year after year. For the most part, these practices were not consistent with arm's length dealings between suppliers and their stand-alone distributors.

4.2.4 Adjustment Methodology under the 1968 Regulations

The 1968 regulations call for comparisons of gross (or resale) margins earned by comparables and affiliates for purposes of applying the resale price method. Note, however, that a gross margin adjustment would address only a subset of the issues discussed above: the fixity of S's intra-company prices, the fact that they were unduly high in the first instance, and S's lack of supplier-provided price protection. The remaining issues were reflected in S's unduly low net profits,[4] and a lower-than-arm's length volume of sales. Consider next whether and how adjustments for these non-arm's length results should be made.

Sales Volume Adjustments: Income Creation versus Reallocation

In principle, one could adjust S's sales volume upward (by imputing a certain level of sales, and, hence, profits to it), on the theory that it would have acted to stem the rapid decline in its sales volume and market share by switching to another supplier when P cum arm's length manufacturer failed to supply it with marketable products. A strict interpretation of the arm's length standard under the 1968 regulations might arguably have been consistent with this sort of allocation. However, in a more fundamental sense, S's diminishing market share reflected a diseconomy of integration (in the form of ineffective communication between P and S, and the absence of competitive pressures inducing P to respond more promptly and more adequately to S's product requirements), for which an adjustment is

[4] S recorded its exchange losses, its incremental shipping costs, and the expenses associated with its support functions, below-the-line.

not warranted.[5] In a more legalistic sense, the "imputed sales" approach amounts to creating, rather than reapportioning an existing amount of, consolidated income. Under the old regime, the IRS was very reluctant to take such a position. For these reasons, we did not adjust S's income to reflect the fact that it would have been free to change suppliers on an arm's length basis, and would very probably have done so.

Below-the-Line Adjustments

This left the question of how to adjust S's net income for the remaining non-arm's length arrangements between S and P: S's assumption of exchange risks without the benefit of potential exchange gains, its excessively high shipping costs, and (possibly) its advertising and warranty responsibilities and associated expenses. We approached the first two of these issues by separately quantifying the incremental costs and foregone revenues associated with each, and adding the indicated below-the-line adjustments to the above-the-line resale margin adjustments described below. Incremental shipping costs were split evenly between S and P, the most conservative arm's length arrangement we observed. We accepted the taxpayer's assignment of exchange risks to S, but allocated both the gains and the losses associated with this risk to S. Our choice of comparables (for purposes of calculating arm's length resale margins) dictated the approach we took regarding S's advertising and warranty outlays.

Prospective Comparables

Consider next our choice of comparables for purposes of determining arm's length resale margins. Broadly speaking, there are two distinct types of distributors in the industry at issue: industrial distributors and OEM distributors. Industrials sell products bearing the

[5] In fact, the potential for such diseconomies itself violates an implicit assumption underlying the arm's length standard, which presupposes that the individual entities comprising a controlled group could perform the same set of functions on a stand-alone basis that they perform within the context of the group, and that the combined income of these hypothetically stand-alone entities would exactly equal the consolidated income of the controlled group.

names and marks of their unrelated supplier/manufacturers. OEMs sell products manufactured by others under their own brand name. Accordingly, the first order of business is to determine whether the sample of comparables should be drawn from the ranks of industrial or OEM distributors. Each type of distributor operation is described briefly below.

Industrial Distributors: Industrial distributors are in the business of buying from manufacturers in large volume, and parcelling bulk supplies into smaller quantities for resale to entities further along the distribution chain (other distributors and dealers), or directly to end-users. Typically, industrials carry a large number of products, which are sold under their suppliers' brand names.

An analysis of a number of such distributors' 10-K filings with the Securities and Exchange Commission indicates that manufacturers of home entertainment products typically provide industrial distributors price protection on products held in inventory for a certain period of time. Moreover, industrials generally keep products in inventory for very short periods, further limiting their exposure to risks of price variability, along with their inventory financing costs. Insofar as they do not sell products under their own name, they do very little advertising. Finally, these types of distributors almost never have a service liability.

OEM Distributors: OEM distributors are a very different, and much more unusual, breed.[6] They conduct extensive competitive analysis, provide detailed specifications of product requirements to their suppliers, sell under their own name, perform a range of warranty and advertising functions for which industrials are not generally responsible, and assume commensurately greater business risks.

Unlike industrial distributors, OEM distributors are not price-protected. Further, they must make fairly firm volume commitments for intervals of several months, and provide reasonably accurate forecasts of annual product requirements. (These annual projections are

[6]We obtained much of our information on OEM distributors from in-depth third party interviews with industry experts.

generally in terms of the number of units, allowing for new model introductions over the course of the year, not the annual requirements for specific models.) OEM distributors limit their exposure to the risk of end-user price declines on given product models in two ways: first, effective competitive analysis enables them to anticipate price and technology trends and, assuming their suppliers are responsive to their requirements, to phase out individual models before they become obsolete and introduce new product innovations on a timely basis. Second, OEM distributors' purchase prices are often tied to their suppliers' production costs, which in turn are determined in part by the volume of production and the cost of components and other resources used to produce home entertainment products.[7] To the extent that end-user price declines are also driven by production cost declines, this cost-based pricing provides a degree of *de facto* price protection (in that distributors' purchase and selling prices tend to move in step).

Industrials versus OEMs as Potential Comparables

Thus, industrial distributors differ from OEM distributors in that they perform fewer support functions (and, thus, incur lower below-the-line costs), assume lesser risks, and own minimal marketing intangible assets. As a consequence, industrials will earn lower gross margins over a number of periods (although this clearly might not be true in any one period). In considering which type of distributor more closely approximated S during the years in question, all three factors differentiating industrials from OEMs—functions, risks, and marketing intangibles—should be taken into account.

Recall as well that S sold both branded products (that is, products bearing the trademarks and names originally developed by P in its domestic market) to non-OEM distributors and dealers, and unbranded products to OEM distributors, who affixed their own brand names thereto. Inasmuch as S's productive activities differed signif-

[7]Production volume is a factor because manufacturers realize economies of scale in this industry, and pass some part of these cost savings on to their distributor customers.

icantly vis-a-vis these two categories of sales, comparables should be selected separately for each.

***S*'s Unbranded Sales:** With respect to its unbranded product sales to OEM distributor-customers, *S* clearly functioned as an industrial distributor. It incurred minimal advertising expenses vis-a-vis these sales, and warranty services were performed by the OEM distributor-customers themselves. As such, *S*'s associated support costs were minimal. Further, OEM distributors made firm volume commitments to *S* several months out; hence, *S*'s inventory risks on these sales were limited. Nor were OEM customers price-protected. Finally, inasmuch as the products that *S* sold to OEM distributor-customers were unbranded, neither *S* nor *P* contributed significant marketing intangible assets on these sales. Hence, the question of intangibles ownership does not arise.

***S*'s Branded Sales:** Determining the pool from which comparables should be drawn was more complex vis-a-vis *S*'s sales of branded products to non-OEM customers. In a strictly functional sense, *S* was more similar to an OEM distributor than an industrial distributor with respect to these sales, in that it was responsible for both warranty services and advertising. In some respects, *S* incurred even greater risks than OEM distributors on its branded sales to non-OEM distributors and dealers: like OEM distributors, it did not receive price protection from its supplier, *P*, on these sales, although it provided price protection to its non-OEM customers. Moreover—and again, like OEM distributors—it was required to make firm volume commitments well in advance of the required delivery date. However, unlike OEM distributors, it was unable to hedge against the risks these arrangements posed by anticipating price and product trends and positioning itself accordingly, because *P* was unable to supply new product models on a timely basis. Additionally, unlike OEM distributors, it could not respond to this state of affairs by bridging to a more responsive supplier. *P*'s unresponsiveness to *S*'s product requirements also indirectly influenced *S*'s (intra-company) purchase price. Because a number of product lines were ill-suited to the U.S. market, *S* could not sell at a sufficient volume to enable

P to realize potential scale economies, and pass these savings along to *S*. In short, with regard to its sales of branded products to non-OEM customers, *S* was more similar to an OEM distributor than an industrial (albeit inexactly so), in terms of both functions and risks.

Consider next the question of marketing intangibles ownership vis-a-vis *S*'s sales of branded products to non-OEM customers. *S* was responsible for the bulk of advertising expenses in the U.S. market, and individuals in the firm's marketing department believed that *P*'s worldwide advertising efforts had little impact in the United States. One might therefore argue that *S* created and, thus, owned exclusive rights, to the company's trade names and marks in the U.S. market. In this event, *S* was clearly more akin to an OEM distributor than an industrial distributor along all of the relevant dimensions (functions, risks, and intangibles ownership).

However, it is not clear that incurring advertising expenses in a particular geographic market in itself establishes market-specific rights of ownership vis-a-vis trademarks and tradenames that were already recognized elsewhere (even accepting that advertising expenses alone give rise to marketing intangible assets). To begin with, there may be some spillovers to name recognition across markets (*S*'s marketing experts' opinions in this case notwithstanding). Relatedly, as discussed at greater length in Chapter 5, it is far from clear that advertising expenses alone generate marketing intangibles in the form of customer perceptions that one's products meet exceptionally high quality standards.[8]

While *S* enjoyed a reputation for supplying high-quality, highly reliable (if, with regard to certain product lines, imperfectly targeted) products, this reputation derived as much or more from from *P*'s investment in quality control as from *S*'s advertising efforts. Thus, the distinction between marketing and manufacturing intangibles may not be entirely meaningful in this instance. To the extent that *P*'s manufacturing processes and quality control practices gave rise, in whole or in part, to *S*'s reputation for providing durable, high-quality

[8]That is, a reputation for quality and reliability that has no foundation will not persist. However, absent sufficient advertising and marketing effort, it may never be established in the first instance, the fact of higher-than-average quality nothwithstanding.

products, the former had a rightful claim on some portion of the income generated thereby. Both of these arguments—the fact that advertising expenditures in one market have spillover effects in other markets, and that expenses other than advertising play a role in creating certain types of marketing intangibles—point to joint ownership of the U.S. marketing intangible assets at issue. Under this interpretation of the facts, S should be likened to OEM distributors overall, but the income attributable to the firm's U.S. marketing intangible assets shared between S and P in proportion to the expenses deemed to create them.

Alternatively, one might turn the issue around entirely, and question whether the fact of advertising per se confers any intangibles ownership rights on S. Specifically, one might argue that P would have retained exclusive rights to its trademarks and names in the United States if it had dealt with S on a genuinely arm's length basis, and, hence, the fact that it did not do so in a related party context should not be controlling. Under this interpretation of the facts, S would be construed as having performed advertising services on P's behalf, and should be compensated accordingly. In this scenario, industrial distributors would perhaps be better comparables, with the appropriate adjustments for differences between them and S as regards functions and risks.

In summary, S functioned as an industrial distributor vis-a-vis its sales of unbranded products to OEM distributor-customers, and comparables are therefore selected from the population of independent industrials for purposes of determining arm's length resale margins on these sales. On balance, S was more closely akin to an OEM distributor than an industrial distributor with regard to its sales of branded products to non-OEM customers, both in terms of the functions it performed and the risks it assumed. However, because of the ambiguity regarding ownership of marketing intangibles, we computed two alternative gross margin adjustments on this category of S's sales, one primary and the other secondary:

- Under the primary adjustment, S was deemed to own exclusive U.S. rights to the trademarks affixed to its products, and likened to an OEM distributor. (As such, it should properly have incurred the associated advertising expenses.)

- For purposes of computing the secondary adjustment on S's branded sales, we assumed that S did not own trademarks in the U.S. market in its own right. (Accordingly, it should not have incurred the associated advertising expenses.) Thus, comparables were again drawn from the ranks of industrial distributors.

If one concludes that S and P jointly owned the marketing intangibles affixed to products that S sold to non-OEM customers, the appropriate adjustment on these sales should fall somewhere between these two extremes.

Computing the Adjustments

Unbranded Sales: Calculating the adjustment to income on S's sales of unbranded products to OEM distributor customers was a straightforward matter. First, we computed the resale margins earned by comparable industrial distributors, and averaged these margins across firms. This average arm's length resale margin was then applied to S's reported revenues on its unbranded sales, to determine its arm's length gross profits thereon. The adjustment to S's gross income on its unbranded sales was given by the difference between its reported gross income and its arm's length gross income. Adding our separately computed below-the-line adjustments for incremental shipping costs and forgone exchange gains to this resale margin adjustment yielded our total proposed adjustment on S's unbranded sales to OEM distributor customers. (Note that S's below-the-line advertising and warranty expenses related solely to its branded sales to non-OEM customers. Hence, no adjustment for these expenses was warranted vis-a-vis S's sales of unbranded products to non-OEM customers.)

Branded Sales: Given the assumption that S functioned as an industrial distributor on its sales of branded products as well, our adjustment methodology vis-a-vis these sales was very similar to that used to determine S's arm's length income on its sales of unbranded products to OEM distributor-customers. However, in addition to applying an average industrial distributor resale margin to S's revenues on sales of branded products, and adding the separately computed adjustments for incremental shipping costs and forgone exchange gains thereto, we also reduced S's below-the-line costs on these sales by the amount of its advertising and field service outlays (on the theory that S *cum* arm's length industrial distributor would have been compensated for these costs). Our (secondary) proposed adjustment on S's branded sales to non-OEM customers was again given by the difference between its reported income and its estimated arm's length income thereon.

For purposes of computing our primary adjustment, in which S was likened to an OEM distributor vis-a-vis its branded sales, we utilized a large OEM distributor as a comparable. During the audit period, this entity was several years into a long-term OEM contract with an independent Scandinavian manufacturer of electronic home entertainment products. It maintained a network of authorized service dealers, and was compensated by its supplier for the associated costs. Specifically, it had the option of a 90-day warranty, or a 2% overshipment of product (at no additional charge) to cover the warranty expenses that it incurred; it opted for the latter arrangement. Additionally, the stand-alone OEM distributor incurred very significant advertising expenses, for which its supplier did not compensate it. Rather, it undertook this advertising function on its own behalf, with a view to creating marketing intangibles that would enable it to sell its own-brand products at a price premium.

Applying the stand-alone OEM distributor's resale margin to S's revenues on its sales of branded products, we obtained S's estimated arm's length gross profits thereon. Note that the mechanism through which the OEM distributor comparable was compensated for its warranty expenses—the aforementioned 2% overshipment of product—was equivalent to a reduction in its purchase price. As such, the warranty compensation was reflected in its (higher) gross margin. By extension, in applying this higher gross margin to S's branded sales, it was likewise effectively compensated above-the-line for its warranty functions (and no separate below-the-line adjustment was necessary). Similarly, because the OEM distributor's gross margin incorporated a return on its marketing intangibles, S likewise retained the same amount of intangible income per dollar of revenues (and, as noted, it should not have been compensated by P for the associated advertising expenses). Consequently, for purposes of this computation, S's gross margin adjustment was increased only by the amount of our separately computed below-the-line adjustments for shipping costs and forgone exchange gains on its branded sales (as with the adjustment to S's unbranded sales).

In summary, we developed two alternative adjustments to S's combined income on branded and unbranded sales, one primary, and the other secondary. In computing the secondary adjustment, S was likened to an industrial distributor vis-a-vis both branded and unbranded sales. The adjustment to S's gross income on combined sales, determined by applying stand-alone industrial distributors' resale margins to its total revenues, was augmented by (a) the separately computed adjustments for incremental shipping costs and foregone exchange gains on both categories of sales, and (b) the reduction in S's below-the-line costs, by the amount of its warranty and advertising expenses.

In computing our primary adjustment, S was (again) likened to an industrial distributor on its sales of unbranded products, but to an OEM distributor on its sales of branded products. Under this scenario, the adjustment to S's unbranded sales was essentially the same as described above (except that its below-the-line costs were not reduced by advertising and warranty-related expenses, all of which were associated with its branded sales.) However, S's arm's length resale margin on its branded sales was based on the stand-alone OEM distributor's results. Additionally, while the resulting estimated arm's length gross profits were augmented by the separately computed below-the-line adjustments for incremental shipping costs and foregone exchange gains on branded products, no separate adjustment for S's warranty and advertising outlays was necessary on these sales.

4.2.5 Possible Adjustment Methodology under the 1993 Temporary Regulations

Hand in hand with the "best methods" rule, the 1993 temporary regulations lay out a very specific set of conditions under which the resale price method (and other methods) should be applied (see discussion in Chapter 2). Per these regulations, the resale price method is apropos when the tested party purchases and resells tangible property, and does not add substantial value thereto in the process. The tested party will be deemed to have added substantial value if it physically alters the good before resale, or contributes non-routine intangible property.

Recall that, for purposes of computing our primary adjustment to *S*'s branded sales under the 1968 regulations, we assumed that *S* was the rightful owner of the marketing intangibles it utilized in the U.S. market. The stipulation described above—that the tested party will be deemed to have added substantial value if it contributes non-routine intangible property—would appear to rule out this alternative resale price adjustment under the 1993 temporary regulations. Nor would the comparable profits method apply:

> [T]he comparable profits method ordinarily will provide an accurate measure of an arm's length result *unless* [my *emph.*] the tested party, in connection with the controlled transaction, uses valuable, non-routine intangibles that it–
>
> (1) Acquired from uncontrolled taxpayers and with respect to which it bears significant risks and possesses the right to significant economic benefits; or,
>
> (2) Developed itself.

Hence, if *S*'s advertising efforts suffice to confer (partial or exclusive) ownership rights to the company's marketing intangibles in the U.S. market, neither the resale price method nor the comparable profits method can be applied to determine arm's length consideration for the tangible property *S* purchased from *P*. In fact, assuming no comparable uncontrolled transactions could be identified,[9] only the proposed profit split methodologies, all of which presuppose that both parties to the transaction(s) at issue own and contribute non-routine intangible property, are apropos under these circumstances.

[9] In this connection, recall that *P* sold only through *S* into the U.S. market. Hence, internal CUPs did not exist. Nor did we identify any satisfactory external CUPs during the audit period.

Alternatively, if one takes the position that P would have retained exclusive rights to the trademarks and names at issue on an arm's length basis, and that S simply performed advertising services on P's behalf for which it should be compensated, then the first adjustment—in which S was likened to an industrial distributor and the resale price method applied accordingly—would stand.

Which of these very different assumptions regarding intangibles ownership is appropriate under the new rules? In making this determination, the 1993 temporary regulations' "as actually structured" provision discussed in Chapters 2 and 3 is highly relevant, but very inconclusive: it does not detail which specific features of the "structure" of the relationship between S and P IRS and consulting economists are required to take as given for this purpose, and, therefore, which features the allocation of income or expenses should be conditional on. For example:

- Should S's legal claims to the marketing intangibles be the determining factor? If so, and assuming that the U.S. trademarks and names were registered solely in S's name, it should retain all of the income attributable to them and incur all of the associated expenses (including the portion, if any, that P contributed). This basis for determining intangibles ownership would lead to a profit split approach under the 1993 proposed regulations, following a reallocation of expenses (if necessary).
- Alternatively, should IRS and consulting economists condition their allocations of consolidated income on the multinational firm's reported allocation of expenses relating to marketing intangibles, as we did in computing the primary adjustment to S's branded sales under the 1968 regulations? This approach would preclude an allocation of advertising outlays from S to P on the theory that P benefitted therefrom and should have incurred the associated costs (or, for that matter, from P to S, on the theory that S had exclusive legal rights and should have incurred all of the associated expenses). Rather, as before, S would be deemed the partial or sole owner of the marketing intangibles used in the U.S. market (depending on whether one gives weight to the spillover effects of advertising across markets and (or) to the effects that quality control procedures and

other manufacturing-related expenses have in creating marketing intangibles). As described above, this weighting of structural features also points to a profit split approach under the 1993 proposed regulations (without a preliminary allocation of expenses).

- Finally, suppose that one need only accept that S performed the marketing and advertising functions at issue (an indisputable fact) but not necessarily that it should have incurred the associated costs and risks and obtained ownership rights as a result—the reported allocation of advertising and marketing expenses and S's legal standing nothwithstanding. Rather, the determination of how costs, risks, and rights should be allocated would depend on the arrangements between suppliers and distributors dealing at arm's length. If unrelated distributors typically do not perform such functions, or if they are typically fully compensated by their suppliers when they do perform such functions, then S would not be deemed to own the intangibles at issue, and conversely. This was essentially the rationale for our secondary adjustment to S's branded sales under the 1968 regulations, and, as noted above, such a weighting of structural features would point to the same resale price methodology under the 1993 temporary regulations.

The last interpretation of the 1993 temporary regulations' "as actually structured" clause described above seems highly unlikely. In fact, the provision is probably intended to preclude proposed adjustments developed along these lines. As such, the resale price method could probably not be used to determine S's arm's length income on branded sales under the 1993 temporary regulations. Rather, the arm's length allocation of income between S and P would likely be determined under one of the three proposed profit split methods,[10] most likely the residual allocation rule.

Broadly speaking, the "residual allocation" methodology entails assigning market returns to the tangible operating assets that both controlled parties (in this case, S and P) employ in the relevant lines of business, and allocating the residual (intangible) income be-

[10]See Chapter 5 for a discussion and approximate application of the capital employed method.

tween them on the basis of their relative contributions of non-routine intangible assets, along the lines of the *White Paper's* basic arm's length return (or BALRM) with profit split.[11] The relative ownership of intangible assets, in turn, may be approximated by the parties' relative expenditures on intangibles development under some circumstances.[12]

In the instant case, the first step alone is quite complex, inasmuch as P is a highly diversified entity that operates in a number of different industries and uses the same operating assets jointly in many of them. Hence, to apply the residual allocation rule, one must first allocate P's operating assets among its different lines of business on some economically reasonable basis. Then there is the question of determining market returns. One might use realized returns on (tangible) assets reported by companies that are comparable to S and P in terms of production- and distribution-related risks and operate in broadly similar industries, but do not own intangible assets (if such companies can be found). Alternatively, one might work with the CAPM to derive a required return on investment in businesses that have similar (non-diversifiable) risk profiles. Finally, there is the difficult and ambiguous question of determining which categories of expenditures give rise to the marketing intangible assets at issue, a key determinant of the allocation of consolidated income under the residual allocation rule.

4.2.6 Taxpayer's Position

The taxpayers in this composite case study took issue more with our choice of comparables than with our choice of the resale price methodology per se. For example, one of the taxpayers argued against the particular comparable uncontrolled distributors that comprised our sample on the grounds that they distributed products with much more variable prices than those that its captive distributor sold. Consequently, their income streams were commensurately more variable from year to year, making annual comparisons less

[11] See discussion in Chapter 2.

[12] In particular, one can use relative intangibles development expenditures as a proxy for the parties' relative contributions of intangible assets if these expenditures are readily identifiable and reasonably constant over time.

valid and calling into question the premise that the independent industrial distributors and the captive distributor assumed similar levels of (non-diversifiable) risk. In lieu of our comparables, the taxpayer proposed to use a very diverse sample of distributors, most of which were a fraction of the captive distributor's size, many of which were start-ups, and some of which were engaged in a range of activities other than distribution. Moreover, a sizeable subset of the taxpayer's sample of independent distributors were in the throes of a variety of exceptional circumstances during the period at issue that adversely affected their earnings in the short run (e.g., very extensive changes in top management, major restructuring plans to ward off bankruptcy, ongoing merger discussions and preliminaries, etc.).[13] Not surprisingly, the arm's length resale margin based on this sample was significantly smaller than that based on the sample of independent industrial distributors that the IRS had put together.

Among the (possibly small) subset of inbound cases that would still come under the resale price method in the new regime, the 1993 temporary regulations will likely rein in disputes over comparables to some extent. As with the cost-plus method, these regulations are far more explicit as to both the comparability criteria and standards that one should apply for purposes of developing arm's length resale margins, and the potential differences between prospective comparables and tested party that may be "particularly relevant" (and for which one must adjust the comparables' profitability measures).[14,15] As a result, arguments based solely on the suitability of specific com-

[13]Inasmuch as the captive distributor was not faced with similar disruptions, its earnings in a given period should not reflect them.

[14]As discussed in Chapter 2, the 1993 temporary regulations describe a set of broad comparability criteria that apply across methods, including functions, risks, contractual terms, economic conditions, and property or services. For purposes of the resale price method, functions and risks, along with economic conditions, weigh more heavily than the remaining criteria. Particularly relevant differences between comparables and tested party under the resale price method include (but are not limited to) inventory levels and turnover rates; scope and terms of warranties provided; sales, marketing, advertising programs and services offered; sales volumes; the level of the market; foreign currency risks; and extensions of credit and payment terms.

[15]Additionally, the 1993 temporary regulations explicitly sanction multi-year averaging of results, partially ameliorating concerns regarding the greater or lesser variability of comparable firms' earnings streams.

parables may be less effective, and probably figure less prominently in taxpayers' defensive positions, under the 1993 temporary regulations.

On the other hand, the 1993 temporary regulations formalize an existing line of defense that both inbound and outbound companies may use (and have in the past used) with some success to fend off proposed pricing adjustments (the aforementioned arm's length range defense discussed in Chapters 2 and 3) and expand considerably on another defense (the market penetration thesis) that inbound companies in particular invoked fairly commonly under the 1968 regulations. Specifically, with regard to the latter defense, the temporary regulations underscore and legitimize the notion that firms may implement different strategies to the (same) end of long-term profit maximization, and that divergent strategies may justify divergent pricing policies (and, hence, earnings) over some (unspecified) period of time.[16] While technically limited to "market share strategies," in principle, the same line of reasoning can be applied more broadly.

Finally, among those (potentially numerous) inbound cases that appear to come under the 1993 proposed profit split methods, companies likewise have considerable leeway. While these particular profit split approaches have some foundation in economic theory at a fairly abstract level, the allocations of consolidated income that they produce in particular instances depend very much on the way in which one deals with the specific implementation issues that invariably arise.[17]

4.2.7 Resolution

While some inbound cases are settled at the Examination level, most of the cases that make up this composite resale price case study progressed to Appeals. Appeals, in turn, resolved them on terms that ranged from approximately 20% to 55% of the IRS's proposed adjustments.

Would these and similar cases be resolved on terms that leave a

[16]See Chapter 2.

[17]See Chapter 5 for a discussion of these issues.

larger or smaller share of consolidated income in the United States under the new regime? This depends on both the magnitude of the proposed adjustment under the 1993 temporary and proposed regulations, and the change in Appeals officers' assessment of litigation hazards.

The proposed "residual allocation" profit split methodology may or may not produce a larger adjustment than that based on the OEM distributor comparable developed under the 1968 regulations. Recall that the latter owned valuable intangible assets in its own right, and retained the intangible income attributable to them. As such, its resale margins incorporated this return. If the marketing intangibles that S utilized were of comparable value—and this is a fair approximation—it likewise retained the income attributable to its marketing intangibles under our standard resale price application. The amount of combined intangible income that S would retain under the proposed residual allocation rule may be greater or lesser than this amount, depending on the value of combined intangible assets, the accuracy of relative development expenditures as a proxy for relative intangible asset contributions, the allocation of P's joint costs, and the determination of market returns on tangible assets for purposes of determining the residual intangible income to be shared.

When the resale price method applies—that is, when the captive distributor is not deemed to add substantial value by, among other things, contributing valuable, self-developed intangible property—the adjustments under both 1993 temporary regulations and 1968 regulations should be of similar orders of magnitude.

Judging solely from the content of the 1993 temporary and proposed regulations, Appeals officers will likely conclude that litigation of similar cases, whether developed along resale price or profit split lines, poses greater hazards under the new regime as compared with the 1968 regulations. As noted, for the time being, the residual allocation rule is only a proposed methodology. Further, the prominence that the 1993 temporary regulations give to the "market share strategy" defense will make it more difficult for the government to overcome this line of argument in conventional resale price cases. Finally, the "arm's length range" defense may make it more difficult for Appeals officers to sustain proposed pricing adjustments.

4.3 Critique of Resale Price Provisions

Under the 1968 regulations, IRS economists encountered two very common problems in inbound cases:

- How to ascertain which entity, supplier or related distributor, should be deemed to own the trademarks and trade names affixed to products sold in the U.S. market; and,
- Whether to use comparable firms' gross or net profit margins in evaluating the pre-adjustment allocation of consolidated income among these related parties, and in developing pricing adjustments.

The first issue—how to determine ownership of marketing intangible assets used in the U.S. market when the U.S.-based subsidiary incurs substantial advertising expenses—has clearly not been resolved. Further, it has taken on added significance with the proviso that the resale price method applies only when the captive entity does not contribute valuable intangible property. The separate "as actually structured" provision adds another layer of confusion to this issue, inasmuch as the 1993 temporary regulations are unclear as to which specific features one is supposed to take as given for this purpose. Different features of the transaction or relationship may point to different allocations of income, even assuming that the captive U.S. subsidiary has some rights to intangible income by virtue of its advertising efforts. This important point should be clarified in the final regulations.

The confusion with regard to gross versus net profit margin comparisons arose chiefly because the 1968 regulations were framed in terms of gross margin comparisons, while the significant Section 482 pricing issues on inbound cases were often below-the-line. That is, if the captive distributor performed more (or fewer) below-the-line functions, or incurred greater (or lesser) risks, a comparison of net margins was thought to be more informative than the required gross margin comparisons, on the often incorrect assumption that distributors differing along these dimensions would nonetheless earn comparable net margins relative to sales.[18] On this point, the 1993 temporary regulations are unambiguous: they continue to sanction gross margin comparisons, while expressly requiring adjustments for differences in functions or risks that would influence bottom-line performance. As discussed in Chapter 3, however, they provide relatively little guidance as to how these adjustments are to be made.[19] This general lack of specificity, and specific lack of prioritizing among alternative approaches to quantifying significant differences, presents potential problems in this context as well.

In addition to clarifying the IRS's position regarding gross versus net margin comparisons, and perpetuating the general confusion as to how one should establish ownership of marketing intangible assets, the 1993 temporary regulations may also give rise to several new sources of confusion and controversy. As noted above, the 1993 temporary regulations do not specify the period of time during which a market share strategy will justify pricing differentials. This ambiguity is bound to create controversies, and the issue should be addressed more explicitly in the final regulations.[20]

More fundamentally, in cases where the captive distributor is deemed to contribute intangible assets, there is a real danger that the profit split concept will degenerate into an entirely *ad hoc* procedure. To prevent this eventuality, the final Section 482 regulations should incorporate a significantly more fleshed-out version of the 1993 proposed regulations' profit split methodologies. (In particular, this version should explicitly address the wide range of implementation

---

[18]Note that the resale price method suffers from one of the same maladies as the cost-plus method: it sanctions comparisons of profits (whether gross or net) relative to sales, on the theory that two distributors performing comparable functions and incurring similar risks would earn comparable profits per dollar of sales. However, as described in Chapter 3, microeconomic theory suggests only that the distributors' risk-adjusted rates of return would be equalized—and this only when the rates of return are properly measured, and the markets in which the distributors operate are both competitive and in equilibrium.

[19]As under the cost-plus method, they are to be calculated on the basis of some combination of economic principles, industry practice, and statistical analysis.

[20]Perhaps a calendar-based restriction would not be sufficiently general; an alternative may be to frame the constraint in terms of an explicit cost-benefit calculus.

issues that arise when one attempts to apply the proposed profit split methods, some of which are discussed in Chapter 5 following.)

The 1993 temporary regulations also create the very real potential for adjustments that create, rather than simply reallocate, income. Under the 1968 regulations, the IRS rarely raised pricing issues when both supplier and distributor reported losses. However, the 1993 temporary regulations clearly state that such adjustments fall within the scope of Section 482:

> The authority to determine true taxable income extends to any case in which either by inadvertence or design the taxable income, in whole or in part, of a controlled taxpayer is other than it would have been had the taxpayer ...been dealing at arm's length with an uncontrolled taxpayer.
>
> ...[E]ven if two controlled taxpayers realize an overall loss that is attributable to a particular controlled transaction, an allocation under Section 482 is not precluded.

Note that adjustments under these circumstances do not necessarily create income in a meaningful sense. That is, a fixed amount of consolidated revenues, expenses, and aggregate losses is consistent both with an allocation that leaves one entity profitable and the other in a loss position (which necessarily exceeds the overall losses), and another allocation in which both parties report losses.[21] Consequently, one is not necessarily creating consolidated revenues or expenses by reallocating aggregate losses in such a way that only one entity is in a loss position (relative to a pre-adjustment allocation in which both parties individually reported losses). Instead, one might simply be rearranging a fixed amount of consolidated revenues or

[21] Consider a controlled group composed of a supplier and a captive distributor, and a pair of identical firms dealing at arm's length. Suppose that the controlled firms report consolidated losses, and the independent firms' combined returns sum to the same negative figure. However, the independent distributor may report profits which are more than offset by its supplier's losses, while the captive distributor *and* its supplier both report losses. This would presumably reflect the controlled group's efforts to reshuffle revenues and (or) expenses to bring about the desired result.

expenses in such a way as to unravel the presumed non-arm's length allocation that gave rise to joint losses in the first instance.

By the same token, pricing adjustments in these circumstances (that is, when both parties to the controlled transactions at issue report losses) are valid only if one does *not* create consolidated revenues (or reduce consolidated expenses) in the process.[22] Note that, using this criterion, the type of income-creating issue described (but not raised) in the composite resale price case study reviewed above—in which S's rapidly declining market share and sales volume would have been offset by imputing sales to it, on the theory that a stand-alone distributor identical to S would have bridged to a more accomodating supplier when P failed to provide it with products adapted to the U.S. market—is not justified. In particular, such an adjustment would amount to creating revenues (and, therefore, profits) that neither P nor S actually earned. This important distinction should also be made explicit in the final Section 482 regulations.

[22] Consistent differences in combined revenues or expenses between affiliated group members and independent parties may reflect some short- or long-term economies or diseconomies of vertical integration, which the arm's length standard does not, and cannot, address. While in theory one would not expect to see integration on a large scale if such diseconomies persisted, observed practice is another matter entirely.

Chapter 5

Cost-Sharing Agreements

5.1 Background

As discussed in Chapter 2, the 1993 temporary regulations do not contain cost-sharing provisions; hence, for the time being, the 1968 regulations' cost-sharing rules remain in effect. Further, the 1992 proposed regulations' cost-sharing guidelines remain outstanding (in proposed form). In the composite case studies reviewed in this chapter, I compare applications of these two sets of cost-sharing guidelines.

The 1968 regulations condone cost-sharing agreements between related parties that meet certain relatively limited criteria. Broadly speaking, these agreements must be in writing, and the parties must make a good faith effort to divide costs in accordance with reasonably anticipated benefits. The 1992 proposed regulations' cost-sharing rules are considerably more detailed, and somewhat more onerous, than these outstanding guidelines in several respects.[1] As with the 1968 regulations, cost-sharing agreements must be set out in writing. Additionally, participants must maintain adequate records to verify the material provisions of the agreement, and they must be able to use the intangibles ultimately developed in the active conduct of their trade or business. Costs (and, hence, risks) must be

[1]However, they are significantly less onerous than the White Paper's cost-sharing proposals. See discussion of cost-sharing regulations in Chapter 2.

shared in proportion to reasonably anticipated benefits, in return for a specified interest in any intangibles produced. Moreover, cost shares must be adjusted to reflect changes in economic conditions, or the business operations or practices of the participants. Under the 1992 proposed regulations, a cost-sharing agreement is also subject to a presumptive benefits test that compares the U.S. participant's cost-to-income ratio with the collective cost-to-income ratio of the remaining participants. Further, buy-ins and buy-outs are expressly required when a participant enters or exits an ongoing cost-sharing agreement.

Cost-sharing agreements among members of a controlled group are commonplace in a number of research-intensive, high-technology industries. Some related party cost-sharing agreements are akin to genuine joint ventures, with participants fairly evenly balanced in terms of their (complementary) capacities to contribute to the research endeavor. At the other extreme, some are made up of very unequal participants, with members consisting of a U.S. parent that possesses state-of-the-art research facilities and conducts the research undertaking essentially single-handedly, and its offshore manufacturing affiliate, whose sole contribution to the venture is financial.

Cost-sharing agreements of the latter type (which IRS economists are more likely to encounter than the first type) displace the cost-plus methodology in a variety of circumstances in which it would otherwise apply. When an offshore affiliate enters into a bona fide cost-sharing agreement with its parent, it becomes the prospective co-owner of potentially unique and highly valuable intangible property. As such, if and when the research joint venture bears fruit, the affiliate is entitled to a return on the resultant jointly owned intangible assets, as well as on the tangible operating assets that it employs. A straightforward application of the cost-plus method in such cases, where markups over costs are derived from stand-alone firms that do not own comparably valuable intangible assets, will clearly not give the subsidiary its proper due. While in theory one could derive cost-plus markups from stand-alone firms that (a) are functionally comparable to the affiliate cum research joint venturer, (b) assume similar risks, (c) own comparably valuable intangible property, and (d) operate in broadly similar industries, in practice such firms rarely exist. Quite simply, unrelated firms generally do not combine relatively simple assembly or manufacturing operations, such as those performed by some (albeit not all) offshore affiliates that participate in cost-sharing agreements, with rights to state-of-the-art intangible assets.

I review three composite cost-sharing cases in Chapter 5. The first composite case involves a U.S.-based multinational firm with a possessions corporation that assembled electronic components for sale solely to related parties, and a manufacturing affiliate in Scotland that manufactured finished products and sold directly to third parties. This taxpayer made a Section 936(h) cost-sharing election, obligating the possessions corporation to contribute to its parent's R&D efforts.[2] By virtue of this election, and its resultant (ongoing) cost-sharing payment, the possessions corporation was deemed to have ownership rights in its parent firm's (existing) manufacturing intangibles, and could price its products accordingly (whether these products were sold to its parent, other related entities, or third parties). Additionally, the Scottish manufacturing affiliate entered into a Section 482 cost-sharing agreement with its U.S. parent, obligating it to contribute to the latter's R&D outlays in accordance with its anticipated benefits, as noted above. In return, it acquired specified rights in the intangibles that the parent ultimately developed.

Broadly speaking, this fact pattern raises several issues:

- How should the transfer prices of intermediate products that the possessions corporation sold to related parties be determined? As noted above, this is not a straightforward issue to be resolved via the cost-plus method, because one must incorporate a return to the manufacturing intangibles that the possessions corporation was deemed to own by virtue of its cost-sharing contribution;

- How should the possessions corporation's cost-sharing contributions be treated, for purposes of determining the pool of R&D expenses to be allocated between the Scottish affiliate and its U.S. parent?

[2]The magnitude of the possessions corporation's cost-sharing payment was determined by the relative importance of its product sales in relation to the consolidated entity's worldwide sales, pursuant to the Section 936(h) cost-sharing requirements.

- How should the Scottish manufacturing affiliate's cost shares be determined, given the relevant pool of allocable research expenses (as established in the prior step)? Equivalently, how should the (anticipated) benefits deriving from the right to utilize intangibles that may or may not ultimately be developed be measured?
- Should the Scottish affiliate be required to pay a buy-in fee, and, if so, how should the amount of the fee be determined?

The first composite case study addresses each of these points (again, under both the 1968 regulations and the 1993 temporary and proposed regulations).

The second composite cost-sharing case study reviewed in this Chapter also involves a U.S. taxpayer with a possessions corporation, which likewise made a Section 936(h) cost-sharing election. In this case, however, the possessions corporation sold directly to third parties; consequently, the issues raised were quite different:

- The possessions corporation's cost-sharing election did not entitle it to intangible income attributable to marketing intangible assets (as distinct from manufacturing intangible assets) developed by its U.S. parent. Consequently, the different types of intangibles (marketing versus manufacturing) embodied in the possessions product had to be identified; and,
- If both marketing and manufacturing intangible assets were incorporated into the possessions product, it would have been necessary to disaggregate the possessions corporation's profits (on third party sales) into (a) a return on tangible and manufacturing intangible assets, and (b) a return on marketing intangible assets. As a second step, the portion of the possessions corporation's profits that represented a return on marketing intangible assets developed by its parent would have been allocated to the latter.

As it happens, we ultimately concluded that all of the intangible assets embodied in the possessions product were marketing intangibles. As such, the possessions corporation was entitled to a return only on the tangible operating assets it employed, simplifying the process of determining its arm's length income considerably. The relevant insights to be drawn from this composite case study concern the definition and classification of intangible assets between manufacturing and marketing varieties, an issue that promises to become increasingly common under the combination of 1993 temporary and proposed regulations, particularly the latter.

The third cost-sharing case study reviewed in this Chapter features a Section 482 cost-sharing agreement between a U.S. parent and its Asian manufacturing affiliate. This composite case was developed along lines very similar to the capital employed method (albeit before the 1993 proposed regulations were drafted). As such, it points up the many ambiguities that arise in attempting to apply this seemingly straightforward approach to splitting profits, including:

- How should one determine which categories of expenditures yield benefits beyond the current period (and should therefore be treated as intangibles development expenditures), and which subsets of these give rise to particular types of intangible assets?
- Again, how should one divide total intangible assets (or group individual intangibles) into marketing and manufacturing types?
- What are reasonable capitalization and amortization rates to apply to different types of intangible assets?

The allocation of consolidated income between U.S. parent and offshore affiliate in this last composite cost-sharing case study was highly sensitive to the way in which total intangible assets were divided between marketing and manufacturing types. Given the difficulties in classifying intangibles in this way, the sensitivity of results to particular classifications made our proposed adjustments difficult to sustain.

5.2 Cost-Sharing Case 1: Scientific and Analytical Instruments

This cost-sharing case involves a U.S. parent firm and two subsidiaries, one located in a U.S. possessions and the other in Scotland.

They jointly produced a line of specialized scientific and analytical instrumentation products for use principally in research laboratories.

5.2.1 Summary Functional Analysis

The parent firm (P), headquartered in the United States, designed, manufactured, and distributed scientific instrumentation products. Two manufacturing subsidiaries (S_1 and S_2), together with P's manufacturing operations, jointly comprised this multinational firm's worldwide production facilities. S_1 (the possessions corporation) assembled electronic components used as intermediate inputs in the producton of scientific and analytical instrumentation products. S_2 (the Scottish affiliate) produced finished analytical and instrumentation products destined for European markets, while P produced finished products designed primarily for the U.S. market.

Research and design engineering functions were performed exclusively by P in the United States. With regard to S_1, the taxpayer had made a Section 936(h) cost-sharing election. Hence, S_1 was obligated to contribute a certain amount to P's R&D budget (based on its share of worldwide sales). By virtue of this election and its attendent cost-sharing payments, S_1 was deemed to have ownership rights in P's manufacturing intangibles relating to the possessions product, and could price accordingly on its direct sales to its parent, other related entities, or unrelated parties. S_2 participated in a Section 482 cost-sharing agreement with P, likewise obligating it to contribute a certain percentage of the latter's R&D outlays, as determined by its reasonably anticipated relative benefits from the joint research. As a result of its cost-sharing contribution, S_2 obtained certain rights to such intangibles as the joint research venture ultimately yielded (albeit not those that P had already developed, in contrast to the statutory Section 936(h) cost-sharing election).

S_1 supplied components to both S_2 and P; its sales were exclusively intra-company. Similarly, S_2 sold its finished products exclusively to related distributors in Europe. Neither S_1 nor S_2 performed marketing or selling functions, as evidenced by their very limited below-the-line expenses. P sold directly to end-users in the U.S. market, and to unrelated distributors in Asia. Additionally, it supplied products to related selling subsidiaries in Europe when S_2's production was insufficient to satisfy demand from these sources. Both P and its selling subsidiaries in Europe performed a range of marketing and selling functions.

5.2.2 Intra-Company Transfer Pricing Policy

S_1 established its transfer prices via the cost-plus method, charging cost plus 90% on sales of components to both S_2 and P. S_2's transfer prices on the units it sold to related European distributors were the end result of a modified resale price approach that the latter applied. Specifically, the captive distributors that sold S_2's output to end-users projected sales volume and market prices in their respective markets, formulated target resale margins, and backed out an acceptable transfer price (S_2's selling price). These transfer prices were reviewed approximately once a year.

5.2.3 Potential Issues

These transfer prices and R&D cross-charges resulted in the following proportional allocation of before-tax consolidated income among P, S_1, and S_2: S_2, the Scottish affiliate, earned approximately half of these entities' combined before-tax income; S_1 and P split the remainder roughly equally. Yet, P employed fixed assets valued at roughly ten times those utilized by S_2, and more than fifteen times those used by S_1. Hence, as measured by return on assets, both of its manufacturing subsidiaries outperformed P by an enormously wide margin.

In assessing the reasonableness of this allocation of consolidated income, we analyzed:

- The taxpayer's application of the cost-plus method used to price S_1's sales of components to S_2 and P; and,
- The structure of the cost-sharing agreement in effect between S_2 and P, and the reasonableness of S_2's contributions to joint research.

5.2.4 Adjustment Methodology under Section 936(h): Possessions Corporation (S_1) to U.S. Parent (P)

The IRS's proposed reallocation of income from S_1 to P was based on a fairly straightforward revision of the taxpayer's cost-plus application of Section 936(h). As noted above, the taxpayer had established S_1's transfer price on sales of components to P and S_2 via the cost-plus method, marking up cost by 90%. It provided no evidence, empirical or otherwise, to substantiate its contention that this markup represented an arm's length return.

Recall that the 90% markup over costs that S_1 reported should have compensated it for the assembly functions it performed, and embodied a return on the manufacturing intangibles it was deemed to own by virtue of its R&D cost-sharing payment to P. To determine the reasonableness of this reported amount, we first conducted an unsuccessful search for independent companies that were comparable to S_1, incurred similar forms and levels of risk, and had rights to similarly valued intangible property. Having located no such firms, we proposed to determine arm's length consideration separately for the two distinct activities in which S_1 engaged—simple manufacturing and investment in R&D—and compare the combined returns on these activities with the taxpayer's unsubstantiated 90% markup. The costs associated with each of S_1's activities were clearly separable, making this procedure feasible.

As a first step, we derived an arm's length markup from a sample of functionally comparable U.S. companies for the interval corresponding to the audit period. Our sample was comprised of four autonomous, publicly held entities. Averaging across firms and years, these entities earned a gross markup over their cost of goods of slightly more than 20%. Next, we adjusted S_1's cost base upwards to reflect its labor savings relative to U.S. factor costs (in keeping with Section 936(h)), and applied the 20% arm's length markup to this adjusted cost base. Finally, we added S_1's labor savings to the resulting estimate of its arm's length gross profits on assembly activities, again, in keeping with Section 936(h).

One can come up with a plausible, if imprecise, estimate of the return to S_1's manufacturing intangibles by determining a reasonable return on its investment therein (via the annual cost-sharing payment it made). This return to research, in turn, can be approximated in a number of ways. If the taxpayer maintained detailed records relating R&D expenditures on a particular project to an outcome (a new product or a process innovation that reduced production costs) some months or years hence, we could have computed an approximate realized return to research on a given project, in a given year, on a consolidated basis.[3] Unfortunately, companies in this industry rarely maintain such records, and this taxpayer was no exception.

Absent information relating the taxpayer's R&D expenditures to specific research results, we looked to a number of published empirical studies to establish an arm's length return to research. Specifically, we relied on a number of econometric analyses of the private return to innovation (based on productivity growth models) and case studies of technical innovations.[4] It should be noted that, in taking this approach, our computations were necessarily broad-brush; further, we guaranteed S_1 a significant annual return on an activity—investment

[3]For an initial period, one would expect these returns to be negative, because the research stage takes time and the commercialization of research results is also a slow process. Upon successful completion of these processes, the returns might be quite high for a time, if competitors did not simultaneously make comparable technical advances. However, as competitors duplicate the initial innovator's advances, the latter's return should decline. Clearly, the length of these stages is key in determining the returns to research in any given year.

[4]The econometric analyses, based on productivity growth models, included: Griliches, Zvi, "Returns to Research and Development Expenditures in the Private Sector," in Kendrick, John W. and Beatrice N. Vaccara, *New Developments in Productivity Measurement and Analysis*, Chicago and London: The University of Chicago Press, 1980; Pakes, Ariel and Mark Schankerman, "The Rate of Obsolenscence of Patents, Research Gestation Lags, and the Private Rate of Return to Research Resources," in Griliches, Zvi, ed., *R&D, Patents and Productivity*, Chicago and London: University of Chicago Press, 1984; Link, Albert N. and Laura Bauer, *Cooperative Research in U.S. Manufacturing: Assessing Policy Initiatives and Corporate Strategies*, Massachusetts and Toronto: Lexington Books, 1989. The case studies of innovation included Link and Bauer, Ibid. (which contains empirical segments); Mansfield, Edwin, John Rapoport, Anthony Romeo, Samual Wagner and George Beardsley, "Social and Private Rates of Return from Industrial Innovations," *Quarterly Journal of Economics*, 91 (May 1977); and, Hippel, Eric, "Increasing Innovators' Returns from Innovation," in Rosenbloom, Richard C., *Research on Technological Innovation, Management and Policy*, Vol. I, Greenwich, Connecticut: JAI Press, Inc., 1983.

in R&D—that was intrinsically risky.

The econometric analyses suggest that returns to research overall have generally ranged from 17% to 45%. One study indicated that firms engaged in both internal and cooperative research earn significantly higher returns on their internal R&D programs than firms engaged exclusively in internal R&D.[5] Additionally, the same study suggested that firms hypothetically engaged exclusively in cooperative research would earn negligible returns on their investment in research. (These firms are hypothetical because virtually no unrelated firms engage solely in cooperative research.) Case studies of the private rate of return to investment in innovation yield estimates that are consistent with those obtained via econometric estimation techniques. In the case studies we reviewed, the authors analyzed a total of 57 innovations. The median private rate of return on these innovations ranged from a low of 25% to a high of 36% across studies.

Drawing on these results, we allowed S_1 a return of 35% on its cost-sharing payment, close to the upper bound of estimated median private rates of return to investment in R&D. In light of the fact that the taxpayer's R&D program was heavily weighted toward product development rather than basic or strategic research, its risks were more limited than many of the firms included in the empirical studies on which we drew. As such, the 35% return on research was probably very generous.

In summary, we adjusted S_1's components transfer price in the following steps:

1. We calculated an appropriate manufacturing markup on costs from a sample of functionally comparable U.S. firms, which amounted to 20%;

2. We applied this margin to S_1's cost of goods, increased by the amount of its labor savings, and again added labor savings directly to the resulting estimated arm's length return on S_1's assembly functions; and,

3. We drew on a number of empirical studies of the private rate

[5] See Link and Bauer, *Op. Cit.*

of return to research to determine a reasonable markup on S_1's cost-sharing contribution.

The sum of these separate adjustments constituted our estimate of S_1's arm's length income. Our proposed adjustment amounted to the difference between its (substantially higher) reported income and its estimated arm's length income.

5.2.5 Adjustment Methodology under the 1968 Regulations: To and from the Scottish Subsidiary (S_2)

Recall that S_2 purchased components from S_1, paid a cost-sharing contribution to P, and charged its related distributor-customers for finished products. Our previously described (downward) adjustment to S_1's components selling price (equivalently, S_2's components purchase price) entailed a concomitant (upward) adjustment in S_2's income. The price that S_2 charged its related distributors for finished instrumentation products was deemed to be arm's length, because the latter earned reasonable resale margins relative to comparable stand-alone distributors operating in the same geographic markets. As such, our additional proposed adjustments amounted to a recomputation of cross-charges from S_2 to P in connection with their cost-sharing agreement. Specifically, we questioned:

- The amount of S_2's ongoing cost-sharing payment; and,
- Its failure to pay a buy-in fee for pre-existing manufacturing intangibles that P contributed to the joint research effort, and that S_2 continued to use directly.

These adjustments are described below.

S_2's Ongoing Cost-Sharing Contribution

First, consider S_2's ongoing cost-sharing contribution. Two basic issues arose in evaluating the reasonableness of this payment:

- How should one measure anticipated benefits deriving from participation in the intra-company research joint venture?

- Should the pool of R&D expenses to which this (proportionate) measure is applied include or net out S_1's cost-sharing payments?

Consider each of these points in turn.

Measuring Benefits—Profits versus Sales: In principle, and under the 1968 regulations, an entity's proportionate cost contribution to a research joint venture should be commensurate with its anticipated relative benefits from the fruits of the shared research: cost-reducing production technology and (or) improved products. Under the taxpayer's schema, the dollar amount of S_2's cost-sharing contribution in a given year was determined by applying its percentage of the group's total sales worldwide to total R&D. S_2's sales and, thus, its proportionate R&D cost contribution, amounted to roughly one-third of group-wide sales during the audit years. However, its percentage share of profits on sales of products embodying the jointly owned technology was approximately one-half. Hence, the crux of this issue: should the benefits to participating in a cost-sharing agreement, and obtaining access to the technology ultimately developed thereunder, be measured by profits or sales?

In considering this question, theory on the one hand, and actual practices between unrelated parties on the other, point in rather different directions. In theory, the relative benefits to jointly owned technology should be measured by the contribution this technology makes to the owners' respective net income streams, not their revenues. In general, the value of any asset, tangible or intangible, is measured by the discounted present value of the net income it is expected to generate. Likewise, the economic benefits deriving from an investment in intangible assets (equivalently, rates of return to research) in the econometric and case studies cited above were effectively measured by the incremental profits earned in consequence, relative to the requisite outlays.[6] More generally, the basic principle of using profits rather than sales as a measure of benefits is compelling from a theoretical vantage point. Microeconomic theory is firmly grounded on the premise that firms are in business to maxi-

[6]See preceding discussion of S_1's allowable income.

mize profits, not sales volume, and their behavior is informed by this objective. In the present context, if an unrelated party were given the opportunity to participate in a research joint venture that would greatly enhance its sales volume, but ultimately yield no additional net profits, one would expect it to decline.

On the other hand, a number of genuinely arm's length cooperative research ventures utilize an altogether different basis for allocating joint R&D expenses. (While none are in the highly specialized field in which this taxpayer operated, the same range of approaches to allocating costs is used across a range of industries in which these ventures are observed.) Specifically, many arm's length research ventures allocate costs simply by dividing them equally among all participants, or on the basis of sales. For example, the Microelectronics and Computer Technology Corporation (MCC), among the largest and best known purely private cooperative research ventures (with members drawn from the U.S. computer and semiconductor industries), divides costs equally because relative benefits (i.e., profits) cannot be foreseen:

> [I]nitially, all the participants in a program pay an equal share [of R&D costs]. (Participants who join later may pay a higher cost ...) Obviously, participants will not benefit equally, but it is difficult to predict the distribution of benefits among participants.[7]

The difficulty in measuring benefits derives in part from the nature of the research that MCC and other collaborative research ventures undertake: relatively long-term strategic research, a number of stages prior to product development.[8] Sponsoring companies' re-

[7] Peck, M.J., "Microelectronics and Computer Technology Corporation," *Research Policy* 15 (1986), 219-231. Also see Dimanescu, Dan and James Botkin, *The New Alliance*, Cambridge, MA: Ballinger Publishing Company, 1986, and Needham, James M. and Yair H. Har el, "What You Need to Know About Joint Ventures," in McAllister, Margaret, ed., *The 1986 Yearbook on Corporate Mergers, Joint Ventures and Corporate Policy*, Boston: Cambridge Press, 1987. The latter authors indicate that ownership allocations are determined not solely by financial contributions in arm's length research joint ventures, but by valuing each partner's total contribution, including technology and know-how, plant, property and equipment, capital, management skills, etc., as one would expect.

[8] This research focus is partly the result of antitrust restrictions.

turns to cooperative research ultimately depend on their own internal research efforts, subsequent to receiving the "research output" of the joint venture. As such, it is exceedingly difficult to project individual participants' benefits to cooperative research per se.

Sematech, a cooperative venture among semiconductor manufacturers financed in equal measure by the government and member firms, sets dues on the basis of sales (or purchases), within upper and lower bounds:

> Members' dues, which are determined on the basis of each company's semiconductor sales and/or purchases, generally range from $1 million to $15 million annually. Under this structure, a small company might pay a greater proportion of its sales than a large company to reach Sematech's minimum dues requirement."[9]

To some extent, arm's length research joint ventures that are partially government-funded, such as Sematech, are less informative than purely private ventures, such as MCC, in that reasonably equal access by small and large firms may be a condition of funding.

In short, arm's length research joint ventures do not necessarily allocate costs on the basis of anticipated increments in profitability, in part because of the difficulty in measuring relative profits attributable to the jointly developed intangible property (either prospectively or even after the fact) and in part because of concerns about equal access when federal funds are involved. However, one can more readily gauge the relative profits attributable to (specific rights in) intangibles that are developed under the auspices of related party research ventures. This is true for a variety of reasons:

- The venture's research "output" does not become an input into individual participants' separate research programs; rather, related party R&D cost-sharing ventures undertake the full gamut of research conducted by the group as a whole, including product development;

[9]Briefing Report to the Chairman, Subcommittee on Defense, Committee on Appropriations, U.S. Senate, *Sematech's Technological Progress and Proposed Research Program*, United States General Accounting Office, July 1992.

- Intra-company cost-sharing agreements can legitimately "carve up" the markets that the controlled group as a whole serves, and assign exclusive geographic rights in the developed intangibles to individual participants. In contrast, antitrust restrictions preclude members of an arm's length research joint venture from imposing measures that inhibit downstream competition in the relevant product markets; and,

- The related participants in an intra-company research joint venture typically combine more similar complementary productive inputs with the process or product innovations resulting from the venture. For example, in the instant case, S_2's manufacturing plant was set up according to the same manufacturing engineering principles. It used tangible assets that were similar in both type and vintage, employed the same quality control procedures, had access to the same pool of managerial and technical know-how, and so forth. Hence, one cannot attribute S_2's higher profits on sales of the same products (in different markets) to superior complementary resources, or more skillful or efficient use of the underlying technology.

As such, in a related party context, it may make more sense to allocate costs based on anticipated relative profits, rather than sales, inasmuch as one may be able to measure the former reasonably accurately (although it may also be necessary to adjust for economies of integration—e.g., cost savings—that benefit the related participants differentially). This is particularly true when the parties are assigned clearly delineated geographic rights to the technology ultimately developed, and the different markets vary fairly consistently in terms of the prices at which products embodying the jointly developed intangibles sell, as was true in the instant case.[10] Further, one finds

[10]Recall as well that P could and did sell into S_2's market when the latter could not satisfy demand for its products, and had sufficient capacity to supply a substantial portion of that market. Thus, in entering into a cost-sharing agreement with S_2, P effectively agreed to limit its sales in the more lucrative overseas markets, concentrating its sales efforts on the less profitable domestic market. A hypothetical unrelated party accepting such conditions and, thereby, a smaller share of the total anticipated benefits from technological innovation, would presumably pay a proportionately smaller share of the associated development costs.

support for this position in both the Conference Report to the 1986 Act and the White Paper. The Conference Report states that:

> In order for cost sharing arrangements to produce results consistent with changes made by the Act to royalty arrangements, it is envisioned that the allocation of R&D cost-sharing arrangements generally be proportionate to *profit* [my *emph.*] as determined before research and development.[11]

The White Paper contains a similar passage:

> Neither units of production nor sales would be an appropriate measure [to use in determining cost shares] if it were apparent (or became apparent during the course of the agreement) that *profitability* [my *emph.*] differed substantially with respect to various participants' rights.[12]

In short, if one interprets the arm's length standard to mean that related party cost shares should be based on the measure of benefits that uncontrolled entities would use if they could, then S_2's ongoing cost-sharing contribution should be based on its anticipated relative profits attributable to the jointly developed technology.

Alternatively, the arm's length standard can be interpreted to mean that related party cost shares should be based on the method of allocating pooled expenses that uncontrolled research joint venturers actually use—in light of the antitrust constraints that limit their research to "pre-competitive" stages and preclude a differential assignment of rights that may inhibit downstream competition. In this event, S_2's ongoing cost contribution should either be (a) based on its relative sales, as it originally was; or (b) determined by dividing the allocable pool of shared R&D expenses equally between S_2 and P. (The choice between these alternatives depends on how much weight one attaches to the fact that sales-based allocations appear to be associated with cooperative research ventures that are partially government-funded.)

---

[11] H.R. Conf. Rep. No. 841, 99th Cong., 2nd Sess. II-6638(1986).

[12] The *White Paper*, *Op. Cit.*

In light of the intrinsic ambiguity of the arm's length standard in this context, we developed two alternative positions in this case. Our secondary position allocated pooled research costs between S_2 and P equally. In our primary position, S_2's share of pooled research expenses was determined by its share of consolidated profits (before deductions for R&D), adjusted (before the cost allocation) to reflect:

- The reduced cost of components that S_2 purchased from S_1; and,
- Below-the-line expenses that we imputed to S_2 solely for purposes of this computation.

The "imputed cost" adjustment described above was necessary because S_2 realized certain savings in SG&A expenses by virtue of the fact that it sold exclusively to related, rather than uncontrolled, distributor-customers. Inasmuch as these cost savings translated into higher profits (relative to P) that were clearly not attributable to its more valuable rights to proprietary technology, their effects should be eliminated before determining cost shares based on profits.

The Costs to be Allocated: Next, consider briefly the proper definition of pooled research expenses for purposes of making the above allocation. Recall that S_1's cost-sharing contributions were determined under Section 936(h), and, as such, represented payment for pre-existing intangibles rather than ongoing research.[13] Consequently, the research expenses to be shared by S_2 and P for the prospective development of intangibles were not actually reduced by the amount of S_1's "contribution."

Accordingly, in determining S_2's cost shares as described above, we applied its proportionate share (its share of consolidated profits, as adjusted, under our primary position, and one-half of the total R&D budget under the alternative position) to the total research budget for the years at issue, before netting out S_1's cost-sharing payments.

[13]In a more legalistic sense, S_1's cost-sharing election was a statutory "device," and its cost-sharing payments were not pursuant to a contractual (intra-company) cost-sharing agreement. See also the discussion of this issue in the White Paper, p. 125.

The Buy-in Payment

Finally, consider the "buy-in" issue. Prior to entering into a cost-sharing agreement with P, S_2 paid P a royalty for the use of its proprietary technology and know-how (pursuant to an intra-company license agreement between them). However, it ceased to pay P for its continuing use of these pre-existing intangibles upon joining the cooperative research venture. Neither S_2's prior royalty payments nor its cost-sharing contributions could be construed as an "installment" buy-in fee. The former were strictly for the contemporaneous use of P's proprietary technology, and they conferred no ownership rights to S_2 cum licensee. S_2's cost-sharing contributions financed concurrent R&D; as such, they did not represent payment for intangible assets that P had already developed. Nor did S_2 make a one-time payment to P for these intangibles.

On the subject of buy-ins in principle, theory and practice are reasonably consonant. In theory, a profit-maximizing firm possessing valuable proprietary technology would clearly not permit an unrelated entity to use its intangibles without receiving adequate compensation. To do so would be to forgo profits unnecessarily, either in the form of royalty payments (or a one-time fee), or as a consequence of increased competition from rivals utilizing the previously proprietary technology. Moreover, the genuinely arm's length research joint ventures discussed above both provide for buy-in payments of sorts. In Sematech's case, "companies wishing to join Sematech currently are required to pay 'back dues' for each year since Sematech's inception."[14] MCC also requires a buy-in fee, although it is proportionately smaller:

> By majority vote, [MCC's] Board approves new members, each of which purchases one non-transferable share in MCC. The Board sets the price of a share; in 1983, the price was $150,000. The price of a share has been increased periodically since then; the 1986 price was $1,000,000. The increases are to reflect the lesser risk

[14]The United States General Accounting Office (July 1992), *Op. Cit.* Note, however, that Sematech's Board of Directors has agreed in principle to delete its back-dues requirement after 1992.

> of latecomers as well as to penalize those who wait to see how the venture fares before joining, though the price of a share is small relative to the annual company contributions made to each of the technology programs which it joins.[15]

One also finds support for buy-in payments in the Conference Report to the 1986 Act:

> To the extent, if any, that one party is actually contributing funds towards research and development at a significantly earlier point in time, or is otherwise effectively putting its funds at risk to a greater extent than the other, it would be expected that an appropriate return would be required to such party to effectively reflect its investment.[16]

Thus, we required S_2 to continue to pay a royalty fee on sales of products that embodied pre-existing intangibles, a conservative estimate of an arm's length buy-in fee. We estimated these sales using information provided by the taxpayer on product life cycles and research gestation lags. The royalty payment due was determined by applying the royalty rate that S_2 paid prior to the cost-sharing agreement to this estimated sales base. Note that the resulting adjustment was far smaller than the annual contributions S_2 would have made for "back dues," using our modified computation of cost shares.

In summary, in calculating our adjustment to S_2's income under the 1968 regulations, we:

- Reduced S_2's (intra-company) components purchase price, consistent with our prior adjustment to S_1's transfer price;
- Recomputed S_2's cost-sharing payment in two alternative ways: (a) by applying its share of profits (with adjustments) rather than sales to a pool of expenditures that was gross of S_1's cost-sharing payment, and (b) by dividing total R&D expenditures

[15] Peck, M.J., *Op. Cit.*
[16] *Op. Cit.*

(again, gross of S_1's cost-sharing payment) equally between S_2 and P; and,

- Imputed a royalty payment from S_2 to P for its continued use of pre-existing intangibles after it had entered into a cost-sharing agreement, in lieu of a one-time buy-in fee.

5.2.6 Possible Adjustment Methodology under Section 936(h) and the 1993 Temporary Regulations: Possessions Corporation (S_1) to U.S. Parent (P)

Despite the fact that S_1 was a possessions corporation and its cost-sharing payment pursuant to a statutory Section 936(h) election, the 1986 Act's *commensurate with income* requirement and the 1993 temporary Section 482 regulations influence the way in which one would go about determining both its transfer price for components and its cost-sharing payment. Under the Section 936(h) cost-sharing provisions, the transfer price for tangible property sold by a possessions corporation to its parent is determined under the Section 482 tangible property provisions (with due regard for the manufacturing intangibles it is deemed to own).[17] Hence, a change in the latter works its way back to Section 936(h) by this route. Equally importantly, after 1986, "...the cost sharing payment by [a] possessions corporation must equal the greater of the amount required under the new commensurate with income standard or 110% of the pre-1986 Act statutory cost sharing amount."[18] The 1993 temporary regulations elaborate on this stipulation:

> If a possessions corporation makes an election under section 936(h)(5)(C)(i)(I), the corporation must make a section 936 cost-sharing payment that is at least equal to the payment that would be required under section 482 if the electing corporation were a foreign corporation. Indetermining the payment that would be required un-

[17] See Chapter 2.

[18] Cited in the White Paper, p. 125.

der section 482 for this purpose, the provisions of sections 1.482-1T and 1.482-4T through 1.482-5T will be applied.

In plain English, the possessions corporation's cost-sharing payment must be set at such a level as to bring essentially all intangible income back to the U.S. parent, in keeping with the *commensurate with income* requirement. Consequently, after 1986, the Section 936(h) cost-sharing election is unambiguously inferior to the profit split alternative, in which consolidated profits (including intangible income) are split equally between U.S. parent and possessions corporation. Practically speaking, then, the pricing issues relating to S_1 in this composite case will probably not arise under the 1993 temporary regulations.[19]

5.2.7 Possible Adjustment Methodology under the 1992 Proposed Regulations: From Scottish Subsidiary (S_2) to U.S. Parent (P)

Consider next the adjustment to S_2's intra-company payments to P under the 1992 proposed regulations' cost-sharing rules. Recall that,under the 1968 regulations, we recomputed S_2's cost-sharing

[19] For the sake of completeness, consider how the pricing of S_1's components and the magnitude of its cost-sharing contribution might be determined if a taxpayer happened to elect cost-sharing under Section 936(h). By virtue of its cost-sharing payment, S_1 would be deemed to own P's manufacturing intangibles, and could legitimately price its tangible product sales to P and S_2 on that basis. (That is, for purposes of setting prices on tangible property—components—S_1 should retain all manufacturing intangible income on its direct sales, whether to its parent, other related entities, or third parties.) If P also owned marketing intangibles (and, in fact, P owned a variety of valuable trade names, marks, and other marketing intangibles), the 1993 proposed Section 482 profit split regulations (as distinct from the statutory profit split provisions under Section 936(h)) would presumably apply, because both related entities would contribute non-routine intangible assets to the product sales at issue. Again, though, the forgoing refers solely to pricing; there is also the cost-sharing payment to consider. That is, in somc form or fashion, the allocation of income that this profit split pricing methodology produces must be reconciled with the separate requirement that S_1's cost-sharing contribution be commensurate with the income attributable to the manufacturing intangibles at issue. Presumably, S_1's arm's length income, as determined by the residual allocation rule, would be reduced by the intangible income portion.

contribution and imputed a royalty payment from S_2 to P in lieu of a one-time buy-in fee. By and large, these issues would likely be raised in essentially the same form under the 1992 proposed cost-sharing rules as well.

In particular, our use of relative anticipated profits to recompute S_2's cost shares has some foundation in the 1992 proposed cost-sharing rules (and might therefore be applied under this regime as well). These proposed rules allow for various measures of anticipated benefits to be derived from prospective intangibles development, among them anticipated gross or net profits. (Other possible measures include anticipated units of production, where there is a uniform unit of production for all participants; anticipated sales, measured at the same level of production or distribution for all participants; and other measures that reasonably reflect benefits.)

Further, the proposed rules state that "[u]nless another method of sharing costs provides a more reliable measure of the participant's reasonably anticipated benefits over time, an allocation may be made by reference to a comparison of the participant's cost/income ratio and the cost/income ratio of the other eligible participants," where "income" in these ratios is operating profits and "cost" refers to R&D outlays.[20]

Additionally, the 1992 proposed regulations explicitly sanction buy-in and buy-out payments. Compensation for pre-existing intangibles must be arm's length under these provisions, and it may take the form of a lump sum payment, a series of fixed installment payments, or a running royalty. Hence, again, our proposed buy-in payment (in the form of a running royalty) has some support in, and might well be raised under, the 1992 proposed cost-sharing provisions.

---

[20]More specifically, the numerator of this ratio is given by the intangibles development costs borne by the participant(s), averaged over the current taxable year and two preceding taxable years; the denominator is given by all operating income that is directly or indirectly attributable to the intangibles development area (gross of development costs), averaged over the current taxable year and two preceding taxable years.

5.2.8 Taxpayer's Position

For the most part, the taxpayers in this composite case study, confronted with the proposed pricing adjustments described above, defended their status quo pricing practices vigorously. The general theme running throughout these counter-arguments was that, while their approaches to establishing arm's length returns in these very grey areas of the regulations were inexact, so too was ours. As such, our approach should not necessarily be accorded a higher priority. With regard to our proposed adjustments to S_1-type possessions corporations, several taxpayers also maintained that the 1968 regulations did not provide for the "return to research" approach we utilized to establish arm's length transfer prices for assemblies, and, therefore, the adjustments we proposed on this basis were inherently arbitrary and capricious. Not surprisingly, the taxpayers faced with recomputed cost shares based on relative projected profits took issue with this particular measure of benefits, arguing that differences in profitability could not be attributed solely to differential rights in proprietary technology.

The "arbitrary and capricious" argument, an easy and effective defense against virtually any proposed pricing adjustment under the 1968 regulations when both (related) parties contributed non-routine intangible property (as in the Section 936(h) pricing issue described above), will likely be somewhat less effective under the combination of 1992 and 1993 proposed regulations and 1993 temporary regulations. While the 1968 regulations simply did not explicitly address such situations, the 1993 proposed regulations do, obviating the need to devise a method that is not expressly condoned (such as our return to research approach).

By the same token, the magnitude of adjustments under the 1993 proposed profit split methods is highly sensitive to the specific ways in which one deals with the numerous implementation issues that arise in applying them (as discussed briefly in Chapter 4, and at greater length subsequently). Consequently, in future cases of this sort, taxpayers may couch their counter-arguments more in terms of the way in which a mutually agreed-upon method should be applied than in terms of the choice of methods per se. It should also be noted that, while this observation applies across a range of pricing issues, the specific context in which it is discussed here—in connection with a Section 936(h) cost-sharing election—will probably not arise very often, if at all, under the new regime. As noted above, after 1986, the Section 936(h) profit split election clearly dominates the cost-sharing election from taxpayers' perspectives.

As regards the proper basis for determining cost shares, taxpayers may still exploit the ambiguous treatment of this issue under the 1992 proposed cost-sharing provisions. As noted, the question of how benefits should be measured is left relatively open-ended under these rules, and taxpayers will not have to overcome a given priority with regard to alternative measures.[21] This lack of prioritizing will probably be an effective argument against proposed changes in cost-sharing contributions based on one or another particular benefits measure, and it will likely remain a point of contention between taxpayers and the IRS.

5.2.9 Resolution

The cases that make up this composite case study were resolved at Appeals, with the pricing issues relating to Section 482 cost-sharing contributions and buy-in fees essentially dropped outright. Nor was the determination of transfer prices via a "return to research" approach deemed consistent with the 1968 regulations; consequently, these proposed adjustments were also dropped.

Under the 1992 proposed cost-sharing provisions, the Section 482 cost contributions and buy-in issues may be resolved on very similar terms, or on significantly less favorable terms (from firms' vantage point). As noted, both of these issues could well be developed along essentially the same lines under the proposed rules, and, hence, involve comparable dollar amounts. While Appeals officers' assessments of the litigation hazards associated with buy-in issues may

[21] While the proposed rules mention that cost shares can be recomputed based on eligible participants' cost/income ratios, as described above, this approach is endorsed very half-heartedly. In particular, taxpayers can overcome such an allocation by demonstrating that "another method of sharing costs provides a more reliable measure of ... anticipated benefits," as noted above.

well diminish, in that the 1992 proposed regulations explicitly condone them, their assessments of litigation hazards associated with revised measures of anticipated benefits from joint research probably won't change significantly. These observations suggest quite similar Appeals settlements of such issues.

By the same token, different allocations of consolidated income, produced by using different benefits measures, are bounded to some (ambiguous) degree by the "presumptive benefits test" under the 1992 proposed regulations, whereby the reasonableness of cost shares can be assessed by comparing the U.S. participant's cost-to-income ratio with the collective cost-to-income ratio of all other participants. If Appeals officers resort to this *ex post* test of the reasonableness of cost shares, the results may be significantly less advantageous to firms, and commensurately more favorable to the government.

5.3 Cost-Sharing Case 2: Specialized Medical Equipment

The parent/subsidiary pair in this second composite cost-sharing case outwardly resembles the parent/possessions corporation pair in the preceding cost-sharing case, in that the subsidiary was likewise a possessions corporation and the taxpayer had likewise made a Section 936(h) cost-sharing election. However, the possessions corporation in this case sold products embodying marketing intangible property, owned by its parent, directly to third parties. In contrast, the possessions corporation in the prior case sold products embodying only manufacturing intangible assets, which it was deemed to own, to related parties. This difference changes the complexion of the case considerably.

After briefly discussing the facts of this case and the potential issues it raises, we describe two broad taxonomies of intangible assets, and the process of attempting to fit the intangibles embodied in the possessions corporation's products into these frameworks, at some length. The general issue of how one should go about dividing up a firm's total intangible assets between broad manufacturing and marketing types will likely become increasingly common under the

1993 temporary and proposed regulations (as illustrated in the last composite cost-sharing case following).

5.3.1 Synopsis of Facts and Circumstances

In the early 1980s, following the lead of one of its rivals, a U.S.-based multinational firm diversified into the manufacture of a particular type of specialized medical equipment for use principally by hospitals. However, the U.S. parent at issue, *P*, learned from its competitor's prior mistakes. The latter had first attempted to distribute the medical product at issue directly to hospitals. After an extended period of consistently disappointing sales, it entered into a long-term contract with one of the three major distributors in the business, in the apparent belief that the equipment could be sold in significantly larger volumes by such a distributor, with proven marketing skills and an established presence in the hospital business. Its sales of the medical equipment increased approximately four-fold upon entering into this relationship, and continued to climb sharply and steadily for several years thereafter before stabilizing at a more sustainable rate of growth.

Having observed this protracted process from afar, *P* determined that a close link with one of the two remaining major distributors was essential to the success of its new business venture, and approached each of them. Coincidentally, *D*, one of the three entities, was experiencing some difficulties with its existing line of comparable equipment, and seeking an alternative supplier. Hence, *P* entered into an agreement with *D*, appointing the latter its exclusive distributor of the medical equipment in the United States and specified foreign territories.

As part of this agreement, *P* granted *D* exclusive use of its product-specific trademark and the non-exclusive use of its corporate name (in connection with the equipment it manufactured). *D* did not compensate *P* monetarily for these rights directly (although it presumably did so indirectly, via higher purchase prices and/or more favorable contract terms). Under the terms of the contract, *D* was obligated to purchase specified minimum quantities of the product, to be manufactured by *P*. (These minimum quantities amounted to a significant share of the U.S. market for the specific equipment at issue.) Moreover, D was precluded from purchasing and distributing competitors' products. The agreement also contained clauses permitting P to adjust prices annually to reflect increased costs for labor, materials, and additional regulatory requirements, and requiring it to pass on a portion of the decreased costs resulting from manufacturing efficiencies created by increased productivity and/or larger volumes of purchases and sales.

In short, as a result of its agreement with D, P obtained access to an established (and extensive) customer base in the hospital business. Moreover, the specific terms of this agreement had the effect of shifting a number of significant business and market risks to D (including variations in the volume of product demanded by end-users, fluctuations in the costs of labor and materials, and potential increases in outlays necessitated by changes in the regulatory environment).

Toward the end of the agreement's initial term of five years, D exercised its right to extend the agreement for another five years. Immediately thereafter, P transferred the business to its possessions subsidiary (S), substituted S's name for its own in the agreement, and made a cost-sharing election under Section 936(h). Hence, S began contributing to P's R&D program, manufacturing the medical equipment covered by the agreement, and selling directly to D. S retained over 90% of the consolidated income earned on these sales. P's residual share was comprised entirely of (a) an intra-company negotiation fee, intended to compensate it at cost for its ongoing negotiations with D (deemed in this new environment to be a service performed on behalf of S); and (b) an intra-company royalty payment for unspecified marketing intangibles.

5.3.2 Potential Issues

Recall that the taxpayer's Section 936(h) cost-sharing election entitled S to retain an arm's length return on its tangible operating assets, and the income (on its product sales) attributable to the embodied manufacturing intangibles that it was deemed to own by virtue of its contribution to P's R&D program. However, S was not entitled to retain the income on its product sales that was allocable to trademarks, names, or any other type of *marketing* intangible developed or acquired by P. The issue in this case was whether the roughly 90:10 allocation of combined income on sales of products produced by S and sold to D (pursuant to the distribution agreement originally negotiated between P and D) was arm's length. Equivalently, did the 90% accruing to S constitute a reasonable return on its tangible operating assets and its manufacturing intangible assets, or did some part of its reported profits represent a return to P's marketing intangible assets? This broad issue, in turn, can be broken down into four distinct, more narrowly defined issues:

1. What intangibles were embodied in, or otherwise associated with, the medical equipment at issue?
2. Which of these should be classified as manufacturing intangibles, and which as marketing intangibles?
3. How should a reasonable return on S's tangible operating assets be determined?
4. How should total intangible income (that is, total profits on sales of the medical equipment to D, less the aforementioned return on S's tangible operating assets) be apportioned between marketing and manufacturing intangibles?

The first three of these questions are addressed in Sections 5.3.3 through 5.3.5 below. Clearly, the allocation of total intangible income between broad marketing and manufacturing intangible asset categories (question 4 above) is necessary only if both types of intangibles were embodied in (or otherwise associated with) the medical equipment that S produced. We argue in Section 5.3.4 that all intangibles at issue in this case should be considered marketing intangibles. Hence, all intangible income was allocated to P.

5.3.3 Intangibles Embodied in the Medical Equipment at Issue

Like any other type of asset, an intangible asset generates benefits beyond the period in which the associated development expenditures are made; however, it has no physical substance. A number of individuals have attempted to develop a comprehensive taxonomy of intangibles, among them Smith and Parr.[22] They divide intangible assets into four broad categories:

1. *Rights* (receiving contracts on favorable terms, and providing contracts, such as mortgage servicing rights);

2. *Relationships* (assembled workforce, customer relationships, distributor relationships);

3. *Grouped intangibles* (goodwill, going concern); and,

4. *Intellectual property* (patents, trademarks, copyrights, and trade secrets or know-how)

In a much earlier analysis, Bain identified the following "barriers to entry" (defined as established producers' advantages vis-a-vis potential entrants in a given industry that permit the former to maintain prices above a competitive level to varying degrees), most of which can be construed as reflecting, or directly constituting, intangible assets:[23]

1. *Absolute Cost Advantages*, including (a) control of production techniques by established firms via patents or secrecy; (b) imperfections in the markets for hired factors of production (labor, materials, etc.) which allow established firms to obtain factors at lower prices, or ownership or control of strategic factor supplies by established firms; and (c) limitations in supplies of productive factors in specific markets.

2. *Product Differentiation Advantages*, including (a) accumulative preferences of buyers for established brand names and company reputations; (b) control of superior product designs; and (c) ownership or contractual control by established firms of favored distribution outlets where supply of further outlets is not perfectly elastic; and,

---

[22]See Smith, Gordon V. and Russell L. Parr, *The Valuation of Intellectual Property and Intangible Assets*, New York: John Wiley & Sons, 1989.

[23]See Bain, J. S., *Barriers to New Competition*, Cambridge: Harvard University Press, 1962.

3. *Economies of Scale*, including (a) real economies of production and (or) distribution; (b) pecuniary economies associated with production and (or) distribution; and (c) real or pecuniary economies of large-scale advertising.

Smith and Parr's classification of intangible assets is not identical to Bain's discussion of entry barriers (in part because not all intangibles constitute barriers to entry), but there are broad areas of overlap: Bain includes some types of Smith and Parr's "relationship" intangibles and some intellectual property in his category of entry barriers that provide absolute cost advantages (including control of production techniques by established firms via patents or secrecy, and potentially the assembled workforce intangible if there are imperfections in the markets for hired factors or limitations in supplies of specific factors). Other types of Smith and Parr's relationship intangibles (distributor relationships), forms of intellectual property (trademarks and names), and possibly goodwill belong in Bain's "Product Differentiation Advantages" category. Bain's discussion includes economies of scale, not an intangible asset as such, but an attribute of particular production technologies—potentially common to both established firms and prospective entrants—that a particular firm realizes by virtue of its dominant market position. Similarly, Smith and Parr include going concern value (avoided start-up costs, including profits forgone, appropriately discounted), by definition not a source of persistent cost advantages to established firms vis-a-vis entrants and, thus, not a credible barrier to entry.

Applying Smith and Parr's taxonomy of intangible assets to the medical equipment at issue, one can identify the following intangibles in this case:

- Among "relationship intangibles," *P*'s agreement with *D* appointing the latter exclusive distributor, locking *D* into distributing only *P*'s products, and assigning certain market risks to it; and,

- Among "intellectual property," *P*'s trademarks (assigned to *D* under the terms of their distribution agreement at no direct pecuniary cost, albeit presumably in exchange for some combination of higher selling prices and favorable contract terms). *P* had registered a number of U.S. patents relating very tangentially to the medical equipment at issue between ten and twenty years prior to the audit period (long before it had entered into the business of manufacturing this medical equipment), and most of these patents had since expired. Further, according to the taxpayer and several of its competitors in this business segment, manufacturing processes were largely standardized. Hence, neither P nor S benefited from intellectual property in the form of superior process technology. If they had existed, exceptional quality control procedures would have constituted a manufacturing intangible in the form of know-how, potentially very important in the business of manufacturing hospital equipment. However, P's quality control procedures—while very impressive—drew on fundamental "quality technology" that was likewise common to all manufacturers of comparable equipment.[24,25]

In terms of Bain's classification of entry barriers cum intangible assets, the product at issue embodied the following:

- Among "product differentiation advantages," accumulative preferences of buyers for established brand names and company reputations. While P did not sell the particular medical equipment at issue directly to end-users, its trademark was prominently displayed thereon. Further, the company was a well-known name in certain other, fairly closely aligned market segments, and enjoyed a reputation for high and consistent quality; and,

- Also included in "product differentiation advantages," P's contractual control of a favored distribution outlet (D), the supply

[24] This information was obtained in interviews with P's senior quality engineers.

[25] The uniformity in quality control processes and know-how across medical equipment suppliers was partly due to the regulatory environment in which these producers operated. The Food and Drug Administration imposes rigorous quality standards on such firms. Moreover, as of January 1992, all firms marketing the equipment in Europe were required to meet stringent quality standards set by the International Standards Organization (ISO). Most manufacturers of the relevant equipment with ambitions to begin or continue selling in European markets after this date had been implementing quality control procedures designed to bring them into compliance with these standards for some time.

> of which was far from perfectly elastic. As P's quality control experts explained it, breaking into the business of distributing the medical equipment at issue was extremely difficult for a variety of reasons. Both D and its very few major competitors in distribution were well-entrenched, each with their own established customer base of hospitals. Hospitals tended to be quite loyal to their suppliers (D and its principal competitors), in part because reliable sources of equipment supplies were critical to their operations. Reliability in supplies, in turn, was greatly enhanced by long-term relationships with established distributor-suppliers. (Hence, the inelastic supply of distribution outlets derived in part from the "accumulative preferences of buyers" not for particular products per se, but for particular sources of supply in the form of established distributors.)
>
> Further, hospitals generally preferred to purchase a wide range of related equipment and supplies from a single source (a distributor), on whom their purchasing departments relied to ensure that particular manufacturers were capable of meeting—and consistently maintained—the requisite quality standards. This single sourcing approach made it all the more difficult for manufacturers of individual types of medical equipment, devices, or supplies to distribute their own products directly, and greatly enhanced the value of a relationship with an established distributor. Note also that D's established market position enabled P (and then S) to realize significant economies of scale in manufacturing.[26]

In summary, combining both Smith and Parr's list of intangible assets and Bain's classification of entry barriers, the following intangibles were embodied in, utilized in the distribution of, or otherwise associated with, the medical equipment in question: (a) a favorable relationship with an established distributor, and (b) an established reputation and associated trademarks and names.

---

[26]Recall that P's agreement with D alluded to potential real and pecuniary scale economies in its discussion of prospective price decreases (manufacturing efficiencies created by increased productivity and/or by larger volumes of sales and purchases), and stipulated that these cost savings were to be divided between supplier and distributor.

Under Section 482 (more specifically, under the 1968 regulations and the 1993 temporary regulations, as distinct from Section 936(h)), an IRS economist might simply treat P's assignment of the agreement originally negotiated between itself and D to its offshore affiliate as a transfer of intangibles for which P was not compensated, and require S to pay an arm's length amount therefor. (On a one-time basis, this amount would presumably be equal to the discounted present value of incremental profits associated with the agreement, in keeping with the *commensurate with income* requirement.) If the (pre-adjustment) amount that S paid P (in the form of an intra-company royalty) for the use of P's trademark satisfied the arm's length standard, no further adjustments would be warranted; if it did not, the royalty rate too would be adjusted accordingly.

However, under Section 936(h) cost-sharing elections (and under the 1993 proposed profit split methods), distinguishing between marketing and manufacturing intangible assets becomes very important. On the face of it, both P's trademark and its distribution agreement with D would seem to be readily classifiable as marketing intangible assets in this case, with the result that all intangible income should have accrued to P alone. However, the taxpayer took issue with this determination, necessitating a more laborious approach to defining and classifying the identified intangibles between marketing and manufacturing types.

5.3.4 Classification of Embodied Intangibles between Manufacturing and Marketing Types

One can conceive of a variety of ways to classify intangibles between manufacturing and marketing types in general, including:

- Whether the intangibles are used in conjunction with manufacturing or marketing activities, and, relatedly, whether they work to reduce costs or increase price;
- Whether the intangibles are created by manufacturing or marketing intangibles development expenditures; and,
- Whether the attributes associated with a given product have a "real" foundation or not.

The merits of each of these possible classification schemes in general is considered briefly below.

Classifications Based on Use and Source of Incremental Profits: As noted, intangible assets can be divided between manufacturing and marketing types by looking to the activities in which they are used, and, relatedly, whether they reduce manufacturing costs or increase product price. Specifically, one might assign all intangibles actively used in, or otherwise relating directly to, the manufacturing process, and which reduce production costs, to the "manufacturing intangibles" category, and those that create, consolidate, or extend the innovating firm's market power and, hence, enable it to increase its selling price, to the "marketing intangibles" category. On its face, this distinction seems clear, and, with regard to some types of intangibles, it is. For example, under this classification scheme, the fruits of all process R&D, which improve production processes and reduce manufacturing costs, should be treated as "manufacturing intangibles."

Unfortunately, it may be somewhat less clear how one should treat proprietary product designs under this classification scheme. Fundamentally, proprietary product designs are the physical embodiment of Bain's "product differentiation advantages," driven by consumer preferences (the demand side of the market). Income attributable to a firm's advantageous positioning in a market with differentiated products likewise derives from its ability to exercise a degree of market power in setting product price, again, as determined by consumer preferences.[27,28] For these reasons, it makes sense to treat proprietary product designs as marketing intangible assets. However, they are also an input into the production process, and

[27]Firms differentiate their products in oligopolistic or monopolistically competitive industries to lessen price competition among themselves, to "carve up" a given market and thereby create downward-sloping demand curves that enable them to price above marginal cost. By the same token, differentiation can take a variety of forms (physical location of production and distribution in relation to buyers, extent of after-sale services, quality, reliability of supplies and rapidity of delivery, etc.), some of which may entail modifications in the production process itself.

[28]In fact, innovative designs may leave production costs unchanged, or perhaps increase them.

could therefore conceivably be treated as manufacturing intangibles under this classification rule. Moreover, one firm's product innovations may be another firm's process innovations, potentially adding considerably to the confusion in related party settings.

Similarly, should cost reductions deriving from scale economies be attributed to the underlying marketing or manufacturing intangibles (or neither) under this classification scheme? Scale effects are generally an attribute of production technology, and, hence, the associated cost savings might legitimately be attributed to manufacturing intangibles. On the other hand, competitors might possess similar process technology, and yet fail to realize scale economies. Stated differently, a firm realizes potential economies of scale only if it has an established market position and a substantial market share—very possibly a function of the "accumulative preferences of buyers" for its product, the very essence of a marketing intangible. By the same token—and complicating matters further—the accumulative preferences of buyers may themselves derive (partially or wholly) from features of a company's proprietary production processes or superior quality control procedures—both clearly manufacturing intangibles.[29]

In short, a classification scheme based on the activities in which intangibles are used, and whether they work to decrease costs or increase product price, does not necessarily lead to an exhaustive and mutually exclusive division of total intangible assets between manufacturing and marketing types.[30]

Classifications Based on the Nature of Associated Intangibles Development Expenditures: Alternatively, one might divide intangibles between marketing and manufacturing categories on the basis of the types of costs incurred to create them. That is, an intangible asset would be classified a marketing intangible if it is created by selling-related costs, and a manufacturing intangible if it is created by production-related costs (as defined below). The advan-

---

[29] See discussion of this issue in Chapter 4.

[30] In fact, the discussion points up the interdependence of various types of intangibles, raising the more fundamental question of whether the marketing/manufacturing intangible distinction is meaningful in any event, at least with regard to certain industries and activities.

tage of this classification scheme, relative to the alternative described above, is that it may be easier to classify development expenditures into manufacturing and marketing types than to classify intangible assets directly.

In an influential work relating to product differentiation first published in the mid-1940s, Chamberlain distinguished between production and selling costs as follows:

> Cost of production includes all expenses which must be met in order to provide the commodity or service, transport it to the buyer, and put it into his hands ready to satisfy his wants. Cost of selling includes all outlays made in order to secure a demand, or a market, for the product...[A] simple criterion is this: of all the costs incurred in the manufacture and sale of a given product, those which alter the demand curve for it are selling costs, and those which do not are costs of production.[31]

Further:

> Selling costs are defined as costs incurred in order to alter the position or shape of the demand curve for a product...Advertising of all varieties, salesmen's salaries and the expenses of sales departments, margins granted to dealers (retail and wholesale) in order to increase their efforts in favor of particular goods, window displays, demonstrations of new goods, etc., are all costs of this type.

However, this approach to classifying total intangibles also raises some difficult issue. As the discussion in Chapter 4 illustrates, it is not always a simple matter to establish the link between specific expenditures on the one hand, and the associated development of particular intangible assets on the other. Further, a given intangible may be the product of a combination of selling- and production-related expenditures. Finally, an expenditure-based classification scheme would very likely give rise to disputes about the nature and function

[31] See Chamberlain, Edward Hastings, *The Theory of Monopolistic Competition*, Cambridge: Harvard University Press, 1946.

of particular types of outlays and, hence, whether they should be deemed selling or production costs.

Classification Based on Real versus Perceived Product Attributes: Some take the view that a manufacturing intangible is something "real," while a marketing intangible, by definition, creates the perception that products are differentiated when in fact they are not. In this schema, suppliers of intermediate goods—often selling into markets characterized by a limited number of large corporate customers with professionally managed purchasing departments that are not easily misled—necessarily possess very limited marketing intangibles; trademarks and names are entirely incidental to product quality/price tradeoffs. It is only in consumer goods industries, where individuals make up the demand side of product markets, that significant marketing intangibles exist. Individuals tend to be less well-informed than corporate customers about product varieties, characteristics, and alternative sources of supply, and may in any case be swayed by the "status content" of products as much as by the price/quality combinations available.

This view, and its obverse, has a parallel in economists' differing views of advertising (in consumer goods markets). As Tirole expresses it:

> We can distinguish two polar views on advertising.
>
> The *partial view* [i.e., favorable view] sees advertising as providing information to the consumers and thus enabling them to make rational choices. Advertising announces the existence of a product, quotes its price, informs consumers about retail locations, and describes the product's quality.
>
> ...The *adverse view* claims that advertising is meant to persuade and fool consumers. It creates differentiation that is not real, rather than reducing real informational differentiation.[32]

[32]Tirole, Jean, *The Theory of Industrial Organization*, Cambridge, Mass.: The MIT Press, 1989, p. 290.

In short, the "advertising is bad" thesis is consistent with the view that manufacturers of intermediate goods virtually never have marketing intangible assets to speak of. Inasmuch as advertising is meant to mislead, such firms have little incentive to invest in it (or in other activities that give rise to marketing intangibles). Conversely, if advertising is meant to inform, it potentially has a role to play in both producer and consumer goods industries. Further, the marketing intangibles that advertising and other expenditures give rise to should then have some value independent of the underlying product characteristics with which they become associated.

5.3.5 Adjustment Methodology under the 1968 Regulations

The different intangibles classifications described above can yield very different divisions of intangible assets between manufacturing and marketing types.[33] Unfortunately, the 1968 regulations did not advocate a specific approach to this problem. However, the White Paper's proposed cost-sharing rules contain a suggestive passage:

> In general, the benefit to be derived under a cost sharing arrangement [covering manufacturing intangibles] is the right to use a developed intangible in the manufacture of a product. Therefore, the [prospective] participant must be in a position to exploit the intangible in the manufacture of products.[34]

[33]Consider, for example, the "installed base" intangible common in several high-technology industries. Using the first classification scheme proposed above (whereby intangible assets are considered manufacturing intangibles if they are actively used in manufacturing activities and reduce costs, and marketing intangibles if they are used in selling activities, to reshape the demand curve and enable firms to charge prices above competitive levels), an installed base is unambiguously a marketing intangible. Under the second, expense-driven classification scheme, an installed base, created by accumulated past sales, would presumably be treated as a combination of marketing and manufacturing intangibles. Finally, under the third classification scheme, an installed base—a very tangible intangible—would presumably be treated as a manufacturing intangible. The switching costs that end-users save by remaining with their original suppliers are real, and products genuinely differentiated in this way from their perspective.

[34]See the White Paper, *Op. Cit.*, p. 118–19.

In equating the benefits derived from rights to manufacturing intangibles with their use directly in the manufacturing process, the drafters appear (admittedly tenuously) to endorse the first approach discussed above implicitly, wherein one classifies intangible assets according to whether they are employed in conjunction with manufacturing or marketing activities. As such, we used it to classify intangibles in the present case under the 1968 regulations.[35]

Clearly, the taxpayer's favorable relationship with D was a marketing intangible according to this classification scheme, in that it related to the distribution of a finished product rather than its manufacture. Similarly, P's established reputation and associated trademark and name were also marketing intangibles. As such, the income attributable to both of these intangibles should have accrued to P.

Given this division of intangible assets between marketing and manufacturing types, the pricing methodology used to determine S's arm's length income entailed (a) determining the consolidated income earned on the production and sale of the medical equipment at issue (the sum of S's income and its intra-company payments to P); (b) deducting a normal return to S's tangible operating assets from this consolidated income via the cost-plus method; and (c) allocating the residual to P.

5.3.6 Possible Adjustment Methodology under the 1993 Temporary and Proposed Regulations

Given the *commensurate with income* requirement that applies to Section 936(h) cost-sharing payments after 1986 (and assuming that the taxpayer continued to make a Section 936(h) cost-sharing elec-

[35]Note that the 1992 proposed regulations' cost-sharing rules take a step back from the White Paper's restriction that cost-sharing participants must be able to exploit the intangible in their manufacturing operations per se (and, thereby, move away from the White Paper's implicit and somewhat tenuous endorsement of intangibles allocations on the basis of field of use (manufacturing versus distribution). Under the proposed rules, an eligible participant must be able to use the developed intangibles in the active conduct of its trade or business. This trade or business is not necessarily limited to manufacturing, but the participant will be deemed to conduct a trade or business only if it carries out substantial managerial and operational activities.

tion going forward—an unlikely eventuality), the post-adjustment allocation of consolidated income between P and S would be independent of the way in which one divides the intangible assets embodied in the possessions product between manufacturing and marketing types. Ultimately, all intangible income (both marketing and manufacturing) would remain with P, as it did (for different reasons) in the proposed adjustment described above.

However, this is not to say that the issue of how one should carve up total intangibles becomes moot under the new regime as a general matter. To the contrary, and as the last composite cost-sharing case following illustrates, the way in which one disaggregates total intangibles into manufacturing and marketing types can play a very significant role in determining the allocation of income under the 1993 proposed Section 482 profit split methods.

5.3.7 Taxpayer's Position

The taxpayers in this (pre-1986) composite case essentially asserted that virtually all of the consolidated income earned on sales of their possessions corporations' products constituted a return to unspecified manufacturing intangibles (to which their possessions corporations had ownership rights), and that the specific intangible assets we had identified were therefore either improperly classified or had minimal value. While this would not be a viable defense under Section 936(h) cost-sharing rules after 1986 (because of the statutory *commensurate with income* requirement), the 1993 temporary and proposed regulations do little to clarify the fundamental issue of how one should classify intangibles into the requisite manufacturing and marketing categories. Consequently, under a Section 482 cost-sharing arrangement, firms may still use the ambiguities surrounding this issue to their advantage.

5.3.8 Resolution

Under the pre-1986 regime, Appeals negotiated settlements with the taxpayers in this composite case that ranged from approximately

15% to 35% of our proposed adjustments. Because the 1993 temporary and proposed regulations do not sanction a specific approach to differentiating between marketing and manufacturing intangibles, there is little reason to think that Appeals officers would assess the litigation hazards associated with similar proposed adjustments, in connection with Section 482 cost-sharing arrangements, differently thereunder.

5.4 Cost-Sharing Case 3: Telecommunications Products

This composite cost-sharing case involves a U.S. parent firm (P) and an Asian affiliate (S). During the years at issue, they jointly produced a range of telecommunications products for private and professional use.

5.4.1 Summary Functional Analysis

The firm's worldwide production facilities were located in the United States and the Far East. S manufactured a line of basic telecommunications products from start to finish, assembling a variety of components and subassemblies in-house as well, both for its own use and for export to P. P manufactured a range of high-end, state-of-the-art telecommunications products, often highly customized to individual buyers' needs. Both S and P sold directly to end-users in their respective markets (in S's case, Asia, and in P's case, the United States and Europe); additionally, S supplied P with low-end telecommunications products as needed. When Asian customers required high-end products, P typically dealt with them directly.

Both S and P provided extensive after-sales support, both directly and, in geographically more distant markets, via service contracts with technically specialized third parties that P trained. P and, to a lesser extent, S, invested heavily in comprehensive market research and competitive analysis as well, charting the direction of the firm's R&D programs and determining pricing policies on this basis. All research, design engineering, and software development functions were performed by P, although S participated in a Section 482 cost-sharing agreement with P, obligating it to pay a proportionate share of P's total R&D outlays and entitling it to an ownership share of the manufacturing intangibles that P ultimately developed. (The cost-sharing amount that S paid was based on its relative sales, as in the first cost-sharing case study discussed above.)

5.4.2 Intra-Company Transfer Pricing Policy

This taxpayer maintained that S and P were joint venturers in the true sense of the term, sharing all of the risks associated with the development, manufacture, and marketing of telecommunications products equally. Moreover, while P and S differed somewhat in their mix of marketing and manufacturing activities (and in their product offerings), the taxpayer also asserted that marketing and manufacturing contributed equally to the firm's profit-making potential. In its view, this set of propositions justified a transfer pricing policy that split projected profits 50:50. In practice, the split often turned out to be slightly more favorable to S and less to P.

5.4.3 Potential Issues

In principle, one could address each type of intra-company transaction in this case—S's sales of components to P, its sales of finished telecommunications products to P, and its cost-sharing contribution—individually. Transfer prices for components would likely be evaluated under the cost-plus method, and transfer prices for finished products, under the resale price method. The adequacy of S's cost-sharing payments would be assessed on the basis of its anticipated relative benefits, as in the first cost-sharing case.

However, such a piecemeal approach had been attempted before, on prior audit cycles of this case and on similar cases, with very limited success. Rather, Appeals tended to accept the joint venture/equal risk-sharing thesis, and the argument that this justified a 50:50 profit split. Consequently, our approach in this case was to accept the taxpayer's basic premises—that S and P shared all of the risks associated with their collective activities equally (a credible claim in this instance), and that marketing and manufacturing contributed equally to the firm's profit potential—and determine whether these propositions implied the division of profits that the taxpayer reported.

5.4.4 Adjustment Methodology under the 1968 and 1993 Temporary Regulations: the Capital Employed Approach

Accepting that S and P shared equally in the primary risks associated with the development, manufacture, and distribution of the firm's telecommunications product offerings, a particular method of adjustment—essentially the 1993 proposed regulations' capital employed method—is indicated.

Broadly speaking, if one assumes that financial, factor, and product markets are competitive, then firms that incur comparable risks (and therefore face the same cost of capital) should earn the same economic rates of return in equilibrium.[36] While it is rarely a simple

[36] Complications arise when the firms being compared operate in different geographic markets, in that world capital markets are not fully integrated, and the risk-adjusted (real) cost of capital therefore not necessarily uniform across countries (an obviously important consideration in a transfer pricing context). Stated differently, two firms operating in different geographic markets would not necessarily earn the same (economic) rate of return, even assuming that they incurred identical risks and both markets were competitive, because their cost of capital would not necessarily be the same. However, individual members of a controlled group do not face separate, market-specific costs of capital in a meaningful sense, inasmuch as "the very feature that distinguishes the multinational firm is that it is integrated worldwide... [and] can obtain funds in one country and employ them profitably elsewhere." See Giddy, Ian H., "The Cost of Capital in the International Firm," *Managerial and Decision Economics*, Vol. 2, No. 4, 1981. Here again, though, the arm's length standard is somewhat ambiguous: for purposes of applying a rate of return analysis for tax purposes, should one work with the market-specific costs of capital that individual group members would pay on a stand-alone basis, or with the uniform cost of capital that guides decision making within a controlled group? There is also a very pragmatic adding-up consideration: at the end of the day, consolidated profits have to be the same before and after the proposed adjustments to individual members' profits. If one works with hypothetical arm's length costs of capital, this adding-up requirement will not be satisfied (for reasons that will become clear in the course of the composite case

matter to fit a given real world industry into the black-and-white paradigms of microeconomic theory, one can make a good case for the proposition that the industry segment in which this (composite) taxpayer operated was reasonably competitive.[37] As such (and given the taxpayer's contention that both entities shared risks equally), on a stand-alone basis S and P should individually earn comparable economic rates of return in equilibrium. We use this basic principle to allocate consolidated income between S and P, by setting their individual (adjusted) after-tax rates of return equal to their consolidated realized return.

Practically speaking, the application of this equalized rate of return (or capital employed) approach for tax purposes requires some significant departures from the rate of return measure suggested by economic theory. Specifically, as indicated above, one would ideally use an economic rate of return, defined as the interest rate that equates the present value of the income stream generated by a given undertaking (i.e., the benefits derived therefrom) with the initial investment required (the cost side of the equation). However, the economic rate of return is exceedingly difficult to work with, because it requires very extensive information about projected revenues and costs related to the (contemplated or actual) undertaking. In its stead, we utilized an accounting rate of return measure, the ratio of current period accounting profits (specifically, operating profits after taxes) to total capital employed. (This is undoubtedly an imperfect substitute, and builds in a degree of inaccuracy. However, in the interest of workable tax laws, it may be justifiable.)

While the procedure of equalizing rates of return on assets sounds straightforward, it raises a number of important questions:[38]

---

discussed above). For purposes of our analysis in this case, we incorporate the fact that S effectively incurred the same cost of capital as P.

[37]Note that this issue was not clear-cut, and that, in general, competitive markets and truly unique intangible assets make strange bedfellows.

[38]Some, albeit a relatively small subset, of these issues are addressed in the 1993 proposed profit split regulations. However, this analysis preceded their release by several years, necessitating an economic justification for the equalized return method as such, and a careful consideration of individual implementation issues. Consequently, the discussion provides some insight into the (somewhat limited) microeconomic foundations of the capital employed method and the implementation issues that the regulations do not address.

- How should the asset base be defined for purposes of calculating these rates of return? In particular, would any asset values be affected by intra-company pricing that was other than arm's length, and, if so, should these assets be excluded? Additionally, should one include both tangible and intangible assets in the asset base, or just the former?
- If intangible assets are included in the base, how should they be valued in total?
- Again, if intangible assets are included in the base, how should they be classified into marketing and manufacturing types? (This classification is necessary because the different types of intangibles may have very different useful lives, and, hence, generate very different amortization allowances.)
- And, finally—and again assuming that intangible assets should be included in the base—at what rate should one amortize the different types of intangibles?

These points are considered in turn below.

The Asset Base

A rate of return on assets can be computed in numerous ways. The asset base may include all assets, current, fixed, and intangible; it may exclude all current assets and/or intangible assets; or, it may be defined to include some combination between these extremes.

Exclusion of Certain Current Assets: In dealing with related entities, it is important to recognize that certain asset values may be distorted via intra-company pricing that is not arm's length, and, hence, should either be adjusted or excluded from the asset base for purposes of establishing or evaluating these prices for tax purposes. For example, accounts receivables and inventories often incorporate intra-company profits. To the extent that transfer prices of products sold by a manufacturing subsidiary to its parent are higher than arm's length, the former's accounts receivables and inventories will be overstated, and its reported (and, potentially, its adjusted) rate of return understated. Similarly, if accounts receivables are outstanding among related entities for a longer period of time than they would normally be between unrelated firms, this too will distort current assets. For these reasons, we eliminated current assets from both S's and P's respective asset bases in applying the equalized return approach.

Inclusion of Intangible Assets: Expenditures on advertising and R&D yield benefits that extend well beyond the period in which these expenditures are made. Hence, logically speaking, such expenditures should generally be capitalized rather than expensed. Economists have long recognized that inter-industry comparisons of rates of return are seriously compromised by the failure to incorporate intangible assets in the rate base. As Kenneth Clarkson expresses it:

> ...Any outlay that brings returns in future periods should be capitalized when we attempt to measure the relative attractiveness of various industries...Since in some industries outlays on intangibles are large relative to outlays on physical assets and in others they are small, the failure to capitalize produces a substantial distortion of asset positions and net worth.[39]

This same distortion can—in fact, very likely would—arise in a transfer pricing context if one allocated consolidated income by equalizing returns, and omitted intangible assets from the asset base. In particular, those members of the controlled group that invest proportionately more in intangible assets (relative to their investments in tangible assets) would be allocated less income than is warranted relative to their total capital employed. Consequently, intangible assets should generally be incorporated into each entity's asset base explicitly for purposes of applying the equalized rate of return allocation method.[40]

[39]See Clarkson, Kenneth W., *Intangible Capital and Rates of Return*, Washington, D.C.: The American Enterprise Institute, 1977.

[40]Note that all of the 1993 proposed profit split methods allocate income on the basis of both tangible and intangible assets. The capital employed method in particular requires an explicit valuation of intangibles, inasmuch as they must be added to tangible assets in determining the proper asset base.

The Mechanics of Determining Rates of Return when the Rate Base Includes Intangible Assets

Including intangible capital in the controlled entities' rate base for purposes of applying the equalized return on assets approach raises a number of issues. Specifically, one must: (a) value the controlled group's total intangible assets; (b) break this total down into its component parts;[41] (c) ascertain which expenditures give rise to each broad type of intangible asset; (d) determine which controlled entity owns each (or, in the case of jointly owned intangibles, determine the parties' proportionate ownership claims); and, lastly, (e) establish reasonable amortization rates for the different types of intangibles.

To see why these elements are important, consider the expression for an (after-tax) rate of return on assets (including intangible assets):[42]

$$r = \frac{[\text{Adj. Operating Income} - \lambda_K(K_t - L_t) - \lambda_r R_t - \lambda_a A_t](1-t)}{K_t + R_t + A_t} \tag{5.1}$$

Where:

Adjusted operating income is *gross* of current R&D, advertising outlays, and the depreciation of tangible assets based on book value;

λ_k = Rate at which tangible assets depreciate;

K_t = Stock of the entity's fixed tangible assets (property, plant, and equipment) at time t, valued at replacement cost;

L_t = Stock of the entity's property at time t, valued at market price;

λ_r = Rate at which R&D capital (manufacturing intangibles) depreciate;

---

[41] Alternatively, one could begin by identifying individual groups of intangible assets and building up to the total, rather than breaking down the total into its component parts. Often a fairly broad grouping will suffice for transfer pricing purposes.

[42] See Grabowski, Henry G. and Dennis C. Mueller, "Industrial Research and Development, Intangible Capital Stocks, and Firm Profit Rates," *Bell Journal of Economics*, Vol. 9, No. 2, Autumn 1978.

R_t = Stock of the related party's manufacturing intangibles;

λ_a = Rate at which advertising capital depreciates;

A_t = Stock of total marketing intangibles; and,

t = The effective tax rate prevailing in the country in which the entity operates.

The first three steps that the decision to include intangibles in the asset base necessitates—how one should value total (group-wide) intangible capital, the breakdown of this total intangibles value into its component parts, and the assignment of specific groupings of intangibles (or proportionate ownership shares therein) to individual controlled entities—determine the intangibles element of individual entities' respective asset bases (the sum of R_t and A_t in the above expression) and their potentially amortizable stocks of manufacturing and marketing intangible assets, respectively (R_t and A_t individually). The assignment of development expenditures to different types of intangibles may be necessary to determine intangibles ownership, but, more generally, if such outlays are deemed to give rise to intangible assets (and these assets are explicitly included in the entity's asset base), they should clearly not be expensed. This means that the intangibles development expenditures that individual entities did in fact deduct in computing their operating income must be added back, increasing their current profits accordingly (before allowing for amortization). Further, the intangible assets that ultimately result from these development expenditures should be amortized over their useful lives (to the extent that these lives are finite). Hence the last issue raised by the decision to include intangible assets in the rate base, the determination of reasonable amortization rates.

Each of these issues is considered below.

Measuring Intangible Capital Stocks: A firm's total intangible assets can collectively be valued as the difference between its market value overall and the sum of its current assets and its tangible assets valued at replacement (as distinct from book) value.[43]

[43]Equivalently, the value of total intangible assets is given by the discounted present value of the income stream that the firm as a whole is expected to gen-

In the instant case, the taxpayer maintained records detailing the replacement value of its tangible assets. Hence, we determined the value of its total intangible assets by netting current and tangible assets, the latter valued at replacement cost, from its market value. The firm's market value, in turn, was determined by averaging its weekly stock market value over the course of the years in question.

Breakdown of Total Intangibles: In order to determine both the intangibles portion of each related party's asset base and the asset-specific amortization allowances therefor, it will ordinarily be necessary to disaggregate group-wide total intangible assets into manufacturing and marketing intangibles, respectively, owned (either individually or jointly) by each entity. (That is, one has to take two "cuts" at total group-wide intangibles, such that they are divvied up both by manufacturing and marketing types, and again—within these categories—by individual group members' ownership rights.) One can divide up total intangibles into marketing and manufacturing types in several different ways, as discussed in the preceding cost-sharing case study. One approach entails valuing the individual intangible assets that compose total intangibles, identifying intangibles development expenditures with particular types of intangible assets (a necessary step in the process of equalizing returns in any case) and determining whether each asset is a marketing or manufacturing intangible based on the nature of the associated intangibles development expenditures. Determining ownership rights, based on an analysis of which entity incurred the associated development costs, is then a simple matter. Alternatively, one might (again) carve out

---

erate, less that portion attributable to tangible and current assets. One might also determine the value of intangible assets by directly projecting the income stream attributable thereto, and discounting it at an appropriate cost of capital. The three valuation case studies discussed in Chapter 7 herein address several of these issues in detail. See also Smith and Parr (1989), *Op. Cit.*, for a discussion of general valuation principles as they apply to intangible assets; Pakes, Ariel, "On Patents, R&D and the Stock Market Rate of Return," *Journal of Political Economy*, Vol. 93, No. 2, 1985, for a discussion of variations in stock market value as a measure of inventive output; and Hirschey, Mark and Jerry J. Weygandt, "Amortization Policy for Advertising and Research and Development Expenditures," *Journal of Accounting Research*, Vol. 23, No. 1, Spring 1985, for an empirical analysis of the factors that determine the ratio of firm market value to replacement cost of tangible assets.

(and value) specific intangibles from the stock of total intangibles, classify them between marketing and manufacturing types based on use and source of incremental profits (the approach taken in the prior cost-sharing case study), and determine ownership rights as a separate step. If one entity owns all marketing intangibles, while all manufacturing intangibles are jointly owned, the proper allocation of particular intangibles follows directly from the classification of identified intangibles into manufacturing and marketing categories.

The 1993 proposed profit split regulations suggest a simpler approach to a similar problem under the residual allocation rule, which may or may not apply, in somewhat modified form, to the equalized return (or capital employed) approach. (Note that we did not use the proposed approach in this composite case, as described below.) Under the residual allocation rule, one can approximate relative intangibles ownership by "the relative value of actual [development] expenditures" when the parties' intangibles development expenditures are "relatively constant over time." While the capital employed method requires an explicit valuation of intangibles, at least in total, one may be able to apply the same principle of dividing up this total block of group-wide intangibles (between marketing and manufacturing types owned by each entity) on the basis of the associated relative intangibles development expenditures here as well (with the same caveat that development expenditures must be reasonably constant over time). This would mean that the laborious process of valuing individual intangibles and grouping them into broad manufacturing and marketing types, and the somewhat less laborious (but still difficult) process of breaking down total intangibles into the same broad manufacturing and marketing categories and valuing these groupings, would be unnecessary. However, it becomes extremely important to distinguish unambiguously between current and capital expenditures (where the latter include intangibles development expenditures), and to associate specific forms of intangibles development expenditures with the requisite groupings of intangibles accurately, if one uses this method of divvying up total group-wide intangibles.

In the instant case, the taxpayer's representation that half of its profits were attributable to its manufacturing operations (that is, to both tangible and intangible manufacturing assets) and half to its marketing operations (again, both tangible and intangible marketing assets) suggested a different approach. An asset's value is given by the discounted present value of the income stream it is expected to generate over its life. Hence, the 50:50 attribution of profits to marketing and manufacturing activities, respectively, implies that the taxpayer's total (tangible and intangible) manufacturing assets combined were equal in value to its total (tangible and intangible) marketing assets combined. Further, as noted, we had reliable estimates of the replacement value of the tangible assets that the firm used in manufacturing and marketing, respectively. The ratio of its tangible manufacturing assets to its tangible marketing assets, coupled with the firm's market value overall, enabled us to determine the implied value of the ratio of its marketing to manufacturing intangible assets. This ratio, in turn, combined with the estimated total value of the group's intangible assets (as calculated above), enabled us to break down this total intangible value into total manufacturing and marketing intangibles, respectively.

Given this breakdown of the taxpayer's total intangibles between manufacturing and marketing types, the next step entailed allocating the different types of intangibles to S and P, respectively. Total marketing intangible assets were divided between them based on their relative advertising and (certain) marketing expenditures (as described below). The cost-sharing agreement between S and P—which had been in effect for a long period of time and spanned a number of product cycles—covered all of the taxpayer's research projects. As such, all of the taxpayer's manufacturing intangibles were jointly owned, with S's and P's respective shares therein equal to their proportionate cost-sharing contributions.

Associated Expenditures: Distinguishing between current and total capital expenditures (including intangibles development expenditures), and between marketing and manufacturing intangibles development expenditures, proved to be highly contentious in this case. The general rule of thumb—that R&D outlays give rise to manufacturing intangibles, and advertising to marketing intangibles—is widely used, but it did not fit the industry at issue. In particular, advertising expenditures were a relatively small subset of total marketing intangibles development expenditures, in our view. Consequently, we argued for, and utilized, a broader definition of marketing intangibles development expenditures, including some of the costs associated with the taxpayer's market research, its sales and marketing staff, and its after-sales service program (in Chamberlain's words, "costs incurred in order to alter the position or shape of the demand curve for a product,"[44] and which could reasonably be expected to have an effect beyond a single period).

Depreciation of Intangible Capital Stocks: Consider next the question of amortization rates. There have been numerous empirical analyses of advertising depreciation rates, and a somewhat smaller number of studies examining the rate at which research and development capital depreciates. In selecting amortization rates for purposes of computing the taxpayer's adjusted rate of return, we relied on several econometric analyses, and on a questionnaire used to construct the U.S. National Accounts.[45]

Hirschey and Weygandt's empirical analysis indicated that amortization rates for advertising range from 30%–60%; that is, advertising expenditures have an effect on sales that persists for 2–3 years. Several other empirical analyses confirm this finding.[46] Hirschey and Weygandt also found that R&D capital depreciates more gradually, between 10%–20%. The questionnaire results conducted earlier were consistent with these findings, indicating that R&D capital depreciates at approximately a 10% rate. Drawing on these and several other studies, we assumed that the taxpayer's marketing intangibles depreciated at a rate of 30%, and its manufacturing intangibles at a rate of 10%. In addition, we assumed that tangible assets (other than land) depreciated at a rate of 20%, and recomputed depreci-

---

[44] *Op. Cit.*

[45] See Wagner, L.U., "Problems in Estimating Research and Development Investment and Stock," in American Statistical Association, 1968, *Proceedings of the Business and Economics Statistical Section*, Washington.

[46] See Hirschey, Mark and Jerry J. Weygandt, *Op. Cit.*; Lambin, J.J., *Advertising, Competition and Market Conduct in Oligopoly over Time*, Amsterdam: North Holland, 1976; and, Peles, Y., "Rates of Amortization of Advertising Expenses," *Journal of Political Economy*, Vol. 79, Sept./Oct. 1971.

ation allowances by applying this rate to replacement rather than book value.

Calculation of Arm's Length Transfer Prices

Rewriting the rate of return expression shown above to incorporate transfer prices of products sold by S explicitly:

$$r_s(t) = \frac{[X+Y](1-t_s)}{K_t(S)+R_t(S)+A_t(S)} \tag{5.2}$$

where

$$\begin{aligned} X &= (t)(Q_r)+(p)(Q_u) - \text{COS} - \text{Adj. Oper. Exp.} \\ Y &= -\lambda_k(K_t - L_t) - \lambda_r R_t - \lambda_a A_t \end{aligned}$$

Where t denotes the transfer price of products that S sold to P, Q_r represents the quantities that S sold to P (in physical units),[47] p denotes the price of products that S sold to third parties, Q_u, S's sales (in physical units) to unrelated parties, and COS, S's cost of goods sold. (Recall as well that adjusted operating expenses in Expression (5.2) above are net of current R&D, advertising outlays, and the depreciation of tangible assets based on book values.)

To determine the arm's length transfer price, we set S's return on assets (the right hand side of the above equation) equal to the taxpayer's consolidated after-tax rate of return on tangible and intangible capital, denoted by r_w:

$$r_s(t) = r_w \tag{5.3}$$

And, lastly, we solved the above equation for t^*, the arm's length intra-company transfer price:

$$t^* = \frac{r_w(K_t(S)+R_t(S)+A_t(S))}{Q_r(1-t_s)} \tag{5.4}$$

[47] Note that t and Q_r shown in the above expression are aggregated for expository simplicity, but disaggregated into different product lines in the actual calculations. This does not generally present a problem, in that one would typically solve for total revenues on intra-company sales, rather than unit transfer prices for the different products.

$$+\frac{[\text{COS} + \text{Adj. Oper. Exp.} + \lambda_k(K_t - L_t) + \lambda_r R_t + \lambda_a A_t - (p)(Q_u)]}{Q_r}$$

Our proposed pricing adjustment was determined by comparing S's actual and estimated arm's length revenues on its intra-company sales to P, as determined above. This rate of return methodology yielded a moderate adjustment of income from S to P.

5.4.5 Taxpayer's Position

The taxpayers in this composite case generally attempted to rebut our proposed pricing adjustments by challenging the various assumptions that we made along the way. For example, one taxpayer argued that the stock market value of a company was not a reasonable means of determining the value of the company's underlying assets (and, thus, the value of total intangible assets), and pointed to both the variability of stock market valuations over time and the many acquisitions in which buyers paid a premium over the target companies' stock price. Another taxpayer maintained that only advertising expenditures, narrowly defined, should be considered marketing intangibles development expenditures, which yielded a much smaller estimate of marketing intangible assets and reduced the firm's parent company's asset base substantially. This firm also challenged the amortization rates that we applied to marketing and manufacturing intangible assets, respectively. Finally, more than one taxpayer contested our premise that rates of return would in fact be equalized at all.

5.4.6 Resolution

While the assumptions we made in applying this equalized return method had a reasonable foundation, they were certainly not unassailable. Further, our proposed adjustments turned out to be fairly sensitive to relatively small variations in the proportionate breakdown of total intangible assets between marketing and manufacturing types. Consequently, in negotiating settlements, IRS representatives at both Examination and Appeals levels tended to be very flexible.

On balance, most of the proposed adjustments developed by equalizing returns were settled either at a fraction of the original amounts, or dropped outright.

Would Section 482 pricing adjustments based on the 1993 proposed regulations' capital employed method founder on the same methodological issues? Very likely, yes. The 1993 proposed regulations' description of the capital employed method is extremely concise, and it addresses very few of the implementation issues discussed above.[48] As noted, and as distinct from the residual allocation rule, the capital employed method requires an explicit valuation of intangibles. However, the 1993 proposed regulations say very little about how one should go about this process of valuing intangibles (en masse and individually), or how one should identify intangibles development expenditures (again, in total and as regards individual types of intangibles) and estimate individual intangible assets' useful lives. The relevant passage states only that:

> Intangibles may be measured by their fair market value, or the capitalized cost of developing the intangibles and all related improvements and updates, less an appropriate amount of amortization based on the useful life of each intangible.

In principle, taxpayers may also argue that the equalized rate of return premise holds only when (a) the markets at issue are perfectly competitive (essentially a theoretical construct); (b) they are in equilibrium (essentially a hypothetical state that one rarely observes in the real world), and, finally, (c) one equalizes economic rather than accounting rates of returns (a virtually impossible measure to work with in practice). Any one of these preconditions would suffice to eliminate the equalized return approach to evaluating intra-company prices for all practical purposes.

In short, the proposed "capital employed" method, as currently described, addresses few of the contentious issues that arose in the composite case reviewed above.

[48] As discussed in Chapter 2, the capital employed method (which applies only if each controlled entity assumes an "approximately equal" level of risk), allocates consolidated income based on "the ratio of the taxpayer's average capital employed... to the total capital employed in the relevant business."

5.5 Critique of Proposed Section 482 Cost-Sharing Provisions

Section 482 cost-sharing agreements give rise to a number of very difficult pricing issues. There are the problems of measuring each participant's anticipated benefits from the prospective technological output (and determining cost shares thereby), determining arm's length buy-in fees, and establishing (or evaluating) intra-company prices when a participant in a related party cost-sharing agreement sells tangible property embodying unique intangibles (in which it has ownership rights) to other members of the controlled group that also own intangible property in their own right.

The 1968 regulations dealt with these issues cursorily, if at all. Most notably, they contained virtually no guidelines as to how one should establish intra-company prices when a cost-sharing participant sold tangible property embodying intangibles to other members of the controlled group. Inasmuch as offshore manufacturing affiliates (both possessions corporations and others) producing intermediate products for sale back to their U.S. parents often participated in intra-company cost-sharing agreements, this was a very common problem. In the absence of clear guidelines, IRS economists improvised by developing a variety of fourth methods, one of which was described in the first cost-sharing case reviewed in this chapter. However, such methods were necessarily inexact, and rather easy to challenge on this basis. Further, the lack of prioritizing among fourth methods made it virtually impossible to argue for one pricing methodology over another, and to resolve disputes when firms and the IRS utilized different approaches to establishing and evaluating intra-company prices, respectively.

The 1993 proposed profit split methods make considerable strides in this regard. In effect, they legitimize a small subset of (previously) fourth methods, ameliorating the choice-of-method problem posed by the above-mentioned lack of prioritizing to some degree. Nonetheless, the fact that the profit split methods are not theoretically compelling in every detail may make adjustments based on them difficult to sustain, absent a clear statement to the effect that they are imperfect but reasonable approaches to the difficult problem of setting arm's length prices when both controlled entities contribute non-routine intangibles, and the prospects of finding serviceable comparables are virtually nil.

However, while perhaps creating more common ground as to the proper choice of pricing methods per se under these circumstances, the 1993 proposed profit split approaches raise far more questions than they answer, as the discussion of the last cost-sharing case reviewed in this chapter demonstrates. For example, under the capital employed method, one may have to:

- Value total intangible assets owned collectively by the related parties at issue;
- Break this total down into broad marketing and manufacturing intangibles types, (possibly) value the groupings individually, and ascertain which categories of expenditures give rise to each;
- Assign the different intangibles to the parties based on their ownership rights; and,
- Establish useful lives (and, thus, reasonable amortization rates) for the different types of intangibles.

The 1993 proposed regulations' description of the capital employed method contains only the briefest mention of these issues. Yet, under this method, variations in any of these elements—in total intangibles valuations, in the breakdown of intangibles between marketing and manufacturing types, in the identification of associated intangibles development expenditures, and in estimates of amortization rates—can yield dramatically different allocations of consolidated income among members of a controlled group.

Similarly, the proposed residual allocation rule raises another (overlapping) set of implementation issues that revolve around expenditure allocations:

- How should horizontally diversified firms' joint costs and assets be allocated across their different lines of business?
- How should one distinguish between current outlays and intangibles development expenditures, particularly those that create marketing intangible assets?

Different allocations of common costs and physical assets used jointly in a firm's different lines of business can potentially produce substantially different estimates of the combined "residual" intangibles income to be divided among members of the controlled group. (An under-allocation to the activities at issue will generally increase the pool of intangible income to be allocated, and conversely.[49]) Likewise, different breakdowns of total expenditures between current outlays, tangible capital expenditures, and intangible capital expenditures can potentially yield dramatically different allocations of a given pool of intangible income under the residual allocation rule.

Hence, while narrowing the scope for disagreements over the choice of pricing methods when both parties to an intra-company transaction own non-routine intangible property, the 1993 proposed regulations may simply shift the battleground to implementation issues. As long experience with Section 338 valuation issues demonstrates, seemingly esoteric methodological fine points can have very significant tax consequences.

The 1992 proposed cost-sharing provisions are similarly unspecific regarding the proper measure of anticipated benefits from rights to prospective technological innovations (developed in the context of a related party cost-sharing agreement) in particular instances—an issue that virtually every Section 482 cost-sharing case raises. Different measures of the benefits to be had from specific rights to prospective innovations can translate into substantially different cost-sharing payments. Consequently, this "benefits measure" question, a fairly common point of contention between taxpayers and the IRS under the 1968 regulations, is likely to remain controversial under the proposed provisions. On the other hand, the 1992 proposed cost-sharing provisions unambiguously endorse buy-in and buy-out payments, another common source of controversy under the 1968 regulations.

On balance, then, the 1992 proposed cost-sharing provisions, in

[49]More specifically, an under-allocation of joint costs such as overhead to the activities at issue will increase the pool of total profits apparently earned on these activities, while the returns on tangible assets should not be affected if tangible assets are not also under- or over-allocated. An under-allocation of tangible assets will result in an under-attribution of returns on tangible assets in the activities at issue, and a corresponding overstatement of residual intangibles income, for a given amount of pooled profits.

combination with the 1993 proposed profit split methods, address several of the important methodological issues that arose under the 1968 cost-sharing rules in fairly broad-brush terms, without resolving them conclusively. Inasmuch as this lack of specificity reflects the broad range of circumstances that the regulations necessarily have to encompass, it is certainly understandable. However, in the interest of reducing controversies and ensuring consistency in the tax treatment of similarly situated multinational firms, it is important to impose some boundaries on both the way in which one should implement the proposed profit split methods in specific instances (along the dimensions discussed above), and on the proper measure of anticipated benefits flowing from participation in cost-sharing agreements, perhaps by means of fairly detailed, conditional "if-then" rules.

Chapter 6

Intra-Company Royalty Agreements

6.1 Background

Intra-company royalty issues potentially arise when one member of a controlled group licenses valuable intangible property to another member. As with other forms of intra-company transactions, intra-company royalty rates must satisfy the arm's length standard. That is, the licensee must pay its related licensor the same royalty rate that it would pay an unrelated licensor for the use of comparable intangible property under similar terms.

On its face, this appears to be a straightforward proposition. However, intra-company license agreements often differ from arm's length license agreements in a number of economically significant ways. Most importantly, a parent company will generally license state-of-the-art technology to its manufacturing subsidiaries, while arm's length agreements tend to involve more dated technology. Thus, comparable uncontrolled licensing transactions rarely exist. As with the intra-company cost-sharing agreements reviewed in Chapter 5 (and, for that matter, the "consignment versus sale of materials" issue raised in the simple cost-plus cases reviewed in Chapter 3), this state of affairs raises a broader question: at what stage should the arm's length standard be applied? Does one take as given the way in which taxpayers have structured their intra-company dealings and apply the standard solely to determine arm's length consideration, or should it be applied to the structure of intra-company transactions as well? If the former, and if uncontrolled entities do not enter into analogous agreements among themselves, the arm's length standard inevitably becomes very difficult to implement (because one is always comparing apples and oranges), and, perhaps more importantly, its meaning can be highly ambiguous.

In the course of applying the 1968 regulations, IRS economists were gradually precluded from questioning the structure of intra-company dealings in general, and the per se validity of intra-company license agreements in particular. This then-unwritten restriction—the product of a series of unfavorable outcomes in transfer pricing disputes at Appeals and Tax Court levels—was in the nature of an informal understanding, passed down from National and District Counsel to Examination. As discussed previously, the 1993 temporary regulations formalized this unwritten rule in a provision requiring the district director to "test the arm's length character of the results of a taxpayer's transaction as actually structured by the taxpayer, and ...not treat the transaction as if it had been structured in a different manner." Hence, when one member of a controlled group licenses intangible property to another under the new regime, the IRS will typically investigate whether the intra-company royalty paid is arm's length, given the fact—and form—of the license agreement.

The 1993 temporary regulations' provisions that one take the structure of intra-company transactions as given, on the one hand, and consider the alternatives realistically available to both buyer and seller in determining arm's length consideration, on the other, could collectively be considered ambiguous as applied to the composite cost-plus and resale price cases reviewed in Chapters 3 and 4. However, by virtue of the statutory *commensurate with income* requirement that applies to intra-company licenses of intangible property, the emphasis is squarely on the alternatives available to licensees and licensors in royalty issues. Further, there is an implicit assumption that, while licensors have many potential "takers," licensees have very limited licensing alternatives, and should therefore be willing to pay a royalty amount such that virtually all income attributable to the licensed intangibles accrues to the licensor.

In the composite royalty issue reviewed in this chapter, I compare methodologies and outcomes under the 1968 regulations' rather amorphous twelve-factor approach[1] and the 1993 temporary regulations' revamped comparable profits method, taking both the fact and form of the intra-company license agreement at issue as given. As discussed in Chapter 2, the 1968 regulations' twelve-factor approach posed several major problems: first, the data necessary to apply even a small subset of the factors rarely existed; second, even if all of the requisite data were freely available, many of the individual factors would only have yielded qualitative, more-or-less-than insights, suggesting whether an intra-company royalty rate should be adjusted up or down relative to some base inexact comparable transaction, but not how large the adjustment should be in absolute (dollar or percentage) terms. Finally, the lack of prioritizing presented major problems from both tax planning and enforcement perspectives.

In lieu of clear and workable guidelines, and in some cases as part of an aggressive tax planning strategy, taxpayers often fell back on "industry norms" to establish royalties, or a broad (and insufficiently substantiated) rule of thumb that divided income between licensee and licensor in 75%-25% proportions (with the larger share accruing to the licensee). IRS economists, contesting these pricing approaches, had little to work with but inexact comparables, with the result that their proposed adjustments were rarely sustained and related licensees frequently retained very large shares of the income attributable to the licensed intangible.

The 1993 temporary regulations eliminate much of this methodological confusion by endorsing the comparable profits method. Under this method, one constructs an arm's length range based on (possibly inexact) comparable stand-alone firms' operating results, and tests the controlled entity's reported income against this range.

[1] As discussed in Chapter 2, the 1968 regulations required one to consider some subset of twelve factors in establishing intra-company royalty rates. These twelve factors included industry royalty rates; competing bids and rates, uniqueness of property, terms of the intangibles transfer, degree of protection afforded by patents covering the transferred property, value of services provided in conjunction with the transfer of assets, prospective profits or cost savings to be realized by the licensee, investment by the transferee in connection with the transferred intangible, substitute intangibles available to the licensee, arm's length rates or prices, the transferor's development costs, and other facts and circumstances.

The comparable profits method essentially sidesteps the difficulties in finding adequate comparables by relaxing comparability standards very significantly. Unfortunately, in doing so, it also creates the spectre of endless wrangling over the relative virtues of different samples of inexactly comparable stand-alone firms.

Relatedly, the results based on any given sample of inexact comparables is likely to be highly imprecise (as judged against a hypothetical "true" arm's length result). More fundamentally, the basic premise that related licensees cum stand-alone firms have no alternative licensing possibilities—which underlies the statutory *commensurate with income* requirement and, hence, the comparable profits method that implements it—is probably untrue to one degree or another in many situations.[2]

On balance, then, the 1993 temporary regulations may well produce results that are more favorable to the government than the 1968 regulations in cases involving royalty issues, but these results will not necessarily be closer to genuinely arm's length royalty rates. The composite case study reviewed herein illustrates these observations.

6.2 An Intra-Company Royalty Issue: Licensed Process Technology

The taxpayer in this composite intra-company royalty case is a large multinational firm that produced several chemical bases used in the manufacture of women's fragrances and cosmetics. The business required a substantial investment in process R&D on an ongoing basis, the fruits of which the developer licensed to its manufacturing affiliates.

[2]However, when the alternatives realistically available to related licensees are far less attractive than the intra-company license at issue, as is often the case, most (albeit not necessarily all) intangible income attributable to the licensed property would accrue to the related licensor on an arm's length basis. As such, this caveat may be of limited practical significance.

6.2.1 Summary Functional Analysis

This composite multinational is comprised of a U.S. parent (P), several manufacturing subsidiaries in Britain, France, and Germany (S_b, S_f, and S_g, respectively), and one partially owned manufacturing affiliate in Brazil (A_b). P conducted extensive process-oriented R&D on an ongoing basis (which it alone financed), manufactured chemical bases in its U.S. facilities, and sold directly to third parties in the U.S., Canada, and parts of South America. Additionally, it licensed intangible property to both its wholly owned European subsidiaries and its partially owned Brazilian affiliate, provided technical support services to both, and performed a wide range of administrative support services for its wholly owned subsidiaries, as described in more detail below.

S_b, S_f, S_g, and A_b all purchased their materials requirements directly from third party suppliers, produced chemical bases using technology developed by P, and sold directly to third parties in their respective markets. Many of these customers were large multinational firms; others were relatively small, specialized niche operations.

The taxpayer competed with a limited number of other producers in this business. However, unlike itself, all of its rivals were vertically integrated, producing and marketing fragrances or cosmetics in addition to the intermediate chemical base products at issue. Further, the taxpayer's technology was widely acknowledged to be far superior to that used by its rivals, yielding base products of consistently higher quality at a slightly lower cost than its integrated competitors. This competitive advantage was reflected in its significant share of both domestic and foreign external markets.

6.2.2 License Terms and Intra-Company Charges

P licensed all of its intangibles, manufacturing and marketing intangible assets alike, to each of its wholly owned subsidiaries. The licenses were exclusive within each entity's respective market. Apart from the implied restriction on the geographic markets in which each related licensee could sell, S_b, S_f, and S_g were otherwise unconstrained in their use of P's intangible property. Further, under the terms of its agreements with these entities, P was called upon to perform a variety of "special services" (the aforementioned technical support services, specifically including engineering, supervision of plant construction, operating and technical assistance, etc.) at the subsidiaries' request.

Each wholly owned subsidiary paid a uniform royalty rate of 6% for rights to P's marketing and manufacturing intangible property and expertise. P levied no additional charges for the special services that it provided by request, nor for the administrative support services that it provided on an ongoing basis.

Under the terms of its license agreement with P, A_b had an exclusive license to use all patents owned or controlled by P in Brazil. However, it was expressly precluded from using P's registered or common law trademarks.

P charged A_b separately for special services, at a fee determined by marking up the wage and salary costs of the personnel directly employed in providing these services by a specified percentage. Additionally, A_b paid P a running royalty of 7% of sales.

6.2.3 Potential Issues

The IRS economist originally assigned to this case determined that many of the administrative support services that P performed, the costs of which it deducted for tax purposes, benefited its wholly owned subsidiaries. As such, he proposed a services adjustment that shifted these costs to the latter. The economist did not investigate or challenge the firm's 6% intra-company royalty, in deference to the case manager's predilections and the scheduled closing date, and the taxpayer agreed to attempt a negotiated settlement at the Examination level on this basis.

In the course of these settlement negotiations, however, the taxpayer raised the issue of intra-company royalties by arguing that S_b, S_f, and S_g compensated P for its ongoing administrative support (as well as the technical support services it provided and the intangible assets it licensed) via their royalty obligations, pursuant to P's intra-company license agreements with them. Having inherited this case in midstream, my task was to determine whether *P*'s intra-company royalty charges constituted arm's length consideration for the combination of manufacturing and marketing technology that it transferred, specialized services that it performed (ancillary to the technology transfer), and administrative services that it provided on an ongoing basis. Note that I was precluded from raising a royalty issue at this stage, pursuant to the Examination team's understanding with the taxpayer. Rather, I was simply attempting to determine the reasonableness of the initial proposed services adjustment. This limited approach simplified the analysis considerably, in that it required only a qualitative, "more or less than" comparison of arm's length and intra-company charges:

- If genuinely arm's length royalty rates for inferior intangible property (and services ancillary to the technology transfer[3]) were:

    1. higher than or comparable to the intra-company rates that *P* charged, then the latter clearly did not adequately compensate *P* for its intangible property alone; nor did they cover the costs of ongoing services unrelated to the technology transfer. (This result would support the original proposed services adjustment.)

    2. lower than *P*'s intra-company rates, one could not say conclusively whether *P*'s rates were sufficiently high to compensate it for intangible property and both specialized technical and ongoing administrative services on the basis of this limited evidence. (Hence, this finding would neither support nor detract from the original proposed services adjustment.) However, the costs of *P*'s ongoing administrative support could then be netted out of its royalty fees, and the recomputed royalty rates—representing compensation for intangible property and technical services alone—compared with the third party rates for inferior technology. If *P*'s adjusted rates were comparable to or lower than the third party rates, one could reasonably conclude either that its original (unadjusted) royalties did

[3]Albeit not ongoing administrative services, in that arm's length license agreements rarely provide for such services.

not cover the costs of administrative services, or that the element of royalties that represented payment for intangible property was not arm's length.

Note also that these same conditional observations hold if the intangible property transferred in arm's length agreements was a subset of, albeit comparable in quality to, the intra-company intangible property transfers, or if the property transferred in controlled and uncontrolled agreements was similar in both kind and quality, but the unrelated licensees' rights were more circumscribed than the related licensees' rights (or, more generally, if the terms were otherwise less favorable).[4]

- If genuinely arm's length royalty rates for similarly valuable intangible property were:

  1. comparable to P's intra-company rates (and the terms

---

[4] Royalty payments are a means of splitting the profits attributable to licensed technology between licensee and licensor. If one assumes, as some have, that the ratio of royalty payments to profits—in effect, the "rental price" of licensed proprietary intangibles—remains fairly constant across agreements within (if not necessarily across) industries, royalty rates as a percentage of sales (as they are usually expressed) will *increase* as a licensing opportunity becomes more valuable (whether because the proprietary property is intrinsically more valuable, or because the licensee acquires more advantageous rights to comparable technology). To see this, convert a royalty payment expressed as a percent of sales into a royalty payment expressed as a percent of profits (that is, the share of profits accruing to the licensor):

$$\frac{\text{royalties}}{\text{sales}} \times \frac{\text{sales}}{\text{profits}} = \frac{\text{royalties}}{\text{profits}}$$

As the profit margins earned on sales of products embodying the licensed technology increase, their reciprocal (sales to profits)—the second term in the above equation—declines. Assuming that the ratio of royalties to profits remains constant across licenses, this would necessitate an offsetting increase in the ratio of royalties to sales—in other words, an increase in the royalty rate, expressed as a percentage of sales. If one relaxes the (largely unsubstantiated) assumption that the split of profits between licensor and licensee remains fairly constant across license agreements, and allows for the possibility that licensors retain a larger share of profits in more lucrative licensing situations (a more plausible scenario, in keeping with the opportunity cost framework), increases in the profitability of a license agreement (again, either because the property itself is intrinsically more valuable or because the licensee obtains more valuable rights thereto) would have a larger effect on the royalty rate expressed as a percent of sales.

of these transfers similar), one could reasonably conclude that the related licensees adequately compensated P for the licensed property, and for services ancillary to the technology transfer, but not for ongoing services unrelated to the transfer. (Again, this would support the proposed services adjustment.)

2. higher than P's intra-company royalty rates, then these rates adequately compensated P neither for technology and ancillary technical services nor for ongoing administrative support (again, supporting the services adjustment).

3. lower than P's intra-company royalty rates, then some portion of ongoing administrative support costs would have been covered via the royalty, undermining the original services adjustment. (In this event, it would be important to obtain a reasonably precise estimate of an arm's length rate for intangible property comparable to P's, in that the difference between this arm's length rate and P's intra-company rates would indicate how much of the services costs were paid via the royalty mechanism.)

- If genuinely arm's length rates for superior intangible property (or comparable property on more favorable terms) were:

  1. lower than or comparable to P's intra-company royalty charges, then the related subsidiaries were compensating P adequately for the licensed intangible property, and paying some share of service-related expenditures via their royalty fees. (Here again, a more precise estimate of arm's length rates for P's licensed intangibles would be necessary.)

  2. higher than P's intra-company royalty charges, again, one could not draw any firm conclusions regarding the services question.

6.2.4 Adjustment Methodology under the 1968 Regulations

To support its claims that the royalty rates which P charged S_b, S_f, and S_g adequately compensated P for transferred intangible property, specialized services, and ongoing administrative support, the taxpayer provided the IRS with a number of very inexact comparable uncontrolled transactions involving intangible property. More specifically, the taxpayer provided three distinct sets of "comparable" uncontrolled transactions:

- Several license agreements between parties that were neither related among themselves nor to the taxpayer;
- P's license agreement with A_b; and,
- A number of related party license agreements between members of other controlled groups, to which P was not a party.

Our analysis of this taxpayer's intra-company royalties under the 1968 regulations entailed comparing a subset of these inexact comparable uncontrolled transactions with the intra-company agreements, arguing whether, why, and in what direction the royalty rates should differ, and drawing some plausible conclusions as to the reasonableness of the taxpayer's claims that ongoing administrative services costs were embedded in the intra-company royalty charges.

Consider first the relative merits of these different types of inexactly comparable uncontrolled license agreements in general. Related party license agreements are clearly of no use in assessing the reasonableness of intra-company royalty rates. The logic in applying the arm's length standard, simply stated, is that unrelated parties generally do not have an incentive to shift income among themselves. Thus, using transactions between unrelated parties as a reference, one can get a good sense of how comparable transactions between related entities would be structured, and compensation determined, absent tax considerations. However, there is no logical basis for applying the terms of one intra-company agreement to another, inasmuch as one is not removing the potential incentives to shift income.

Arguably, one can use agreements between partially owned entities as a measure of the reasonableness of intra-company royalties when the quasi-related licensor has no incentive to shift intangible income to the licensee[5] (absent compensating payments from the other co-owner(s), or if there are no channels through which such compensating payments can be made.[6]) However, license agreements between unrelated parties are clearly the most compelling source of information,[7] assuming they are sufficiently similar. Unfortunately, such agreements are extremely rare.

In the subsections below, the taxpayer's license agreement with A_b and its sample of agreements between unrelated parties (to which it was not a party) are evaluated with regard to their suitability as (inexact) comparable uncontrolled transactions, fitted into the typology of less valuable, comparable, and more valuable intangible property and terms described above, and P's claim that its intra-company royalty charges included compensation for its ongoing administrative support tested on this basis. (For the reasons given above, the license agreements between members of other controlled groups were given no weight.)

[5]Consider when a licensor, dealing with a partially owned licensee, will not have an incentive to shift intangible income: loosely speaking, the licensor can refrain from shifting intangible income to its partially owned affiliate (by charging an arm's length royalty rate), and, hence, report its arm's length share of this income in its own jursidiction, where it will be taxed at a higher rate. Alternatively, the licensor can shift intangible income to its partially owned affiliate (by charging a lower than arm's length royalty rate), pay a lower average tax rate, but retain a smaller share of the (higher) total after-tax intangible income (as determined by its ownership share in the licensee). The incentive to shift income under these circumstances thus depends on the relationship between the licensor's ownership share in the partially owned affiliate cum licensee, and the ratio of effective tax rates (more accurately, the proportionate after-tax income retained) in the licensor's and partially owned licensee's jurisdictions. Note that this simple description disregards the fact that the partially owned affiliate's income will eventually be repatriated, complicating the comparison somewhat and reducing the incentive to shift intangible income.

[6]Transactions between the joint owners of the licensee, or cross-licensing agreements between the licensor and its partially owned affiliate, may constitute such channels. Alternatively, if both co-owners contribute intangible property to their jointly owned affiliate, they could be undervaluing them to the same degree.

[7]This is particularly true in the case of "internal" CUPs, in which the same entity licenses (the same) intangible property to both related and unrelated entities on comparable terms.

License Agreements between Uncontrolled Parties

The third party agreements that the taxpayer submitted were all between firms operating in allied, albeit different, industries than P. These third party agreements, all of which provided for running royalties in the 2%–6% range, differed from P's licenses with S_b, S_f, and S_g in a number of important respects:

- All of the third party license agreements involved inferior manufacturing technology, as measured by vintage and, relatedly, the availability of substitute technologies and projected cost savings;

- As noted above, P permitted its wholly owned licensees to use its trademarks and other product designations. In contrast, none of the genuinely arm's length agreements which the taxpayer supplied allowed the licensees to utilize their respective licensors' trademarks and names. In two third party agreements, the licensees were permitted to convey the information that their products were produced under license by their respective licensors. While this stipulation conferred some value, it was not comparable to the value associated with rights to use the licensors' product designations outright. Further, these two licensors' marketing intangibles were significantly less valuable than P's marketing intangible assets.

- One third party agreement stipulated that the licensee's production levels could not exceed a specified maximum per annum. The taxpayer's license agreements with its wholly owned entities contained no such restrictions.

- Several of the arm's length agreements supplied by the taxpayer called for forms of payment other than, or in addition to, a simple running royalty applied to sales volume. For example, one required the licensee to pay a fixed sum in lieu of a running royalty, and two required the licensees to pay a lump sum in addition to a royalty stream. The most complex form of payment required the licensee to issue the licensor a specified share in its business at the outset, pay lump sums annually for six years, and subsequently pay a running royalty based on sales volume.

- Finally, none of these third party license agreements called for services other than those that were clearly incidental to the technology transfers (in particular, the licensors did not provide ongoing administrative support) and, hence, provided for a very limited period of time.

In contrast to the remaining differences identified above, one can adjust for differences in the types and levels of services that P and the taxpayer's unrelated licensors provided in a simple and straightforward manner. Specifically, inasmuch as S_b, S_f, and S_g benefited from a range of ongoing administrative support services that the uncontrolled licensees did not receive, the associated costs should be deducted from their royalty payments before comparing them with the genuinely arm's length rates. These recomputed rates, net of administrative support costs, were significantly lower than the 6% intra-company rates that P charged overall: S_b (P's British manufacturing subsidiary) paid an adjusted royalty rate of 2.5%, S_f (its French manufacturing subsidiary) 2%, and S_g (its German manufacturing subsidiary) 3%.

What conclusions can be drawn by comparing the third party license terms and royalty rates described above with P's intra-company agreements and adjusted royalty rates? As already noted, the unrelated licensees all operated in different industries than P's related licensees. Hence, the first order of business is to consider when one can legitimately compare license terms and royalty rates across industries.

Briefly stated, if two licensors operating in different industries, licensing intangible property with comparable profit potential under the same terms and conditions, would charge their respective licensees the same royalty rate, such cross-industry comparisons are valid. (That is, one could then attribute variations in specific license terms and conditions to differences in royalty rates, even though the licensees operated in different industries.) In general, this will be true if licensors in the different industries retain the same share of their respective licensees' profits (as would be the case if the often-cited

75%-25% "rule of thumb" regarding the division of income between licensor and licensee applied consistently across agreements and industries, or if the pairs of licensors and licensees whose license agreements are being compared each had comparable opportunity costs), and the licensees earn the same profit margins on their respective sales of products embodying the licensed intangibles (as determined by such factors as market structure, the capital intensity of the businesses, and so forth). For purposes of this discussion of uncontrolled license agreements supplied by the taxpayer, I assume that both of these prerequisites are satisfied.

On balance, the third party agreements that the taxpayer supplied provided little support for its contention that *P*'s 6% royalty rate compensated it for marketing and manufacturing intangible assets, technical support, and ongoing administrative services. Equivalently, judging from these agreements, the adjusted 2%–3% intra-company royalty rates—the low end of the 2%–6% range of arm's length royalty rates that the inexact comparable transactions established—did not adequately compensate *P* for its intangible property and interim technical services. Inasmuch as the third party agreements involved unambiguously inferior manufacturing technology and virtually no marketing intangible assets, an unrelated licensee would be expected to pay a lower royalty rate for rights thereto than it would have paid for *P*'s superior technology and marketing intangible property. Hence, *P*'s intra-company royalties should be higher than those provided for in the third party agreements, all other things equal. Similarly, one would expect an unrelated licensee to pay a higher royalty for the more extensive set of rights transferred under the related party agreements at issue, all other things equal. Finally, to the extent that the third party license agreements provided for forms of payment in addition to a running royalty, one would expect offsetting reductions in the latter, all other things equal.[8]

In short, all of the differences in property, terms, and conditions between controlled and third party licenses pointed to the same conclusion: the arm's length rates should have been lower than *P*'s

[8]Stated differently, direct comparisons of the arm's length royalties with the intra-company rates were uninformative and potentially misleading, in that they understated the unrelated licensors' total compensation.

intra-company rates, net of services costs. The fact that they were not suggested either that P undercharged S_b, S_f, and S_g for the intangibles it licensed, or that the costs of P's ongoing administrative support had not been factored into its royalty fees. Given our working assumption that P's royalties were arm's length, the logical conclusion was that P had not been compensated for its ongoing administrative services.

P's License Agreement with Its Partially Owned Entity

Next, contrast P's license agreements with A_b, its partially owned Brazilian manufacturing affiliate, and its wholly owned European subsidiaries, respectively. Under the terms of A_b's license agreement, A_b cum licensee had exclusive rights to use all patents owned or controlled by P in the manufacture of the chemical base products at issue in Brazil. Recall, however, that it was expressly precluded from using P's resistered or common law trademarks and names, and that P charged it separately for technical services provided. A_b's royalty—which covered only the "rental price" of the licensed intangibles—was 7%. Thus, A_b paid a substantially higher royalty rate for the use of P's manufacturing intangibles alone than the 2%–3% adjusted royalty rates that P's wholly owned subsidiaries paid for the use of its manufacturing and marketing intangibles, together with comprehensive technical support on an as-needed basis.[9] Hence, this comparison suggests that S_b, S_f, and S_g paid less than arm's length royalties for P's manufacturing technology alone, and that their royalty payments incorporated no compensation for either marketing intangibles or ongoing services.

In summary, under the 1968 regulations, the (unadjusted) royalty rates that P charged its wholly owned subsidiaries did not appear sufficient to cover the costs of its ongoing administrative and periodic technical support services, and compensate P adequately for the intangible assets (both marketing and manufacturing) that it transferred via intra-company license. Both the agreement between P and

[9] Again, because A_b's royalty was net of administrative support costs, the point of comparison should be this 7% quasi-arm's length rate and the 2%–3% royalties that S_b, S_f, and S_g paid, net of ongoing administrative services costs.

its partially owned manufacturing affiliate and those between entities that were neither related among themselves nor to the taxpayer cast doubt upon the taxpayer's arguments to the contrary. Consequently, the original proposed services adjustment appeared to have been warranted.

In general, these comparisons would also suggest that the intra-company royalty rates themselves should have been revised upward. However, leaving aside the Examination team's understanding with this (composite) taxpayer that the IRS would forgo potential royalty issues and focus exclusively on services, it would have been extremely difficult to establish an arm's length royalty in absolute terms on the basis of this sample of highly inexact "comparable" transactions (as distinct from determining whether the reported intra-company rate was relatively higher or lower than an arm's length rate, as in the instant case). Specifically, one would have to quantify the effects of individual differences—in the intangible property itself, in the permissible scale of production, in the industries and markets in which products embodying the licensed technology were sold, and in the forms of compensation—on arm's length running royalty rates.

In principle, such quantifications are feasible, given a sufficiently large sample of third party agreements that vary along all of these dimensions. In practice, however, neither taxpayers nor the IRS have the resources necessary to value the multitude of material and minor differences between controlled license agreements and the inexactly comparable agreements used to evaluate them in (the numerous) pricing cases involving royalty issues. Hence the frequent resort to industry norms and simple rules of thumb (which often biased the allocation of intangible income in favor of the licensee under the 1968 regulations), and, ultimately, hence the *commensurate with income* requirement and the comparable profits method that implements it under the 1993 temporary regulations.

Taxpayer's Position

The taxpayers in this composite case study raised several objections to the foregoing analysis. One argued that its wholly owned licensee would have earned above-normal returns on its operating assets had the manufacturing intangibles it utilized been as valuable as the IRS maintained. Averaging operating returns on total assets across subsidiaries and tax years, this taxpayer contended that these results demonstrated that the licensed intangibles were of minimal value. As such, the argument went, the U.S. parent cum licensor's intra-company royalty charges represented compensation partly for marketing intangible assets,[10] but primarily for technical and ongoing administrative services. Another taxpayer maintained that its subsidiaries cum licensees were not in a position to pay additional amounts—either in the form of royalty payments or service fees—and to require them to do so would put them in a loss position. Finally, a third taxpayer maintained that the parent firm's return on expenses incurred to earn the royalty income at issue, calculated by averaging its R&D expenses over the tax years and dividing concurrent royalty revenues by this figure, was sufficiently high (in some absolute sense) that it could not justifiably be challenged.

Resolution

Ultimately, the cases in this composite case study were settled—some at the Examination level, and some at Appeals—at between 30% and 40% of the original proposed services adjustments.

6.2.5 Possible Adjustment Methodology under the 1993 Temporary Regulations: The Comparable Profits Method

As reviewed in Chapter 2, with the 1986 Act, related licensees' royalty payments must be "commensurate with the income attributable to the [licensed] intangible[s]." Under the 1993 temporary regulations, the *commensurate with income* requirement is satisfied by applying one of the approved intangibles pricing methods: the "compa-

[10] This taxpayer contended that its trademarks and names were of minimal value, inasmuch as both the U.S. parent and its manufacturing subsidiaries were in the business of manufacturing intermediate products for sale to sophisticated corporate customers whose buying decisions were guided solely by "real" quality and price considerations.

rable uncontrolled transactions" method, or the "comparable profits method."[11]

Choice of Methods

While the choice between the comparable uncontrolled transactions method and the comparable profits method is to be determined under the best methods rule per the 1993 temporary regulations, one can still clearly discern an underlying preference for the former:

> [T]he comparable uncontrolled transaction method, when it can reasonably be applied on the basis of available information, ordinarily will provide the most accurate measure of an arm's length charge for the transfer of intangible property.[12]

However, under the 1993 temporary regulations' version of the comparable uncontrolled transactions method, controlled and uncontrolled transactions must involve "comparable" intangible property (with substantially the same profit potential),[13] and take place under comparable circumstances (where "circumstances" encompass contractual terms).[14] These very high standards of comparability greatly restrict the applicability of the comparable uncontrolled transactions method as a practical matter.

---

[11]As noted in Chapter 2, the 1993 temporary regulations also provide for "other" methods under limited circumstances.

[12]See Section 1.482-4T.

[13]More specifically, two items of intangible property are considered comparable if they are in the same class of intangibles, relate to the same types of products, processes, or know-how within the same general industry or market, and, as noted, have substantially the same profit potential. See Chapter 2.

[14]Two transactions will be considered to have taken place under comparable circumstances if the terms of the transfer are similar, where terms encompass the exploitation rights granted in the intangible, the exclusive or non-exclusive character of any rights granted, any restrictions on use, or any limitations on the geographic area where the rights may be exploited; the stage of development of the intangible; rights to receive periodic updates; the uniqueness of the property; the duration of the license, contract or agreement, and any termination or renegotiation rights; economic and product liability risks assumed by the licensee; the existence and extent of any collateral transactions or ongoing business relationships between the transferee and transferor; and the functions to be performed by the transferor and transferee, including any ancillary or subsidiary services.

Further, while one can adjust for differences in circumstances (such as license terms) under the 1993 temporary regulations, it appears that differences in intangible property per se effectively rule out a given prospective comparable uncontrolled transaction:

> The intangible property involved in an uncontrolled transaction is comparable to that involved in the controlled transaction if ... [the listed requirements for determining comparability of property] are met. The circumstances involved in an uncontrolled transaction are comparable to those of a controlled transfer if any differences can be accounted for....[15]

As such, none of the taxpayer's prospective comparable license agreements would pass muster under the 1993 temporary regulations, adjustments for differences notwithstanding. First, the manufacturing intangible property exchanged in the controlled and uncontrolled transactions, respectively, had very different profit potential, and related to different products sold in different industries. Second, as noted in the preceding discussion, most of the taxpayer's prospective comparable arm's length agreements involved only manufacturing intangible property, while the controlled transactions involved marketing intangible assets as well. Finally, the terms (and, hence, the circumstances) of the uncontrolled transfers differed significantly from the controlled transfers (in that the former contained a number of restrictions on use that had no parallel in P's license agreements with S_b, S_f, and S_g, and required forms of payment other than, or in addition to, a simple running royalty rate).

In lieu of satisfactory comparable uncontrolled transactions, intracompany royalty rates would ordinarily be determined (implicitly) under the comparable profits method, per the 1993 temporary regulations.

The Comparable Profits Method: General

Recall that the comparable profits methodology entails building up an "arm's length range" from a sample of stand-alone firms' prof-

[15] *Ibid.*

itability measures, or "profit level indicators." Determining the arm's length range and evaluating or establishing intra-company royalty rates on this basis is a multistep procedure:

1. In the first step, one selects a "tested party" from among the related entities participating in the transaction(s) at issue (typically the licensee).

2. In the second step, one puts together a sample of reasonably comparable stand-alone firms. Under the comparable profits methodology, these firms "need be only broadly similar [to the tested party], and significant product diversity and some functional diversity between the controlled and uncontrolled transactions is acceptable."[16]

3. If there are economically significant differences between the tested party and the stand-alone firms selected, one has the option of adjusting the latter's profitability accordingly (to incorporate the bottom-line effects of these differences).[17]

4. Given this sample of reasonably comparable stand-alone firms (with or without adjustments for differences between them and the tested party), one calculates a series of "constructive operating profits" from them, using a single "profit level indicator" (e.g., rates of return on capital employed, financial ratios such as operating profits to sales, gross profit to operating expenses, etc.). More specifically, one computes the selected profit level indicator for each stand-alone firm used as a comparable and applies each of the resulting ratios to the tested party's relevant base (assets, operating expenses, sales, etc.), as determined by the denominator of the profit level indicator used. Each resulting dollar amount constitutes a "constructive operating profit."

5. If the stand-alone firms from which these profit level indicators are derived are sufficiently comparable to the tested party in the first instance, or if one has adjusted for the significant differ-

---

[16] See 1.482-5T.

[17] Note that these adjustments are not *de rigueur* under the comparable profits method, as they are under other pricing methods. However, whether one makes these adjustments or not has implications for the breadth of the arm's length range, as described subsequently.

ences between them, the arm's length range is coincident with the range of constructive operating profits. If the stand-alone firms are only broadly similar to the tested party, and adjustments for differences are not made, the arm's length range is a subset of the range of constructive operating profits (specifically, the interquartile range). In this event, the 1993 temporary regulations also require a minimum of four comparable stand-alone firms.

6. If the tested party's reported operating profits are within the arm's length range, the consideration paid for transferred intangibles will be deemed arm's length.
7. If the tested party's reported operating profits are outside the arm's length range, the district director may make allocations that shift its adjusted profits to any point within the arm's length range. However, the tested party's post-adjustment position "will ordinarily be...the midpoint of the range."

In contrast to the twelve-factor approach sanctioned under the 1968 regulations, which often indicated only whether intra-company royalty rates should be adjusted up or down in relative terms, the comparable profits method yields a specific dollar adjustment that implicitly incorporates a "constructed" arm's length royalty rate.[18] Further, this constructed arm's length royalty rate will generally shift *all* intangible income back to the related licensor (as required by the statutory *commensurate with income* standard) if the stand-alone firms used as comparables neither own nor license intangible property.[19] (In this event, the independent firms' profits—and,

[18]One can solve for this embedded royalty rate by netting out the following items from the tested party's total revenues (on sales to both related and unrelated entities): (a) its cost of goods sold; (b) its operating expenses other than intra-company royalty payments (where operating expenses are defined in the 1993 temporary regulations as "all expenses not included in cost of goods sold except for interest expense, foreign income taxes, and domestic income taxes"); and (c) the constructive operating profit deemed to constitute an arm's length profit under the comparable profits method, and dividing residual royalty payments through by revenues. If the IRS adjusts intra-company prices or costs other than the royalties, these separate adjustments should be incorporated prior to computing the embedded royalty.

[19]As described subsequently, this statement presupposes that the "comparable" firms used to derive profit level indicators are in fact fairly closely comparable.

hence, the tested party's constructive operating profits—will embody a return on tangible assets alone.) Conversely, if the stand-alone firms used as comparables either own or license intangible assets, their profits—and, again, the tested party's constructive operating profits—will likely incorporate some return on intangibles as well, and the constructed arm's length rate will leave some portion of intangible income with the related licensee.

The Comparable Profits Method as Applied to this Composite Taxpayer

Consider next how one might apply the comparable profits method in the instant composite case. Recall that all of the taxpayer's competitors were large, vertically integrated firms, manufacturing and marketing fragrances or cosmetics in addition to the intermediate chemical base products at issue. Moreover, several were multinational companies, with geographically dispersed production and marketing operations. As such, unadjusted profit level indicators drawn from any of the prospective comparable companies operating in the taxpayer's industry will reflect their significantly more diverse activities and their different geographic loci. Further, they will incorporate a return to the vertically integrated firms' intangibles—both their (inferior) manufacturing intangibles and (in some cases) the very valuable marketing intangibles associated with their final cosmetics and fragrance products.

In short, unadjusted profit level indicators will provide very little insight regarding the return that P's manufacturing subsidiaries cum stand-alone firms, manufacturing only intermediate chemical base products, operating in a single geographic market, and presumably having no claims to intangible income (per the *commensurate with income* requirement), should earn. How, then, should one apply the comparable profits method under these circumstances? There would seem to be two options:

- One can attempt to allocate the vertically integrated firms' total operating profits between their chemical base manufacturing activities on the one hand, and their perfume and cosmetics manufacturing and marketing operations on the other, and derive profit level indicators from the former segment only. (In general, it will not be feasible to segment operating profits on a geographic basis reliably, using only publicly available information.) Or,

- One can select "comparable" firms from other industries with similar market structures and similar demand and cost characteristics. Per the 1993 temporary regulations, these stand-alone firms should perform similar functions and incur similar risks as the tested party (in both form and amount), and, in keeping with the *commensurate with income* requirement, they should neither own nor license intangible assets. (Depending on the profit level indicators used, additional comparability criteria should—but, under the regulations, may not—be applied, as described below.)

The relative merits of these alternatives are considered briefly below.

Segmenting Vertically Integrated Firms' Profits: Consider first how one might segment vertically integrated firms' profits between their (intermediate) chemical base manufacturing activities and (final) cosmetics and fragrance manufacturing and marketing activities. While there were no independent companies other than the taxpayer that produced only intermediate chemical base products during the period at issue, there were several stand-alone companies that produced only fragrances or cosmetics. In principle, one can use profit level indicators drawn from these stand-alone firms to segment the vertically integrated companies' total operating profits between intermediate and final stages of production and marketing, respectively.[20]

[20]Note that, under the 1993 temporary regulations, one must be able to determine the division of "operating profits and related assets and liabilities" across both comparables' and tested parties' industry segments "reliably." The first application of the comparable profits method described in this chapter may or may not satisfy this standard. Note also that, with regard to firms that are horizontally diversified rather than vertically integrated, an allocation of assets to different industry segments based on sales will generally be misleading. In using sales to allocate assets, one implicitly assumes that sales per dollar of assets are uniform across business activities. In fact, it is far more likely that some activ-

For example, using the rate of return profit level indicator, one would:

1. Derive rates of return on operating assets from each of the stand-alone entities that produced only final products (cosmetics or fragrances);
2. Segment the vertically integrated companies' operating assets between intermediate (chemical base) and final (cosmetics or fragrance) products (if necessary, by reference to the composition of assets employed by the stand-alone firms producing only final cosmetics or fragrance products);
3. Apply the (average of) rates of return profit level indicators calculated in step 1 above to the operating assets that each of the vertically integrated firms used in the production of fragrances and cosmetics;
4. Deduct the dollar amount computed in step 3 above (which represents vertically integrated firms' estimated operating profits on cosmetics and fragrances) from these firms' total profits; and,
5. Divide the residual operating income (which represents vertically integrated firms' estimated operating profits on chemical base products) by the assets that each of these firms used in manufacturing chemical base products.

The rate of return profit level indicators obtained in step 5 above are the magnitudes that one would apply to the tested parties' asset base to determine their constructive operating profits.

Alternatively, one could use a different profit level indicator (e.g., the ratio of gross profits to operating expenses) derived from (and averaged across) the stand-alone firms that produced only fragrances and cosmetics to segment vertically integrated firms' profits and derive profit level indicators on their chemical base businesses alone.[21]

---

ities are more capital-intensive than others, with the result that a sales-based allocation will underestimate the value of assets necessary to carry out the more capital-intensive activites.

[21]Analogously, one would apply this (average) ratio of gross profits to operating expenses to each of the vertically integrated companies' operating expenses

The choice of specific profit level indicators for this purpose should generally be based on the availability of the requisite segmented base data for the vertically integrated companies.

Clearly, these allocations of vertically integrated comparables' profits across their stages of production, and, hence, the relevant profit level indicators, will be inexact to some degree. Consider some of the possible inaccuracies one builds into computations of arm's length constructive operating profits via this allocation procedure. First, suppose that the independent firms producing only fragrances or cosmetics possessed marketing or manufacturing intangible property that was uniformly less valuable than the vertically integrated firms' marketing or manufacturing intangibles. In this case, one will underestimate the profits attributable to the latter's fragrance and cosmetics business by using the former's profit level indicators, in that a portion of marketing or manufacturing intangible income associated with the vertically integrated firms' final fragrance and cosmetics products will incorrectly be allocated to their intermediate chemical base manufacturing activities. Hence, the profit level indicators derived from their chemical base business, which would ultimately be applied to *P*'s manufacturing subsidiaries' financial data, will be unduly high, and the tested party's arm's length income overstated. (Stated differently, this combination of circumstances yields an implicit constructed arm's length royalty that is too low.) The converse holds as well: if the independent firms producing only fragrances or cosmetics possessed more valuable marketing or manufacturing intangible assets than their vertically integrated counterparts, the manufacturing subsidiaries' profits will be underestimated (equivalently, the constructed arm's length royalty will be overstated).

Apart from these and other potential distortions that arise because of differences between the vertically integrated companies and the stand-alone firms (that produced only cosmetics and fragrances) used to segment their profits, there were also potentially significant

associated with the manufacture and marketing of final fragrance and cosmetics products. The resulting dollar amount constitutes an estimate of the vertically integrated firms' gross profits on the manufacture and marketing of final products, and the difference between this amount and total profits, an estimate of their gross profits on the manufacture of chemical base products.

differences between the vertically integrated firms' chemical base businesses and those of S_b, S_f, and S_g, some of which were alluded to above. The fact that the integrated comparable firms were multinational companies, composed of parents and subsidiaries that may not have been dealing with one another at arm's length, is not overly concerning in itself, in that the profit measures derived from them would be based on consolidated results. (Consequently, they would not be "tainted" by non-arm's length intra-company pricing.) However, the integrated companies' consolidated profits would reflect both the various product prices prevailing in, and the location-specific costs associated with, the different geographic markets in which they operated. In contrast, each manufacturing subsidiary produced and sold in a single geographic market. (This might work to individual taxpayers' advantage or their disadvantage in a given instance, depending on the relative magnitudes of the manufacturing affiliates' sales prices and manufacturing costs, and the weighted average of integrated companies' product prices and manufacturing costs.)

Further, to a firm, the vertically integrated companies' chemical base operations were substantially larger than those of S_b, S_f, and S_g. Consequently, to the extent that there are economies of scale in the production of chemical base products, the manufacturing subsidiaries' estimated arm's length income, calculated via profit level indicators derived from the vertically integrated comparables, would be higher than it should have been.

Finally, as noted above, all of the vertically integrated firms possessed some manufacturing intangible assets related to their chemical base businesses. While these manufacturing intangibles were inferior to P's, they nevertheless had some value. As such, profit level indicators derived from the vertically integrated comparables would incorporate a return on these intangibles, as would the tested parties' constructive operating profits—a result that is presumably incompatible with the *commensurate with income* requirement.

On balance, then, the results produced in this particular case via the comparable profits method, using vertically integrated firms as comparables, would likely overestimate the manufacturing subsidiaries' arm's length income and underestimate the implicit arm's length royalty rate. To some extent, such biases arise because the proposed comparables were dissimilar to S_b, S_f, and S_g in several important respects, independent of the fact that they were vertically integrated—a drawback that is likely to be present in many, if not most, applications of the comparable profits method, given the lax comparability standard applied in conjunction with it.[22] However, because the comparables were vertically integrated, necessitating that their profits be segmented by stage of production (by reference to yet another set of inexact comparables), these inevitable inaccuracies in estimated arm's length royalty rates would be compounded.

Further, the fact that one would look to the interquartile range of constructive operating profits derived from these firms (rather than the entire range)[23] does little to ameliorate the potential distortions identified above. The vertically integrated firms all differed in many of the same ways from the tested parties; for example, all owned manufacturing intangibles, all were significantly larger, and so forth. Consequently, each of the "data points" comprising the entire range of constructive operating profits—and, hence, the interquartile range and the midpoint thereof—would incorporate the same distortions.

Utilizing Comparable Firms Drawn from Other Industries: The alternative to segmenting vertically integrated firms' profits to derive profit level indicators in this case entails drawing prospective comparable uncontrolled firms from different industries altogether, a procedure that is sanctioned under the comparable profits method, within limits. If such firms can reasonably be expected to earn similar returns as the tested party in a given period (relative to assets, operating expenses, or sales), this liberty is harmless.[24] However, the fact that the comparable profits method can in principle be applied when the markets at issue are not strictly competitive, combined

---

[22]Note that, while in this instance, the net result was an over-estimate of arm's length income, the reverse situation is probably equally likely.

[23]The upper and lower bounds of the range of constructive operating profits would be eliminated because the standard of comparability necessary to justify using the entire range under the 1993 temporary regulations would presumably not be satisfied.

[24]In fact, the first cost-plus case reviewed in Chapter 3 argued for exactly this procedure.

with the lax comparability standards applied in conjunction with it and the range of approved profit level indicators, make this "similar returns" premise untenable.[25]

Consider the return on assets measure of profitability. Two stand-alone firms drawn from different industries should earn comparable (economic) rates of return (in equilibrium) if they both operate in competitive industries and incur similar risks. Analogously, prospective comparables and a tested party cum stand-alone firm operating in different (competitive) industries can reasonably be expected to earn similar economic rates of return if they incur similar risks (and utilize only tangible assets and "routine" intangibles, if any). Hence, applying the rate of return profit level indicator, and assuming that the controlled tested party operates in a competitive market, comparables should be selected on these bases.[26] Inasmuch as the comparable profits method fails to screen out comparable uncontrolled firms that incur different levels and types of risk than the tested parties, operate in imperfectly competitive markets, or own valuable intangible property, it will likely produce inaccurate results relative to the arm's length standard.[27]

---

[25]While the assumption that a controlled tested party and comparables will earn similar returns is unlikely to be satisfied *within* a given product market that is not competitive, where profit ratios other than a return on assets measure are used, and when the firms being compared do not incur similar risks, it is all the more implausible when comparables are drawn from different industries and these prerequisites are not satisfied in one or both markets.

[26]As discussed in Chapter 5, the rate of return profit level indicator is an accounting measure. While it is economic rates of return, rather than accounting rates of return, that should be equalized across firms incurring comparable risks and operating in competitive markets, again, the extrapolation from economic to accounting rates of return may be reasonable, if not precisely accurate, in the interest of workable tax regulations.

[27]Note also that realized returns in any given period vary around expected returns, and tax laws are applied on a year-by-year basis. As such, it would ideally be useful to rely on a moving average of realized rates of return, and to scale back the sample of prospective comparables selected on the basis of risk and intangibles ownership to include only those firms that manufacture products with similar demand characteristics as the tested parties, and utilize similar inputs in their manufacturing processes. In this event, variations in the cost of inputs and fluctuations in demand should affect comparables and controlled firms cum stand-alone entities similarly. For example, in the composite case described above, the taxpayer manufactured intermediate products, the demand for which was derived from demand for the final products that incorporated them. Consequently, the

The comparability requirements for other profit level indicators should be still more stringent to ensure that the tested parties' resultant constructive operating profits reasonably approximate arm's length income levels.[28] For example, if one uses gross margins relative to sales (or costs) as a profit level indicator, prospective comparable stand-alone firms should incur comparable risks, and employ roughly the same below-the-line factors of production (including tangible capital) per dollar of revenues (or costs), in roughly the same proportions, as the tested party. (This last prerequisite is not likely to be satisfied if the comparables operate in distinct factor markets and face different relative factor costs, or if they utilize substantially different technologies—differences that are all the more likely, and likely to be more pronounced, if comparables are drawn from different product markets.) Again, if the comparable profits method fails to screen out firms that differ from the tested parties in these respects—a very likely scenario, given the comparability standard that are currently to be applied—it will generally produce inaccurate results relative to the arm's length standard.

In short, the comparable profits method, combined with the relaxed standard of comparability applied in conjunction with it, ma frequently produce results that are inconsistent to one degree or an other with both the arm's length standard and the *commensura with income* requirement. The relative merits of segmenting ve tically integrated firms' profits by stage of production or drawi comparables from other industries—the choice in this case—depe

relevant demand characteristics in this case pertain to final demand. Presumab the demand for high-end fragrances and cosmetics is correlated to some deg with the demand for luxury personal hygiene products, such as specialty soa skin and hair care products, etc. Hence, suppliers selling intermediate inputs manufacturers of such products—again, in particular, those that incur compa ble risks and own very limited intangible assets—would be logical comparab candidates in such cases if one utilizes a rate of return profit level indicator.

[28]The 1993 temporary regulations make this same point: "Since financial ra do not directly relate operating profit to the level of investment and risk in a tr or business, more stringent comparability is ordinarily required than when a r of return on capital is used as a profit level indicator." However, it is difficul know how this stipulation will be balanced against the more global statement t uncontrolled firms "need be only broadly similar [to the tested party under comparable profits method], and significant product diversity and some functi diversity between the controlled and uncontrolled transactions is acceptable.

largely on the magnitudes of the additional distortions one builds into estimated arm's length incomes under each procedure. On the one hand, there are the incremental inaccuracies that result from allocating the vertically integrated entities' profits, based on a second set of inexact comparable firms' results; on the other, there are the incremental inaccuracies produced by utilizing "comparable" firms that operate in different industries, potentially with different market structures, different technologies, different risk profiles, and so forth.

6.2.6 Comparison of Results under the 1968 Regulations and the 1993 Temporary Regulations

How are proposed royalty adjustments and resolutions under the 1993 temporary regulations likely to compare with those under the 1968 regulations? Recall that, under the 1968 regulations, the royalty rates that *P* charged its wholly owned subsidiaries did not appear sufficient to cover the costs of ongoing administrative services and interim technical services, and compensate *P* adequately for the intangibles that it transferred. In fact, its adjusted royalty rates for intangible property and ancillary technical services alone appeared to fall significantly short of arm's length rates. However, one could not say with confidence precisely what the "true" arm's length royalty rate would have been on the basis of the comparables that the taxpayer supplied, or the limited information that was publicly available. In situations of this sort, the IRS frequently had a very difficult time substantiating significant proposed adjustments to taxpayers' intra-company royalty charges under the 1968 regulations (although minor adjustments were sometimes sustained). As a result, royalty rates that were probably substantially below the hypothetical "true" arm's length rate often went unchallenged, or, if challenged, were ultimately sanctioned (perhaps with minor adjustments) via the negotiated settlement process.

Under the 1993 temporary regulations' comparable profits method, the (implicit) constructed royalty rate might be higher or lower than the "true" arm's length rate, potentially by a wide margin. Moreover, the constructed rate may well be inconsistent with the

commensurate with income standard in any given instance (in the sense that it shifts more or less than 100% of the intangible income attributable to the related licensor's intangibles). These shortcomings notwithstanding, royalty issues may be more sustainable under the new rules than they were under the 1968 regulations, for the simple reason that the comparable profits methodology yields specific dollar adjustments rather than "more or less than" approximations. By the same token, it may be easy to challenge a proposed royalty adjustment simply by assembling another set of "comparable" firms, with very different operating results, that point to a smaller—or no—adjustment. Again, the fact that the comparability standards applied in conjunction with the comparable profits method are very lax means that it will be difficult to rank different samples of inexactly comparable firms unambiguously, in terms the accuracy of allocations that they produce.

6.2.7 Critique of the Comparable Profits Method

Long experience under the 1968 regulations underscored the need for more conclusive guidelines as to how one should establish or evaluate intra-company royalty rates paid by licensees to their related licensors for rights to proprietary intangible property. Truly comparable arm's length transactions virtually never exist, because intra-company license agreements generally differ from their arm's length counterparts in a number of significant ways (among other things, the transferred property is frequently state-of-the-art in controlled licenses, and the restrictions on use often minimal). Moreover, arm's length licenses themselves are often fairly idiosyncratic affairs. Consequently, a comparable transactions-based approach to determining arm's length royalty rates is of limited practical utility (and leads almost inevitably to the use of industry norms and unsubstantiated rules of thumb to allocate intangible income).

The 1993 temporary regulations attempt to resolve the methodological problems posed by this dearth of comparable transactions in much the same way that the 1968 regulations addressed the analogous problem vis-a-vis tangible property: they incorporate a profits-based method of determining intra-company royalty rates. Taking the statutory *commensurate with income* requirement as given (and, hence, leaving aside the important question of whether it is consistent with the arm's length standard for purposes of this discussion), there are three overriding drawbacks with the comparable profits method (as currently constituted):

- The associated standard of comparability is unduly lax. As the composite royalty case reviewed in this chapter illustrates, inexact comparable firms will produce inexact results (just as inexact comparable uncontrolled intangibles transactions will yield arbitrary allocations of intangible income);
- A variety of profit level indicators (including several financial ratios, such as gross income to operating expenses and operating profits to sales) can be used to construct the arm's length range under the 1993 temporary regulations, given a sample of quasi-comparable stand-alone firms. However, microeconomic theory points only to a systematic relationship between profits and capital employed, contingent on market structure; and,
- While applications of the comparable profits method are not restricted to markets that are effectively competitive, there is little theoretical justification for supposing that two functionally similar firms will earn comparable risk-adjusted rates of return if one or both of them operates in (the same or different) imperfectly competitive markets.

Stated differently, if stand-alone firms that incur different forms and levels of risk, utilize intangible property, or operate in (the same or different) imperfectly competitive product markets are used as comparables, or if profit level indicators other than rates of return are used to construct the arm's length range, the allocation of income from licensee to related licensor may bear very little relationship to the total intangible income actually attributable to the licensor's proprietary intangible property. All of these "ifs" are well within the realm of possibility under the 1993 temporary regulations' comparable profits method.

Nor do the 1993 temporary regulations' requirements that arm's length ranges be based on at least four stand-alone firms when comparables are inexact, and that the range be a subset of constructive operating profits in this event, resolve the problem. It may well be that all four (or more) of the quasi-comparable firms differ from the controlled tested party in ways that bias the constructed royalty rate in the same direction (coincidentally or intentionally), with the result that potential distortions are not necessarily averaged away. Further, the same lax standard of comparability is very likely to produce endless controversies between taxpayers and the IRS over the relative merits of different samples of stand-alone companies, with neither having a clearly superior position.

These shortcomings would be significantly diminished (again, taking the *commensurate with income* requirement as given) if the standard of comparability applied under the comparable profits method were raised, its application limited to effectively competitive markets, appropriate measures of risk defined clearly, and the profit level indicators restricted primarily to rates of return on operating assets. (However, inasmuch as many multinational firms operate in imperfectly competitive markets, these refinements would also necessitate the development of an alternative intangibles pricing methodology that would apply to such firms.)

Chapter 7

Valuation of Intangible Assets: Section 338

With the release of the 1993 proposed profit split regulations, the valuation of intangible property will likely figure more prominently in transfer pricing issues. In particular, when both parties to the controlled transactions at issue possess non-routine intangible property in their own right, such valuations may be necessary, as the last composite cost-sharing case reviewed in Chapter 5 illustrated.[1]

[1] As noted in Chapter 5, it may or may not be necessary to value individual classes of intangible assets (e.g., marketing versus manufacturing types) explicitly, via the income, cost, or market comparison methods, under the capital employed method. If the total stock of jointly owned intangibles, explicitly valued via the residual method, can be divided up on the basis of relative intangibles development expenditures (and the explicit value of intangibles owned by each related party approximated in this way), it will not be necessary to value individual groupings of intangibles directly. However, if relative intangibles development expenditures cannot be used to carve up the combined value of total intangibles under the capital employed method, individual classes of intangibles—and, perhaps, individual assets themselves—will have to be valued directly. Similarly, if intangibles development expenditures are not relatively constant over time, explicit valuations of intangibles groupings may be necessary under the residual allocation profit split method as well. Further, even when the valuation of individual classes of intangibles is not required by the regulations, taxpayers may opt to do so if this more complicated procedure yields significantly more advantageous transfer pricing results than the more approximate measures based on relative development expenditures.

Additionally, intangibles valuations may be called for, in a more cursory sense, to support the use of a particular uncontrolled intangibles transaction under the comparable uncontrolled transactions method, in that the intangible property exchanged is required to have substantially the same profit potential as that licensed in the controlled transaction.

As described in Chapter 2, prior to the 1993 Act (which added Section 197 to the IRC), companies acquiring businesses via a qualified stock purchase, and electing to treat the stock purchase as a purchase of the acquired firm's assets under Section 338, confronted a similar valuation problem. In particular, they had to allocate the (deemed) purchase price paid for the acquired company across each of four classes of assets (cash and similar items; certificates of deposit, marketable securities, and similar items; tangible and intangible assets other than goodwill and going concern; and goodwill and going concern value). In many cases, it was also necessary to value individual assets within these groupings.

As a general rule, taxpayers electing Section 338 prior to the 1993 Act had an incentive to maximize the value of acquired amortizable intangible assets, and minimize the value of acquired goodwill and going concern (both of which were then non-amortizable).[2] For transfer pricing purposes, taxpayers may have an incentive to maximize the value of intangible assets possessed by affiliates in relatively low-tax regions (depending in part on the pricing method that is apropos given their specific facts and circumstances). Despite these relatively superficial differences, however, the history of Section 338 cases prior to the 1993 Act—the methodologies that firms used to value intangible assets for tax purposes, the IRS's assessment of different valuation approaches, and the ways in which such issues were resolved—may yield some very useful insights into the closely analogous valuation issues that could begin to surface in the transfer pricing arena.[3]

In this chapter, I briefly review three composite valuation issues.

---

[2]See Chapter 2.

[3]Moreover, the residual allocation method—one of the proposed profit split approaches—raises many of the same cost allocation issues that regularly arose in connection with intangibles valuations under Section 338.

In essence, one overriding methodological theme emerges: valuing individual intangible assets via the income approach is an extremely imprecise business. When it can be applied, the replacement cost methodology is generally more reliable, and, hence, preferable.

7.1 Valuation of Patient Relationships

7.1.1 Introduction

In the mid-1980s, Company "Y" acquired a chain of specialized health clinics, collectively referred to as Company "X." Having elected to treat these stock acquisitions as purchases of X's assets, Y was required to allocate the total purchase price of each acquisition to individual assets, both tangible and intangible. An unrelated appraisal company, denoted by "V," undertook these valuations on Y's behalf. At the time X changed hands, it had an established base of patients with a common disorder, who regularly visited the clinics for treatment. According to V, these "established patient relationships" constituted the bulk of X's total intangible assets. These relationships (collectively a "customer-based intangible") are the focus of the following discussion.[4]

As described in the appendix to Chapter 2, the IRS's primary position on customer-based intangible assets, prior to the 1993 Act, was that they were inseparable from goodwill, and, hence, could not be amortized.[5] This, then, was the thrust of our primary position in the instant composite case, which entailed disallowing amortization benefits associated with patient relationships entirely.

However, the IRS's primary position was not entirely persuasive in this instance. In general, a contractual relationship between buyer and seller would have been considered separate and distinct

[4]Customer-based assets are defined as "those intangible assets which are closely associated with continuing the customer relationships developed by the acquired business." See page 1, *ISP Coordinated Issue Paper: Customer-Based Intangibles*, Internal Revenue Service, January 1990.

[5]This will clearly change vis-a-vis Section 338 issues raised after the 1993 Act, in that the latter expressly provides for the amortization of both acquired customer-based intangibles and goodwill.

from goodwill.[6] While the patient relationships at issue in this case were not contractual, they were very stable. Treatments were not optional; rather, patients required care on a regular basis. Stated differently, while these relationships were "terminable at will" as a matter of law, they were not readily terminable as a matter of fact. For this reason, and in anticipation of the possibility that the Appeals officer ultimately assigned to the case might not have been persuaded that patient relationships were inseparable from goodwill (or perhaps concluded that the hazards of litigation precluded holding the line on this position, its intrinsic validity notwithstanding), we developed an alternative position that entailed assigning the "patient relationship" intangible asset a specific value, and recalculating amortization allowances on that basis. Hence, the problem in this case: how should one value a set of patient relationships, assuming that they have a finite life?

The choice of a particular valuation methodology—income approach, replacement cost approach, or market comparison method—is generally dictated fairly unambiguously by the availability of data and the facts and circumstances of a given issue. The income method is indicated when the asset cannot readily be reproduced, and when it generates an identifiable income stream. (When this second condition does not hold, the requisite allocation of joint income to individual assets is likely to lead to distorted valuations. If too much income is allocated to a particular asset, the valuation will be excessive; if too little income is allocated, it will be unduly low.) Realistically speaking, the market comparison method is rarely an option vis-a-vis customer-based (and many other) intangible assets, because they are rarely bought and sold individually (that is, independent of the acquisition of a going business). The replacement cost approach entails summing the (explicit and opportunity costs) associated with reproducing rather than purchasing the asset in question. It is gen-

[6]For example, the Appeals court in *Newark Morning Ledger Co. v. U.S.* noted that, "if the [paid] subscribers [the customer-based intangible at issue] were contractually obligated to continue subscribing for some period of time, Morning Ledger [the taxpayer seeking to amortize the 'paid subscriber' intangible] clearly would be permitted to depreciate the value of those contracts over that time period. In such an event, continued patronage would not be a mere 'expectation,' but a contractual right...."

erally the most suitable when the asset can be reproduced, in that it requires far fewer assumptions than the income approach.

In this case, V employed a version of the income approach to value X's patient relationships. In section 2 below, this methodology is described. Ultimately, we concluded that V's application of the income approach could not be salvaged given the facts of the case, for reasons described in section 3. As such, we recomputed the value of patient relationships using a replacement cost method.

7.1.2 Appraisal Firm's Methodology

Revenue Projections: In valuing X's patient relationships, V began by calculating the expected remaining commercial life of this source of revenue, using survivor curve analysis and clinic-specific data. Survival rates, in combination with data on patient revenues per period, were used to project revenues over the predicted remaining life of each patient relationship. This magnitude represented total projected revenues jointly attributable to all of the assets used in the business of treating existing (as distinct from future) patients. According to V, patient relationships and "requisite assets," consisting of net working capital, fixed assets, and an assembled workforce, collectively constituted total assets. (Hence, V implicitly assumed that goodwill and going concern had no value separate and apart from existing patient relationships.)

Given V's projection of total revenues, it remained to:

- Translate this figure into projected operating profits (by projecting costs associated with the treatment of existing patients, and netting them out of revenues); and,
- Carve up total projected profits, jointly attributable to all assets used to treat existing patients, into segments attributable to individual assets, including patient relationships, and discount each segment at an appropriate capitalization rate.

Cost Projections: Hence, the second order of business was to project operating expenses, and net these projections out of projected revenues. Per patient variable costs were calculated on the basis of historical financial data, and the decline in these costs attributable to patient retirements based again on statistical survival rates. Additionally, V reduced each clinic's fixed costs by the proportion of unused capacity at the acquisition date, and thereafter assumed that the taxpayer would consolidate treatment centers and forego the repairs necessary to maintain redundant assets[7] in working order as existing patients retired (due to death, geographic relocation, new forms of treatment, etc.). Stated differently, V allocated the capital expenditures necessary to maintain redundant requisite assets in working order to prospective future patients (rather than to the base of patients in place on the acquisition date).

Segmenting Total Projected Profits: Next, V had to carve up total projected profits, calculated above, and attribute individual segments to individual requisite assets and patient relationships. It did so by valuing all of the requisite assets that it identified, other than patient relationships (again, net working capital, tangible assets, and an assembled workforce) on a replacement cost basis, and assigning individual required returns to each. Specifically, V allowed for a (before-tax) return of 10% on working capital, 15% on fixed assets, and 25% on the "assembled workforce" intangible. These returns were then deducted from total projected profits. Finally, netting out taxes and discounting the resulting after-tax income stream attributable to patient relationships at a discount rate of 10%, V arrived at its estimate of the value of patient relationships.

7.1.3 Critique

The IRS challenged V's valuation of patient relationships on several grounds. First, V underestimated the costs associated with providing care for existing patients, in that it effectively treated fixed costs as variable. Further, its estimates of the potential cost savings from clinic consolidations were highly unrealistic, given the nature of the taxpayer's business. For these reasons, V's projections of total profits

[7]That is, assets that became redundant relative to the diminishing pool of existing patients.

associated with existing patients, to be allocated among individual requisite assets and patient relationships, were overstated. Second, and more fundamentally, the way in which it went about allocating this pool of profits across requisite assets and existing patient relationships was inherently arbitrary. Lastly, and equally fundamentally, V's implicit assumption that X had neither goodwill nor going concern independent of existing patient relationships as of the acquisition date was questionable. Each of these issues are taken up briefly below.

Fixed Costs: In general, economists and accountants alike distinguish between fixed and variable outlays. As the term suggests, variable costs vary with the volume of output or level of services provided; fixed costs, in contrast, do not.[8] Recall that V reduced fixed costs as of the acquisition date by the proportion of unused capacity at each clinic, for purposes of projecting the costs of providing the medical services in question to existing patients. By doing so, V effectively treated certain fixed costs as variable, and understated them substantially as a result.

One might make a case that hypothetical fixed costs would be lower than actual fixed costs, if the existing pool of patients was substantially smaller than the number of patients one ultimately expected to serve (and had allowed for in building the clinics), and if the requisite fixed assets were divisible to some degree such that a smaller clinic size was feasible. However, for purposes of determining actual projected profits, the IRS argued that actual fixed costs should have been used, in lieu of either capacity-adjusted or hypothetical fixed costs.

Capital Expenditures and Clinic Consolidations: V's argument that some portion of capital expenditures should be allocated

[8] For example, the cost of requisite capital equipment is fixed; to produce one unit of output or the maximum feasible volume of output given the plant or clinic size, one must incur this expense. However, the fuel costs of running the equipment are variable. If one produces no output, there are no fuel costs; if one produces at half capacity, additional fuel is required, while at full capacity, still more is necessary.

to future patients had some merit, accepting the premise that existing and future patients can be distinguished for valuation purposes in a meaningful sense. Likewise, its position that the taxpayer would consolidate clinics to reduce costs as existing patients retired, absent new patients (a hypothetical assumed for the purpose of allocating costs between existing and future patients), made sense.

However, in our view, *V* had greatly overestimated the scope for clinic consolidations. The acquired clinics were geographically dispersed over several states, and the patients were not exceptionally mobile. Stated differently, the taxpayer would have had to maintain more clinics than *V* had assumed, in order to serve the declining patient pool. Consequently, *V* underestimated the requisite capital expenditures properly attributable to existing patients by omitting those necessary to keep the additional clinics up and running. Its underestimate of fixed costs, described above, also translated into an additional understatement of requisite capital expenditures allocable to existing patients.

Arbitrary Allocation of Projected Profits among Requisite Assets and Patient Relationships: Equally to the point, *V*'s assignment of asset-specific rates of return to individual requisite assets was largely unfounded. As described briefly in Chapter 2, the capital asset pricing model, or CAPM—which is widely used to establish required returns on investments—is based on a conceptualization (and measure) of risk as the variability of a stream of returns produced by the group of assets comprising a given investment (and used in tandem), relative to the variability of returns one would earn by holding a "market portfolio," comprised of all traded stocks and weighted in accordance with the market as a whole. It is difficult to see how this conceptual framework can be used to establish the"riskiness" of (and, hence, the required return on) an individual asset that does not generate income in itself. Absent an economically defensible means of determining returns to individual assets, the segmentation of total projected profits to individual assets by this means is entirely arbitrary.

No Goodwill and Going Concern: Finally, V implicitly assumed that X, the acquired company comprising the clinics at issue, had no going concern value and goodwill separate and apart from the existing "patient relationship" intangible, without actually demonstrating or even expressly arguing this point.

However, X was clearly a going concern on the acquisition date, and Y simply stepped into its proverbial shoes. To the extent that going concern value can and should be distinguished from patient relationships, its separate value should be disentangled. Likewise, goodwill, defined by case law as "the expectancy of continued patronage," presumably encompasses the likelihood that future patients (as distinct from those which were already affiliated with the clinics at the acquisition date) will choose these clinics for treatment. Its value, too, should therefore have been disentangled from the "existing patient relationship" intangible. Note, however, that under the income approach, there was no convincing way to separate out the value of patient relationships from the collective remaining value of goodwill and going concern, a more general issue that the next composite valuation case reviewed illustrates.

In short, V's valuation of patient relationships via the income approach did not bear up under close scrutiny, in that the general standard of reasonable accuracy was not satisfied, and both goodwill and going concern value were collapsed into the patient relationship intangible. In its stead, we developed an alternative valuation based on the replacement cost approach, using data that V had relied on in computing its income-based valuation.[9]

[9]It should be noted that this replacement cost value was a very small fraction of V's income-based valuation, providing additional support for it (even leaving aside the specific methodological flaws in V's valuation described above): faced with the choice of purchasing an asset at a given price, or reproducing it at a substantially lower cost (where "cost" includes both explicit and opportunity costs, as noted above), a third party would clearly opt for the latter course of action. Stated differently, a willing buyer would not pay more, and a willing seller could therefore not charge more, than replacement cost. The differential between income-based and replacement cost valuations in this case also lent credence to our view that V incorporated elements of going concern and goodwill in its valuation of the "patient relationship" intangible.

7.1.4 Resolution

The Examination teams working on the valuation issues that make up this composite case study did not request variances from the IRS industry specialists overseeing these types of issues. Hence, in all cases, our primary position was based on the IRS's *Coordinated Issue Paper on Customer-Based Intangibles*, whereby such intangibles were considered part and parcel of goodwill essentially by definition.[10] However, in most cases, we put forth the replacement cost approach as well, as an alternative position. Most of these issues were resolved at the Appeals level, with Appeals typically rejecting our argument that a replacement cost approach was clearly superior to the income approach that the taxpayers generally relied on, but incorporating some of the specific methodological points we had raised concerning these income valuations in working out a compromise.

7.2 Valuation of Advertiser and Subscriber Lists

7.2.1 Introduction

In the late 1980s, Company Y acquired a firm engaged principally in publishing from Company X. Y elected Section 338 in connection with this acquisition, requiring it to allocate the total purchase price to individual assets composing the acquired entity. An unrelated appraisal company, again denoted by "V," undertook these valuations on Y's behalf. Collectively, subscription lists, advertiser lists, noncompete agreements, and trademarks constituted the bulk of total intangible asset values owned by the acquired company. In this discussion, I focus principally on acquired subscription and advertiser lists, both customer-based intangibles.

The valuation approach that V employed in this composite case was very similar to that used to value patient relationships in the prior valuation case study. Hence, the methodological issues are very similar, with one important difference: in the instant case, V

[10] See appendix to Chapter 2.

attempted to value two separate intangibles via the residual income method, necessitating a division of residual projected profits between them. Additionally, the business of the acquired company—in this case, publishing—was such that current expenditures had an effect on both current and future business. As such, V was faced with the difficult task of determining how the taxpayer's total expenditures broke down between current and capital outlays.

7.2.2 Appraisal Firm's Methodology

V valued the subscriber and advertiser lists that Y acquired from X using the income approach. Accordingly, as in the prior valuation case, it began by determining the estimated useful lives of advertiser and subscriber lists using Iowa curve techniques.

Clearly, neither subscriber nor advertiser lists alone generate income. To attract subscribers and advertisers in this medium, one must publish periodicals. Publishing, in turn, requires property, plant and equipment, materials inventories, etc. Hence, as a second step, V projected the revenues and costs to be generated by the acquired company's publishing-related assets, used in combination, over their estimated lives. As in the previous composite valuation case reviewed, the third step entailed isolating the portion of this total projected income stream that was attributable to both advertiser and subscriber lists, by a process of elimination. To this end, V assigned required rates of return to individual assets other than advertiser and subscriber lists, applied these rates of return to the assets (valued at replacement cost), and deducted the resulting dollar returns on individual assets from total projected profits jointly attributable to all assets. The residual, in V's estimation, constituted income attributable to both advertiser and subscriber lists.

In order to value subscriber and advertiser lists individually—a necessary step because they had different estimated useful lives—V had to allocate the residual projected revenues and costs between them as a fourth step. Revenues were readily separable between the two types of intangibles: subscriber revenues included both those earned on sales of the acquired firm's publications through outstanding subscriptions, and list rentals; all revenues on the sale of advertising space constituted advertising revenues. However, allocating costs was more problematic: as *V* recognized, certain direct costs (such as editorial and production expenses), and virtually all indirect costs (such as general and administrative expenses), were attributable to both subscribers and advertisers. *V* made the simplifying assumption that shared costs should be allocated on the basis of relative revenues.

The allocations of residual projected revenues and costs described above yielded total projected profits attributable to advertisers and subscribers, respectively. In *V*'s estimation, however, some portion of the costs assigned to advertisers represented an investment in future business (and, hence, should not have been included in the costs associated with current subscribers), and, likewise, some portion of the costs assigned to subscribers constituted a form of intangibles development expenditures aimed at attracting future subscribers. Hence, yet another allocation of costs, between current and future advertisers and current and future subscribers, respectively, was necessary.

V allocated subscriber-related costs between present and future subscribers, and advertiser-related costs between present and future advertisers, by analyzing the nature of individual cost items and applying percentages that were subjectively determined. For example, with regard to advertiser-related costs, *V* concluded that 90% of executive salaries, 75% of sales promotion expenses, 90% of both mailing and market research expenses, and 75% of marketing expenses related to obtaining and maintaining new advertiser relationships. It applied a similar proportional allocation to individual subscriber-related expenses as well.

After netting out the proportion of advertiser- and subscriber-related costs attributable to future business from total projected advertiser and subscriber costs, as determined above, *V* arrived at its estimate of the income attributable to existing advertiser and subscriber lists, respectively. It remained only to capitalize these projected income streams at an appropriate discount rate to determine the estimated values of these intangibles. *V* utilized a discount rate of 10% to this end.

7.2.3 Critique

Many of the same methodological criticisms raised in connection with the valuation of patient relationships, discussed in the first composite valuation case study, can also be levelled against the valuation of advertiser and subscriber lists described above: both valuations made a number of questionable assumptions in projecting costs;[11] both assigned arbitrary required returns to individual assets in segmenting total projected profits; both presupposed that the acquired company possessed neither goodwill nor going concern separate and apart from the customer-based intangibles at issue, etc. In addition, in valuing advertiser and subscriber lists, *V* applied a very inexact sales-based allocation of joint costs, and broke down total projected advertiser- and subscriber-related costs, respectively, between present and future business in a highly subjective (and potentially self-serving) manner.

7.2.4 Resolution

Again, with regard to the cases that make up this composite case study, we proposed replacement cost valuations in lieu of the discounted cash flow approach on which the taxpayers relied. As before, the replacement cost method generally yielded substantially reduced (and—in the IRS's view—significantly more reliable) valuations. In several cases, the Examination team sought and obtained a variance from the industry specialists overseeing these issues, and attempted unsuccessfully to settle a settlement directly. Ultimately, all of the cases progressed to Appeals. Where the proposed valuation adjustment was one of a number of issues that the team raised in its audit of the taxpayer at issue, one adjustment was frequently traded off against another in the course of settlement negotiations—often the way that an agreement is reached. In the end, the taxpayers' original valuations of customer-based intangibles were typically reduced in a very back-of-the-envelope fashion, and the taxpayers permitted to amortize these intangibles.

[11] These have not been detailed with regard to the instant case, but they were quite similar to those raised in the prior case.

7.3 Valuation of Product Endorsements

7.3.1 Introduction

In the early 1980s, Company Y acquired 100% of Company X's capital stock from its parent, Company Z. X produced a range of high-end fitness equipment, sold directly to health and fitness clubs and indirectly to individual end-users through a variety of independent retail outlets. Pursuant to this acquisition, Y elected Section 338. As with the prior composite valuation cases reviewed above, Y procured the services of an unrelated appraisal firm, V, to allocate the total purchase price to individual acquired assets.

Acquired tangible assets in this case included land, buildings and improvements, machinery and equipment, and lab equipment. Y also obtained a variety of current assets (cash, accounts receivables, etc.) in the transaction. According to V, acquired intangible assets consisted of a number of product endorsements by health care professionals, in-place wholesale distribution systems, computer software, an assembled workforce, patents, trademarks, and goodwill. By V's reckoning, total intangible assets amounted to approximately four times the value of tangible assets. Among intangible assets, product endorsements accounted for over three-quarters of the total.

I focus on product endorsements in the analysis of V's valuation approach below. As with the composite valuation cases reviewed above, V employed an income approach to value these intangibles. Consequently, the same choice-of-method issue arises. However, the discussion herein underscores the kinds of distortions that can arise, and their potential orders of magnitude, when unsound applications of the income approach are used to value intangible assets.

7.3.2 Appraisal Firm's Methodology

As noted above, V utilized the income approach to value acquired product endorsements. Specifically, it discounted the projected earnings attributable to these endorsements (by its calculation) by the risk-adjusted opportunity cost of capital. It computed projected earnings, in turn, as the sum of:

- All profits earned on those sales of fitness equipment that resulted directly from (existing) endorsements by health care professionals (by V's estimation, a substantial fraction of total sales, albeit not all);
- The cost savings attributable to the acquired product endorsements. According to V's analysis, X's closest competitor in the fitness equipment business chose not to pursue professional endorsements as a means of facilitating sales, but, rather, opted to establish and maintain its position in the relevant market segment by launching a major media advertising campaign. V maintained that X realized substantial cost savings by virtue of its reliance on endorsements over major media advertising, and argued that these cost savings (per dollar of sales) were equal to its competitor's major media outlays (per dollar of sales). And, lastly,
- The tax benefits that resulted from amortizing acquired endorsements over their remaining useful lives (again, estimated via Iowa curves), a function of the two preceding components of "economic benefits" associated with product endorsements.

7.3.3 Critique

V's valuation of X's product endorsements incorporated two fairly egregious errors: first, V effectively double-counted a substantial portion of the value of certain requisite assets other than endorsements in its overall valuation, overstating the value of existing product endorsements by the amount of this double-counting (while understating the value of trademarks by the same magnitude). Second, V dramatically overestimated cost savings attributable to endorsements, and double-counted them as well. These issues are addressed in turn below.

As described above, V attributed all profits earned on sales generated by endorsements to endorsements. However, these profits (as well as those earned on the portion of sales that were not endorsement-generated) were jointly attributable to all of the tangible and intangible assets employed in developing, manufacturing, and marketing the fitness equipment, not just to product endorsements. Consequently, V overestimated the value of product endorsements by the amount of profits on endorsement-generated sales that should have been attributable to the remaining (tangible and intangible) productive assets, appropriately discounted.[12] By the same token, V also valued each of these other requisite assets individually via the replacement cost approach, double-counting a portion of them thereby, while collapsing the double-counted portion into endorsements.

While this double-counting significantly overstated the value of product endorsements, it paled in comparison to V's second methodological miscalculation. Recall that V added cost savings to its projected profits on endorsement-generated sales in valuing endorsements, on the theory that X gained a competitive advantage by relying on endorsements rather than major media advertising to generate sales, and that it permanently avoided certain costs thereby. Further, it quantified these cost savings by equating them to its competitor's major media outlays (per dollar of sales). Note that cost savings calculated in this way were approximately two times the amount of projected profits on endorsement-related sales.

Even accepting V's argument that endorsements were a less costly means of differentiating one's products and generating demand, and that competitors were effectively precluded from taking the same approach,[13] V's quantification of cost savings was substantially overstated. Furthermore, the cost savings were also double-counted.

Cost savings should be calculated as the difference between the higher cost option (by assumption, major media advertising) and the lower cost option (again, by assumption, professional product endorsements). By calculating cost savings simply as the total cost associated with the higher cost option, V implicitly assumed that existing endorsements could be established and maintainedat no cost.

[12]This represented a substantial portion of the value of these other requisite assets, albeit not all, both because the profits at issue were projected out only over the estimated life of the product endorsements, while many of the remaining requisite assets were longer-lived, and because profits on sales that were not endorsement-generated were netted out of the projected income stream.

[13]If this were not the case, such cost savings would presumably be bid away through competitive pressures.

This was clearly not the case, as attested to by the composition of X's costs.

Further, and more fundamentally, inasmuch as product endorsements actually generated cost savings, they were already incorporated into the projected profits earned on endorsement-generated sales. (Similarly, if the endorsements had enabled X to charge a price premium for its fitness equipment relative to competitors' comparable products, this economic benefit, too, would have been reflected in its realized profits.) Consider an individual firm producing an undifferentiated product that sells at a uniform price in a competitive market. If this firm possesses superior technology (or some other sustainable advantage) that reduces its manufacturing costs relative to its competitors' costs, it will earn higher profits than its competitors by the amount of its cost savings. Likewise, consider a firm that produces a product that is perceived, accurately or otherwise, to be superior to its competitors' products, with production technology that is comparable to its competitors' technologies. Again, this firm will earn higher profits than its competitors, because it will be able to sell at a price premium.

Thus, while one might legitimately add price premia or cost savings realized by the advantaged firm to the (normal) profits earned by its competitors (that do not possess superior manufacturing technology or exceptionally valuable marketing intangibles) in estimating the advantaged firm's profits, if one works with the latter's realized (or projected) profits in the first instance, cost savings or price premia are already incorporated.

In short, by adding estimated cost savings to X's realized profits, V double-counted them. Moreover, in doing so, V arrived at a value of endorsements that substantially exceeded the income attributable to them (even leaving aside the fact that it attributed no income to other requisite assets, as described above). Clearly, a rational investor contemplating the purchase of a given asset would pay no more for it than the discounted present value of the income that it is expected to generate. To do so is tantamount to investing in a project guaranteed to lose money.

7.3.4 Primary and Alternative Positions

As in the preceding composite valuation cases, the IRS Examination team's primary position in the cases that make up this composite held that customer-based intangibles (including product endorsements) were inextricably bound up with goodwill, and could not be amortized for that reason. Again, as an alternative position, we developed replacement cost valuations in these cases as well. However, in several instances, our attempts to revalue the specific customer-based intangibles at issue via the replacement cost method were hindered by firms' refusals to respond to any information requests that were not strictly factual in content. As such, we arrived at our (undoubtedly imperfect) estimates of the acquired intangibles' replacement value via publicly available information and interviews with the acquired firms' competitors.

From a tactical standpoint, the IRS Examination team felt that it was also important to revise the acquiring firms' income-based valuations, in the event that Appeals officers rejected both our primary and alternative positions, and concluded that the taxpayers' income-based valuation approaches were warranted as a general proposition. To the end of revising specific applications of the income method, we argued that the economic benefits directly attributable to individual customer-based intangibles per se—either price premia (where pertinent) or cost savings (or both)—should constitute the basis for an income approach.

7.3.5 Resolution

By and large, these cases were settled at the Appeals level, with minimal intervening discussions at the Examination level. The Appeals officers typically split the difference between the taxpayers' versions of the income approach to valuing their respective customer-based intangibles, and our revised income-based valuations based on projected price premia or cost savings.

Chapter 8

Conclusions and Policy Recommendations

The foregoing composite transfer pricing case studies illustrate how and why both the 1968 regulations, and the 1993 temporary and proposed regulations that superseded them, will sometimes fail to produce arm's length results, and may give rise to inconsistent applications across firms and IRS districts. Similarly, under Section 338 (prior to the 1993 Act), intangible assets were often valued in ways that were at odds with basic economic and financial principles. This, too, made for inconsistent tax treatment across cases and districts (and may increasingly drive the uneven treatment of multinational firms under the 1993 temporary and proposed transfer pricing regulations).

In the short term, corporations generally benefit from this state of affairs—albeit differentially—in that they often pay less taxes than they would if the arm's length standard were implemented more effectively (and, relatedly, assets consistently valued in accordance with widely accepted valuation principles). However, rational tax planning is extremely difficult in such uncertain environs, the potential for penalties looms large, and a basic principle of tax equity—that similarly situated firms should be treated uniformly—is sometimes violated. Moreover, the disparity between statutory legislation and administrative practice is enormously costly in a very tangible sense, both from the standpoint of individual firms and the government. Such a system induces firms to engage in a variety of unproductive activities in an effort to reduce their expected tax liabilities, and forces the government to devote still more resources to its largely futile enforcement efforts. Finally, less concretely but perhaps even more importantly, the fairly pervasive under-assessments of corporate tax liability with respect to transfer pricing create real incentives to integrate vertically and diversify geographically, which may not be "welfare improving" from a broader, societal perspective.

The disparity between statutory principles and adminstrative practice is caused in part by ambiguities in the interpretive regulations, and by the institutional context in which transfer pricing and valuation disputes have been played out. As such, Section 482 legislation and administrative practice can be brought closer together (and some of the costs enumerated above reduced) either by:

- Reformulating the interpretive guidelines and modifying certain institutional features such that actual corporate tax liabilities under Section 482 conform more closely to those implied by tax legislation; or,
- Reworking the legislation itself, such that it conforms more closely to actual practice.

In this connection, the 1993 Act's addition of Section 197 to the IRC can be interpreted, rather convincingly, as an attempt to modify tax legislation to accord with actual practice *vis-a-vis* the valuation of acquired intangible property. (The relatively modest revenue estimates associated with this statutory change attest to such a conclusion.) However, unlike the primarily domestic tax issues that Sections 338 and 197 address, transfer pricing is intrinsically a multijurisdictional matter. As such, Congress' hands are tied, to some degree, by the extensive network of bilateral tax treaties endorsing the arm's length standard (to say nothing of the fact that the United States has historically championed this basic principle). Accordingly, for purposes of this discussion, I assume that current Section 482 legislation will remain in place, and that attempts to reduce the gap between legislation and practice will be directed to reformulating the interpretive guidelines and modifying certain (limited) aspects of the institutional context in which transfer pricing issues are currently raised and resolved. To the extent that these changes reduce some of the still-pervasive ambiguities in transfer pricing methodologies and the variability in negotiated resolutions, they should also be useful to multinational firms seeking to avoid the new Section 482 penalties. This chapter pulls together the methodological and issue-specific recommendations made in Chapters 3 through 6, and proposes several concomitant institutional changes touched on briefly in Chapter 3.

8.1 The 1993 Temporary Regulations: Two Steps Forward, One Step Back

In this section, I briefly summarize the ways in which the 1993 temporary regulations clarify and improve on the 1968 regulations, the issues that they leave unresolved, and the new questions that they raise, for each broad pricing method analyzed in the prior case studies.

8.1.1 The Cost-Plus Method

Under the 1968 regulations, corporate taxpayers tended to challenge the IRS's applications of the cost-plus method primarily on two grounds:

- The comparability of the particular uncontrolled firms that the IRS used to derive arm's length markups over cost; and,
- The composition of the cost base to which these markups were applied.

Questions of comparability revolved around the relative levels of risk that controlled entities and comparable stand-alone firms incurred. On the subject of the cost base, taxpayers and the IRS differed both in how materials that the manufacturing affiliate purchased from its parent outright, but which the latter would probably have consigned on an arm's length basis, should be treated, and how location-specific cost savings should be allocated between parent and offshore manufacturing affiliate.

The 1993 temporary regulations address two of these issues head on.

1. Comparability Criteria under the Cost-Plus Method: The 1993 temporary regulations flesh out the comparability criteria and standards to be applied in conjunction with the cost-plus method very substantially, potentially reducing disputes over proposed pricing adjustments thereby. Additionally, they unambiguously elevate substance over form in weighing risk, a clarification that became necessary in light of a number of decided Section 482 cases that placed considerable weight on the content of intra-company agreements, and very little weight on actual practice.

   However, the 1993 temporary regulations do not adequately define risk; nor do they propose a sufficiently precise measure of risk. Further, their more specific comparability requirements (under the cost-plus method) may be overshadowed by the possibility that some cases which would have been developed along cost-plus lines under the 1968 regulations will be relegated to the comparable profits method under the 1993 temporary regulations, which imposes much less stringent standards of comparability. In such instances, Appeals officers will have a very difficult time ranking alterative sets of comparable stand-alone companies, and many of the potential benefits to be had from more rigorous comparability standards—more consistent tax treatment across firms, results that are closer to arm's length, etc.—will not be realized. The arm's length range concept, in principle a sensible tool, may likewise be used to circumvent the cost-plus method's higher comparability standards.

2. Composition of the Cost Base: The 1993 temporary regulations address the question of whether offshore manufacturing affiliates should retain location-specific "cost savings" (relative to U.S. costs) clearly and unambiguously. In keeping with the arm's length standard, this determination is to be made with reference to the relative competitive positions of (related) buyer and seller cum stand-alone entities.

However, the associated "materials issue"—whether IRS economists can legitimately treat materials that one member of a controlled group sold outright to another as if they had been consigned—is (indirectly) dealt with ambiguously. The twin provisions that IRS representatives take the actual structure of intra-company dealings as given, and that they consider the alternatives available to both buyer and seller in determining appropriate compensation in the context of this actual structure, have a reasonably unambiguous interpretation from a purely economic standpoint: The related entity selling materials and purchasing finished products embodying them (often the U.S. parent) should be willing to pay no more for the right to sell materials outright rather than consign them—either in the form of a price premium or a side payment—than the value of the economic benefits it derives thereby. (In general, this will probably amount to its savings in inventory financing costs.) However, the legal interpretation of these "as actually structured" and "alternatives available" provisions would likely differ significantly from this economic interpretation, with relatively more weight placed on actual structure, and less on alternatives available.

8.1.2 The Resale Price Method

Two methodological issues arose fairly regularly under the 1968 regulations' resale price method, as applied to "inbound" cases:

- How should one establish ownership of potentially valuable marketing intangible assets (and, if the U.S. subsidiary was deemed to own these intangibles, how should one determine arm's length resale margins); and,
- Should one work with gross or net margins in deriving arm's length results from stand-alone distributors. (This was an issue whenever the controlled U.S. distributor performed more, or different types of, below-the-line functions than typical independent U.S. distributors in the same market segment.)

The 1993 temporary regulations clearly endorse gross margin comparisons, with appropriate adjustments for those differences (in functions or risks) between tested party and comparables that would be reflected below-the-line. Hence, this source of confusion and controversy should be eliminated, albeit differences of opinion as to how the requisite adjustments should be quantified may well take its place.

On the broader question of how one should determine ownership of intangible property, the 1993 temporary regulations make little headway. Moreover, with the explicit restriction that the resale price method can be applied only when the tested party (typically the U.S. distributor) does not contribute intangible property, the issue becomes all the more important. Here, too, the requirement that IRS representatives take the actual structure of intra-company dealings as given may add to the confusion: It is unclear what specific features of the interaction between parent and subsidiary that bears on intangibles ownership one should hold fixed. For example, legal ownership may lead to the conclusion that marketing intangibles development expenditures should be reallocated from one entity to another; alternatively, the observed allocation of intangibles development expenditures may be precisely the element that one should take as given (and, hence, determine ownership rights on that basis).

Finally, the 1993 temporary regulations raise the spectre of pricing adjustments that literally create income for tax purposes. Pricing adjustments that create income from the vantage point of a subset of related entities, while leaving consolidated losses unchanged, would seem to be entirely consistent with the arm's length standard. In principle, multinational firms can shift revenues or expenses within the controlled group such that each group member shows a loss for tax purposes, whereas a subset of individual group members would earn a positive return on a stand-alone basis (and the remaining members would bear a commensurately larger share of the same aggregate loss on a stand-alone basis). Under these circumstances, an allocation of revenues and/or expenses is clearly warranted. However, a pricing adjustment that creates income on a consolidated basis effectively penalizes vertically integrated firms, by treating them differently, for tax purposes, than comparable groupings of independent firms. This is incompatible with the spirit of the arm's length standard. The 1993 temporary regulations do not distinguish between adjustments that create income on a consolidated basis, and those that create income from the vantage point of a subset of group members while leaving consolidated losses unchanged.

8.1.3 Cost Sharing

Under the 1968 regulations' cost-sharing provisions, taxpayers and the IRS often parted company over the way in which benefits deriving from specified rights to prospective intangible property should be measured (and, hence, the way in which pooled costs should be allocated). Taxpayers often measured individual participants' benefits by their (anticipated) share of group-wide sales,[1] and allocated pooled costs accordingly. IRS economists took issue with this sales-based cost allocation on occasion (particularly when some cost-sharing participants obtained exclusive rights to sell in markets that commanded consistently higher profit margins), arguing instead that cost shares should be determined on the basis of relative profits. The IRS also raised buy-in issues fairly regularly under the 1968 regulations, whereby a related party joining an ongoing cost-sharing undertaking was required to contribute "back dues," or an entity contributing pre-existing intangibles to a new cost-sharing agreement would be compensated therefor. Taxpayers often challenged this buy-in approach on general principle, with some success.

In addition to these ambiguities concerning benefits measures and buy-in payments, the 1968 regulations did not provide adequate guidance as to how one should establish intra-company prices when one member of a related party cost-sharing agreement sold tangible property embodying the jointly developed intangibles to another member, or to a related non-member that possessed intangible property in its own right. This latter lacuna led to a morass of "fourth method" applications, none of which could unambiguously claim a higher priority than any other, with the result that Appeals officers had little basis for evaluating the relative merits of the IRS's proposed adjust-

[1]Where "sales" here refers to sales of products that would embody the manufacturing intangibles to be developed jointly.

ments and a given taxpayer's rationale for its reported allocation of consolidated income.

The 1992 proposed cost-sharing provisions, combined with the 1993 proposed profit split regulations, clarify two of these sources of confusion and controversy: The former clearly sanction buy-in payments, and the latter propose three pricing methodologies to be applied (only) when both related parties to the transactions at issue own valuable intangible property in their own right (that is, intangible property that was either self-developed or acquired from third parties). In effect, then, the 1993 proposed profit split regulations elevate a small subset of approaches, previously considered "fourth methods," above the alternatives, ameliorating the problems associated with the previous lack of prioritizing among them.

By the same token, these proposed profit split approaches are described in very broad-brush terms. Consequently, they may simply shift the focal point of disputes between taxpayers and the IRS from methods per se to the way in which the particular proposed profit split approach that applies in a given case should be implemented. Further, such implementation issues may well prove to be fertile ground for taxpayers: The allocation of consolidated income across related entities under the proposed profit split methods can differ dramatically, depending on methodological fine points that seem, at first blush, to be rather esoteric: how total intangible property should be divided between broad marketing and manufacturing types, the rate at which different intangible assets should be amortized, and so forth.

Finally, the 1992 proposed cost-sharing provisions will do little to moderate disputes about the proper measure of benefits deriving from prospective intangibles development.

It should also be noted that cost-sharing issues may well arise more frequently in the future than they have arisen in the past, because the *commensurate with income* requirement will likely make cost sharing a more attractive option than intra-company licensing of intangible property in some instances. Consequently, these lacunae in proposed cost-sharing and profit split regulations may be increasingly problematic.

8.1.4 Intra-Company Licenses of Proprietary Intangible Property

Intra-company licenses of intangible property rarely involve assets with comparable profit potential, and take place under comparable circumstances, as uncontrolled licenses. Consequently, the price-based comparable uncontrolled transactions method—the preferred method under both 1968 and 1993 temporary regulations—can rarely be used to establish arm's length royalty rates, raising the difficult issue of how one should go about establishing or assessing intra-company royalty charges. The 1968 regulations' answer to this predicament was the amorphous twelve-factor approach discussed in Chapters 2 and 6. Unfortunately, the individual factors that companies and the IRS were to consider in determining arm's length royalty rates were not assigned any particular priority. Many simply indicated whether the intra-company rate should be adjusted up or down (vis-a-vis some inexact comparable rate) in a purely relative sense, and the data necessary to apply a substantial number of the twelve factors rarely existed in any event. In response to this regulatory vacuum, companies resorted to industry norms and broad rules of thumb in establishing intra-company royalty rates, and IRS economists made the best of very inexact comparables in evaluating (and, in some instances, challenging) these fairly ad hoc methods. The net result, in many such cases, was that related licensees often retained very substantial shares of intangible income.

The 1993 temporary regulations set out in much more detail the comparability criteria that must be satisfied by prospective comparable uncontrolled transactions in intangible property. Because these comparability standards are quite high, the 1993 temporary regulations will probably do away with such expedients as industry norms and rules of thumb. For the same reason, however, there will be very few occasions when the comparable uncontrolled transactions method can be applied. Anticipating this implication, the 1993 temporary regulations provide for an alternative, profits-based approach, the "comparable profits method."

From a purely practical standpoint, the comparable profits method may solve some of the IRS's methodological and data problems in contending with intra-company licensing issues. However, there is no assurance, nor even a reasonable likelihood, that the imputed royalty rate that this method yields will be any closer to the "true" hypothetical arm's length rate than industry norms or broad-brush rules of thumb (although the comparable profits method may err on the high side more often than the latter approaches, which tended to err on the low side fairly consistently). Nor is it clear that all intangible income will remain with the developer/licensor under the comparable profits method, as required by the statutory *commensurate with income* standard.

8.2 Proposed Revisions to the 1993 Temporary and Proposed Section 482 Regulations

As the above discussion suggests, there is room for improvement in both the 1993 temporary Section 482 regulations and the 1993 proposed profit split regulations. On the broadest level, the 1993 temporary regulations' "case study" approach, whereby one attempts to find individual comparable firms with which the controlled tested party can be directly compared (and their operating results equated) should be reconsidered, and greater weight placed on statistical methods. Statistical analysis effectively obviates the need for perfect comparables, in the sense that one can extract the information necessary to "construct" such comparables from a (sufficiently large) sample of inexact comparables. Briefly stated, this is done by estimating—via statistical techniques—the precise relationship between profitability (the "dependent variable") on the one hand, and specific firm and market characteristics (the "explanatory variables") on the other.

With such an estimation in hand, one can simply fit the controlled tested party into this more general relationship between profitability and both firm and market characteristics, given its particular profile of explanatory variables. One of several benefits associated with this statistical approach over the current case study methodology is that it will be significantly more accurate (if the statistical analysis is done correctly). Additionally, it enables one to separate out random variations in profitability from variations caused by factors that influence profits systematically and predictably. Moreover (and again, unlike existing methods), a statistical approach yields estimates of the degree of uncertainty associated with one's conclusions. (While this description of the basic features and virtues of statistical analysis relates to firm-level comparisons, the same basic approach can be applied to transactions-based methodologies.)

Short of a fundamental shift in emphasis from the current case study-type focus on small sets of close comparables to the statistical analysis of large samples, both the 1993 temporary and proposed regulations could more effectively achieve their (presumed) ends—moderating the often acrimonious and unproductive disputes between the government and multinational firms on transfer pricing issues, bringing the post-adjustment allocation of income across related parties more in line with the arm's length standard, and ensuring greater consistency in the tax treatment of multinationals across firms and districts—if they were modified in the following ways:[2]

- The meaning and measure of risk should be elaborated on and defined much more precisely in both 1993 temporary and proposed regulations.[3]

---

[2]Note that, at least as a first cut, it is more important to reduce or eliminate the ambiguities identified than to refine the suggested clarifications to the nth degree.

[3]Probability theory and the capital asset pricing model are very useful starting points in this regard. As a general proposition, economists conceptualize the risk associated with a given undertaking as the variance in its possible outcomes. Measures of variance incorporate both the range of possible outcomes (operating results in the present case) associated with a given undertaking and the probability that individual outcomes will be realized. The 1993 temporary regulations do not provide an overarching definition of risk (but, rather, enumerate specific forms of risk, describe how one should determine whether a given controlled entity in fact incurs individual forms of risk, list the documentation necessary to substantiate a given allocation of risks, and require that risk be allocated consistently). The 1993 proposed regulations include the following, very ambiguous statement regarding risk: "Risk is measured as the probability of gain or loss rather than a measurement of total potential gain or loss from an activity." If one interprets the probability of gain or loss as pertaining specifically to the probability that individual outcomes will be realized, and the measurement of total potential gain or loss as the expected value, this is an incomplete or incorrect definition of variance or risk. Rather, as noted above, the range of possible outcomes and the probability that individual outcomes will be realized should both enter into an

- The final regulations should clarify how the "as actually structured" and "alternatives available" provisions balance out. If the drafters of the 1993 temporary regulations intended to endorse an opportunity cost framework, this should be done less ambiguously, and the general approach described in such a way that transfer pricing experts across a range of disciplines would bring the same conceptual framework to bear.

- The regulations should be more specific as to which features of the "structure" of intra-company interactions one should take as given, for purposes of evaluating transfer prices;

- They should explicitly address the question of how one should determine ownership of marketing intangible property;

- Pricing adjustments that create income on a consolidated basis should not be sanctioned. However, adjustments that reallocate a given consolidated loss across entities, such that one or more shows a profit, and the remaining group members incur a commensurately larger share of the (fixed) consolidated loss, should be permitted to the extent that they are justified by comparisons with comparable independent firms.

- The final regulations should clarify when specific approved measures of anticipated benefits flowing from participation in a related party cost-sharing agreement should be used.

- The comparable profits method's comparability requirements should be tightened up substantially, and, if the present range of approved profit level indicators is retained in the final regulations, these comparability criteria should be tailored more explicitly to individual profit level indicators. If rate of return profit level indicators are used, degrees of risk should constitute the key comparability criterion; if other profit measures are used, the list of comparability criteria should be significantly more comprehensive, such that the below-the-line (explicit and imputed) payments to productive factors (including capital) can reasonably be expected to be uniform across comparables

---

appropriate measure of risk.

and tested parties.[4] Alternatively, the approved profit level indicators should be scaled back to include only rates of return on assets. In principle, the comparable profits method should also apply only when the product markets at issue (in which both tested party and comparables operate) are effectively competitive.

- The approaches that one can use to quantify the inevitable differences between comparables and tested party (statistical methods, commercial practices, and economic principles) should be ranked in order of priority. Where commercial practices point unambiguously to a particular quantification, they are presumably the best gauge of arm's length practices. If commercial practices yield ambiguous conclusions, or information concerning them is unavailable, statistical analysis is a logical second choice. If the data necessary to apply statistical techniques are unavailable, broad economic principles should be used.
- The 1993 proposed profit split methods should be fleshed out in much greater detail than presently. In particular, they should explicitly address how one should:
  - value total intangible assets collectively owned by the related parties at issue;
  - break this total down into broad categories of marketing and manufacturing intangibles;
  - distinguish between current and (tangible and intangible) capital expenditures overall;
  - ascertain which categories of intangibles development expenditures give rise to individual types of intangible assets;
  - establish reasonable amortization rates for the different types of intangibles; and,

[4] With these tighter comparability criteria, the arm's length range defense can play a very useful role.

  - allocate horizontally diversified firms' joint costs and assets across their different lines of business.

While this list is fairly lengthy, the proposed clarifications would narrow the scope for disagreement between the IRS and corporate taxpayers on transfer pricing issues considerably. These suggestions can be implemented in a variety of ways. However, the overriding concern—at least initially—should be to eliminate the ambiguities identified, rather than to perfect the particular way in which this is done.

8.3 Lessons from Section 338

As described in Chapter 5, the valuation of intangible property may become increasingly important under the 1993 temporary and proposed regulations, just as Section 338 intangibles valuation issues are receding in importance (in the wake of the 1993 Act). However, the history of Section 338 intangibles valuation issues may yield some useful insights into the ways in which taxpayers have gone about valuing intangible assets for tax purposes, how the IRS has weighed the different approaches, and how intangibles valuation issues have been resolved. These insights should be of interest to the drafters of the final regulations, and to multinational firms attempting to implement these regulations.[5]

A number of common themes emerged in the Section 338 valuation cases reviewed in Chapter 7:

- Corporate taxpayers' method of choice for valuing certain types of intangibles is typically some variant of the income (or discounted cash flow) approach.

- Aggressive taxpayers can potentially inflate asset valuations

[5]Recall, however, that the valuation of individual intangible assets—generally necessary under Section 338, and the stuff of which disputes thereunder were usually made of—may or may not be called for under the 1993 proposed profit split regulations, depending in part on the specific facts and circumstances of a given case.

substantially under the income approach,[6] through a variety of mechanisms that are dressed up in technical jargon, and, as such, may be difficult to recognize.

- Even if one is not motivated by tax considerations in choosing the income method, and applies it in good faith, the computations it necessitates are very involved and highly inexact, often leading to over- or undervaluations.

- Intangible assets are over- or undervalued via the income approach (intentionally or otherwise) for a variety of reasons that tend to recur from case to case:

  - Determining the total projected profits jointly attributable to intangibles and other requisite assets is no small feat in itself, inasmuch as these projections require forecasting revenues and costs far into the future. (Further, where a taxpayer opts for an aggressive tax position, revenue and cost projections can potentially be manipulated to over- or understate future profits, and, hence, asset values.)

  - If the intangibles at issue have finite useful lives,[7] one has to break out total projected revenues and costs between those that will be earned and incurred, respectively, within the intangibles' useful lives (and in connection with business that is concluded during this period), and those that relate to future business. While this procedure may be fairly straightforward as regards revenues, the allocation of fixed and variable costs—some of which will generally be joint between existing and future business to one degree or another—is a difficult, highly inexact (and potentially self-serving) procedure.

  - On occasion, magnitudes such as separately computed

[6]In *Newark Morning Ledger Company v. U.S.*, for example, the customer-based intangibles at issue—"paid subscribers"—were valued via the income approach at $67.8 million; the IRS, employing a replacement cost method, put their value at $3 million. (If this $3 million accurately represents replacement cost, it is very difficult to argue that a willing buyer would pay over twenty times this amount for pre-existing subscribers.)

[7]Recall that acquired intangible assets could be amortized only if they were finite-lived, among other things, under Section 338.

price premia or cost savings are added to projected profits for purposes of valuing intangible assets via the income method. Inasmuch as these items are already included in projected profits, this procedure double-counts the separately computed profit elements. (More generally, the value of an asset, intangible or otherwise, should never exceed the discounted present value of projected profits associated with it, inasmuch as rational investors should be unwilling to pay more than this amount.)

- Given a plausible projection of total profits jointly attributable to intangibles and other requisite assets over the relevant time frame, it remains to assign individual slices of this income stream to individual groupings of assets, including the intangibles at issue, that may not generate income in themselves. Taxpayers and valuation specialists have approached this problem in a variety of ways,[8] all of which are essentially ad hoc.

In short, valuations of intangible assets via the income method are generally based on a long list of interlocking assumptions, many of which are inevitably ad hoc (and, potentially, manipulable). As such, if the income method is widely used under the final Section 482 regulations to value intangible assets, it could well contribute significantly to the inconsistent tax treatment of multinational firms. Further, it would likely perpetuate the disparity between transfer pricing resolutions in Appeals and "true" arm's length results. Hence, while the 1993 temporary Section 482 regulations have moved away from a fixed priority of pricing methods by incorporating the best methods rule, a fixed priority of valuation methods makes some sense, in that they can be ranked on the basis of objective criteria. In several important respects, the replacement cost approach is unambiguously preferable to the income method. Consequently, it should ideally be given first priority, to be applied unless the intangible at issue cannot be reproduced.

When an intangible is non-reproducible, and a variant of the in-

[8]For example, by assigning fairly arbitrary rates of return to all assets other than the intangibles at issue, by implicitly assuming that all assets other than the intangibles have no value, etc.

come method is apropos, the final profit split provisions should contain more detailed instructions as to how it should be implemented. Where possible, the specific price premia or cost savings allocable to the intangible asset(s) at issue should be estimated and projected separately, and the asset(s) valued by discounting this segment of income, rather than by projecting total profits jointly attributable to all assets together, and then segmenting this total projected income stream via the asset-specific required return device that was widely used in connection with Section 338 valuations. Alternatively, the final profit split provisions should provide specific guidelines as to how total projected profits jointly attributable to intangibles and other requisite assets over the former's useful life should be apportioned among each asset grouping.[9]

8.4 Proposed Institutional Changes

In addition to these suggested changes in the transfer pricing regulations, several institutional changes would also help to make the resolution of pricing issues more consistent across firms and districts, and more faithful to the arm's length standard.

Ideally, the mediating role that Appeals officers with expertise in accounting, tax, and legal matters, but rarely economics, currently play in resolving transfer pricing disputes should be assumed by individuals with a stronger grounding in economics. This would presumably mean segregating Appeals-level issues by type, and maintaining a small staff of economist Appeals officers to deal with transfer pricing matters. Such a step would significantly enhance the consistency of Appeals decisions in this area and reduce the likelihood that unsupportable pricing adjustments will be sustained, inasmuch as most economists bring a very specific analytical framework to

[9] As noted, the asset-specific required return approach is unduly arbitrary. One alternative might be to assume, for valuation purposes, that all requisite assets other than the intangibles at issue are leased rather than owned, and compute total projected profits (which would then be attributable to the intangibles alone) on that basis. This approach would be preferable if one is able to determine the cost of leasing requisite assets more easily, and more accurately, than the hypothetical slice of joint income attributable to individual requisite assets that do not generate income in isolation.

bear on product and asset pricing issues.[10] This is not to say that economists will always develop a given issue in the same way. To the contrary, given the open-ended nature of both 1968 and 1993 temporary Section 482 regulations on some fairly major points, there is a good deal of room for interpretation, and a clear need for more effective coordination among economists across districts on transfer pricing issues, as argued below. However, on fundamental principles, economists generally see eye to eye.

Along the same lines, in the interest of bringing transfer pricing resolutions in Appeals more in line with the arm's length standard and ensuring greater consistency in these resolutions—again, by assumption, the government's objectives—Appeals officers should be in a position to forward more cases to district counsel (where the issues under consideration have merit, and should in principle be sustained). Absent a credible threat that the government will litigate, taxpayers with very weak cases have little reason to compromise on, or concede to, proposed pricing adjustments, and will hold out for very favorable Appeals settlements.[11] To the extent that the pressures on Appeals to settle cases stem from limitations in litigating resources, they can be alleviated by increasing such resources.

The limited mechanisms for coordinating case development and Appeals resolutions within and across districts obviously contributes significantly to the inconsistent tax treatment of similarly situated firms as well.[12] On international tax matters in general, and transfer

[10] Relatedly, having economists function as Appeals officers would give substance to the notion that transfer pricing and valuation guidelines need not—and in fact cannot—allow for every eventuality, but that their application to a range of highly specific fact patterns over time should build up a body of coherent and mutually consistent precedents. By and large, this has not happened, again, because decisions on transfer pricing and valuation issues—which are fundamentally economic in content—have been made by individuals with extensive backgrounds in law and accounting, but limited training in economics.

[11] After the fact, penalties simply reinforce these incentives, by increasing the costs of compromising.

[12] As regards valuation issues, the appointment of industry specialists and the dissemination of coordinated issue papers on specific intangibles represented an important effort to ensure consistency in case development. However, because Appeals was not bound by these coordinated issue positions, such efforts did not translate into consistent resolutions across issues and districts—the bottom line, from the vantage point of taxpayers.

pricing issues in particular, the IRS has recently taken a number of important steps to coordinate case development. Beginning in FY 1992, the IRS established a number of *Issue Specialist* positions covering such areas as Sections 482 and 936, Subpart F, financial products, and the foreign tax credit, under the umbrella of a new *International Field Assistance Specialist Program.* The incumbents in these positions (previously international examiners) function as advisors to their counterpart technical specialists in the field, and convey information from field to National Office (and National Office to field) on issues that arise in the course of applying the pertinent IRC provisions. The program is intended to improve coordination between the National Office and individual IRS districts, and to facilitate communication between districts, on the covered international tax issues. By all accounts, it has already had a very positive effect.

However, these laudatory efforts to coordinate on transfer pricing (and other international tax) issues have focussed largely on international examiners to date. For the most part, economist groups in different districts do not communicate with one another on a regular basis. This lack of ongoing communication creates the potential for—indeed, almost the certainty of—inconsistent applications of the transfer pricing regulations. Accordingly, institutional mechanisms that coordinate among economist groups, ensure that the requisite level of quality in economic analysis is achieved and maintained, and provide for greater inter-district consistency on recurring pricing issues, should be put into place. More effective coordinating mechanisms on transfer pricing issues are also clearly called for at the Appeals level.

Index

1968 regulations, 11
- cost-sharing, 18
- intangible property, 16
- loans, 20
- services, 19
- tangible property, 13

1992 proposed regulations, 32
1993 proposed regulations, 53
1993 temporary regulations, 40
Advance pricing agreements, 65
Alternative minimum tax, 64
Amortization rates, 195, 202
APA, 65
Arbitration, 72
Arm's length range, 35
Arm's length research joint ventures, 163
Asset base, 195
BALRM, 28, 44
Basic Arm's Length Return Method, 28, 44
Bausch & Lomb, 117
Buy-ins, 30–31, 154–55, 168
Capital Asset Pricing Model, 80
Capital employed method
- 1993 proposed regulations, 55
- asset base, 195
- application, 155, 196
- critique, 206–209, 269–270.

CAPM, 80
CAT, 34
Classifying intangible assets, 175, 195, 199, 275
Commensurate with income, 24–25, 44, 58, 212
Comparable adjustable transactions method, 34
Comparable profit interval, 34
Comparable profit split, 55
Comparable profit(s) method
- 1992 proposed regulations, 33–34
- 1993 temporary regulations, 50
- applications, 213–14, 229
- critique, 241, 271

Comparable uncontrolled price method, 13, 46
Comparable uncontrolled transactions method, 44
Comparables, exact and inexact 26–27
Competent authority, 67
Compliance, 1968 regulations, 21
Congressional hearings, foreign-based multinationals, 62
Constructive operating income, 34
Cost-plus method, 49

1968 regulations, 13
1992 proposed regulations, 37
1993 temporary regulations, 42, 49
applications, 91
Cost base, 106, 117
critique, 115, 265
Cost-sharing, IRC Section 482
1968 regulations, 18
1992 proposed regulations, 38
applications, 151, 155
Computation of cost shares, 154–55
critique, 206, 269
CPM, 34
CUP, 13, 46
CUT, 44
Designated summons, 61
Dispute resolution procedures, 67
Enforcement, 1968 regulations, 21
Exact comparables, 26–27
Foreign Income Tax Rationalization and Simplification Act, 64
General Rule, 57
Going concern, 75, 253
Goodwill, 74, 253
Gross valuation misstatement, 60
Inbound, 13, 15, 22–23, 33, 52, 63–64, 123
Income approach, 80, 248–49
applications, 247, 254, 258
critique, 250, 257, 259, 276
Income creation, 52, 130
Inexact comparables, 26–27
Intangible property provisions
1968 regulations, 16
1992 proposed regulations, 33
1993 proposed regulations, 53
1993 temporary regulations, 44
White Paper, 27
IRC Section 197, 73, 77
IRC Section 338, 73
IRC Section 482, 10
IRC Section 936(h), 56
cost-sharing election, 58, 153
profit split election, 58
IRC Section 6038(A), 63
IRC Section 6662, 60
IRS coordinated issue papers, 76, 82
Labor savings, 112
Litigation hazards, 69, 120
Loans, 1968 regulations, 20
Location savings, 53, 58
Market comparison method, 80, 248–49
Market penetration strategy, 52
Marketing intangibles ownership, 135
Matching transactions method, 33
Measuring benefits from cost-sharing, 162, 274
MTM, 33
Mutual agreement procedure, 71
Newark Morning Ledger, 77
Omnibus Budget Reconciliation Act, 56, 60

Opportunity cost, 80, 117, 274
Penalty provisions, 59
Periodic adjustments, 24, 29, 36
Profit level indicators, 34
Policy proposals
  1993 temporary regulations, 272
  institutional changes, 279
Prudent businessman standard, 32
Regulations, transfer pricing, 10
Regulations, valuation, 73
Replacement cost approach, 80, 248–49, 278
Resale price method
  1968 regulations, 13
  1992 proposed regulations, 37
  1993 temporary regulations, 42, 49
  application, 123
  critique, 147, 267
Residual allocation rule, 54, 142
Residual valuation method, 73
Safe harbors, 19–21
Services, 1968 regulations, 19
Significant Business Presence Test, 57
Statistical analysis, 49, 52, 67, 105, 272
Substantial valuation misstatement, 60
Tangible property provisions
  1968 regulations, 13
  1992 proposed regulations, 36
  1993 temporary regulations, 41
Tax Reform Act of 1986, 24
Temporary regulations, 1993, 40
Transfer pricing regulations, 10
  possessions corporations, 56
Two-prong test, 75
Valuation methodologies, 80, 248–49
Valuation regulations, 73
White paper, 26